RAYMOND ROUSSEL AND THE REPUBLIC OF DREAMS

# RAYMOND ROUSSEL
## and the Republic of Dreams

MARK FORD

*faber and faber*

First published in 2000
by Faber and Faber Limited
3 Queen Square WCIN 3AU

Phototypeset by Intype London Ltd.
Printed in England by Clays Ltd, St Ives plc

© Mark Ford, 2000

The right of Mark Ford to be identified as author
of this work has been asserted in accordance with Section 77
of the Copyright, Designs and Patents Act 1988

A CIP record for this book
is available from the British Library

ISBN 0–571–17409–4

2 4 6 8 10 9 7 5 3 1

For my parents

GENEVIÈVE: Parmi tant de merveilles le choix ne pouvait être qu'embarrassant.

TRÉZEL: «Entre les Colonnes d'Hercule» eut en fin de compte sa préférence.

CLAUDE: «Entre les Colonnes d'Hercule»?

TRÉZEL: C'est le titre d'une œuvre profonde dans laquelle Vicherat, à l'imitation avouée de Platon, décrit la république de ses rêves.

CLAUDE: Étrange titre! . . .

TRÉZEL: À la recherche d'un pays chimérique où faire évoluer ses héros, qui lui semblaient d'ailleurs ne pouvoir tirer que profit d'une situation très reculée dans le temps, Vicherat choisit l'isthme qui unissait jadis l'Afrique à l'Espagne.

GENEVIÈVE: Quoi! Il y eut une époque où le détroit de Gibraltar n'existait pas?

TRÉZEL: C'est là un fait unanimement admis.

GENEVIÈVE: Among so many marvels the choice must have been perplexing.

TRÉZEL: *Between the Pillars of Hercules* was his eventual choice.

CLAUDE: *Between the Pillars of Hercules*?

TRÉZEL: It's the title of a profound work in which Vicherat, fully acknowledging his debt to Plato, describes the republic of his dreams.

CLAUDE: A strange title! . . .

TRÉZEL: In search of a fantastical country in which to develop his protagonists, whose actions, it seemed to him, would be best off located in the distant past, Vicherat chose the isthmus which used to connect Africa and Spain.

GENEVIÈVE: What! There was a time when the Straits of Gibraltar didn't exist?

TRÉZEL: *That* is a fact accepted by everyone.

*L'Étoile au front*, Act II, Scene I

# Contents

# Illustrations

All photographs courtesy of the Bibliothèque nationale de France, Paris.

# Foreword

by John Ashbery

It is unlikely that Raymond Roussel ever read John Keats's more-than-accurate prediction: 'I think I shall be among the English Poets after my death.' Yet in his book *Comment j'ai écrit certains de mes livres*, published in 1935, two years after his death, he offers a similarly modest and touching estimate of his work: ' . . . I may perhaps gain a little posthumous recognition for my books.' Both the extravagantly impoverished Keats and the extravagantly wealthy Roussel were destined to die in a foreign land (Italy, in both cases) with a single friend for company and doubtless with little real confidence that their genius would indeed be recognized by posterity.

Keats, however, had a certain measure of fame during his lifetime. Roussel had only notoriety, the result both of the absolute strangeness of his work and the vast fortune he dissipated in trying to draw attention to it. Perhaps he might have been more successful if he had been poorer, but it is more likely that, as with Proust, we should never have heard of him if his means hadn't allowed him the leisure to devote himself entirely to his writing, and, in Roussel's case, to publishing it. Another advantage was that his financial adviser happened to be the father of the future Surrealist writer Michel Leiris, who, beginning in 1935, published a remarkable series of essays on Roussel's work (eventually collected in a volume called *Roussel l'ingénu* in 1987, and reprinted in 1998 in *Roussel & Co.*). Thus his name, at least, was kept alive by the Surrealists and a few others until the 1960s, when a sudden explosion of interest gave birth to what can only be called a 'Roussel industry'. Though the fame that has resulted would have pleased him far more than the attentions of the Surrealists, whose works baffled him, it seems that misunderstanding of a different, albeit benign, sort has supplanted the scorn with which the world viewed him during his lifetime. From being always *le mal aimé*, he became almost too well loved, not only in the domain of literature but by the mass media as well, though it is chiefly his bizarre biography that interests the latter.

Though Jean Ferry's book-length study, *Une Étude sur Raymond Roussel*, appeared in 1953, interest in Roussel had pretty much congealed by 1958, when I decided to do research on him with the aim of producing a doctoral dissertation at New York University. I had already spent three years in France, trying to learn the language chiefly in order to read this writer whose work had fascinated me since 1951, when Kenneth Koch had brought back some of his books after a Fulbright year in France. Even their physical aspect attracted me, published as they had been by the firm of Lemerre, whose heyday in the late nineteenth century had long passed and whose pale-yellow volumes of the likes of Leconte de Lisle and José-Maria de Heredia emitted an appealing air of desuetude. One Roussel book in particular, his *Nouvelles Impressions d'Afrique*, a long poem interrupted by sets of multiple parentheses and illustrated with curiously banal drawings like the ones in my high-school French grammar, intrigued me. It seemed impossible that I would ever be able to read it with any understanding, but for a long time it was the thing I most wanted to do. So I learned French with the primary aim of reading Roussel.

Eventually I began my research by writing to Michel Leiris, who kindly invited me to have a drink at his sumptuous digs on the Quai des Grands Augustins. He produced a stack of postcards from Roussel that he had received over the years, starting in childhood, which I began to devour eagerly – too eagerly, as I later realized. Although I am not exceptionally uncouth, I committed the faux pas of copying down some of the postcard messages, without, as I recall, even asking Leiris's permission. I suppose I thought that he, as the principal guardian of the flame, would welcome the interest of a fellow Roussel enthusiast, or *roussellâtre* as they were called even during the master's lifetime. How could I have been so stupid as to forget that tenders of flames rarely feel the need of outside assistance? After a cordial hour, Leiris withdrew the pack of postcards and announced that they were the only Roussel documents in his possession. This proved to be false, and when I ran into him several years later, after the publication of a volume of Roussel's miscellanea called *Épaves* (Jetsam) that included several other previously unpublished texts from Leiris's collection, he said, 'But you know those were the last papers of his that I owned.'

Leiris did, however, give me the last address he had for 'Madame Dufrène', Roussel's sole companion, who had played the role of his mistress so as to shield his homosexuality from public knowledge. Eventually I was able to find her in 1960 at a public nursing home in Brussels, a far cry from the elegant flat near the Champs-Élysées she had occupied during Roussel's lifetime. During the course of several visits she told me of her platonic relationship with him and gave me a couple of photos – an elegant 'official' portrait of the supposed couple and a passport photo of Roussel. (Soon afterwards I mentioned her destitution to Leiris, who had her placed in a comfortable private residence where she lived till her death in 1968, aged eighty-eight.)

Meanwhile I had begun to pester everyone I could find who might have had a connection to Roussel, to the point where I became known (in the words of Paule Thévenin, a onetime friend of Antonin Artaud) as 'ce fou d'Américain qui s'intéresse à Raymond Roussel' – an indication of the state of Roussel's reputation at that time. Being American was, however, useful in at least one instance, since I was able to establish relations with Roussel's nephew and sole heir, Michel Ney, Duc d'Elchingen, who had hitherto refused to discuss his uncle with anyone, considering him the disgrace of the family. But an inquiry from America was welcomed, since it raised the prospect of possible revenue from Roussel's hitherto unsaleable writings.

In the early 1960s Roussel's stock began to rise. Michel Foucault's first book, a study of Roussel, was published in 1963. Alain Robbe-Grillet and Michel Butor, creators of the *nouveau roman*, acknowledged their debt to Roussel, and essays on him by Leiris, Breton and other Surrealists continued to appear. Michel Ney was now more than willing to talk about his uncle to anyone who would listen. He had remarried in the early 1960s and his new stepson, François Lorin, happened to be a writer who subsequently contributed an essay to a special Roussel number of the review *Bizarre*. Ney had, it seemed, kept nothing in the way of documents or mementos that might be of use to researchers. He did contribute recollections and some family photos to François Caradec's ground-breaking biography of Roussel which appeared in 1972. Meanwhile, Roussel's books were being reprinted by Pauvert, Gallimard and the Livres de Poche series. The Roussel revival was on, but the trail had grown cold. It seemed doubtful that any unpublished writings or further biographical materials would ever come to light. (I had meanwhile abandoned my project of a dissertation and returned to America for family reasons.)

Then in a *coup de théâtre* worthy of Roussel's play *La Poussière de soleils* (which deals, like so many of his works, with a search for hidden treasure), a trunk filled with boxes of manuscripts, letters, photographs and other memorabilia was discovered by accident in a Paris warehouse where it had been deposited shortly after Roussel's death, perhaps by Ney, and had been gathering dust ever since. The warehouse was itself moving house, and the trunk and its contents might well have been discarded had an alert workman not noticed a sumptuously bound volume of Roussel's great novel *Locus Solus*, in which he had specified that it be bequeathed to the Bibliothèque Nationale. The library was notified, and most of the trunk's contents are now in its possession in a specially created Fonds Roussel. (I couldn't help feeling pangs of jealousy – when I was attempting to do research there some thirty years before, the subject index of the card catalogue, consisting of handwritten fiches, had progressed only as far as the letter M and was therefore of limited use to someone investigating a writer whose name began with an R, not to mention the normal bureaucratic roadblocks seemingly set up on purpose to discourage scholars in that once antiquated but now futuristic institution.)

So, valuable new studies of this great and elusive writer are now being made. Publication of the thousands of newly discovered manuscript pages is proceeding, albeit at a snail's pace. Two enormously long, previously unknown early works have already appeared with the firm of Fayard/Pauvert. François Caradec, the grand master of *roussellâtres*, has published a new and vastly enlarged version of his earlier biography. And now Mark Ford has written the first major work on Roussel in English (Rayner Heppenstall's brief and cursory study of 1966 doesn't really count). It's to be hoped that out-of-print translations of the works will be reissued and new ones undertaken, so that a new generation of Anglophone readers can discover what the fuss (created by a small but energetic minority of Roussel freaks) is all about.

I have purposely avoided describing the work since Mark Ford has done it so brilliantly. In particular, his intensive analysis of Roussel's famous *procédé*, the gimmick at the core of his writing, sheds light not only on the passages where it was employed (in so far as they are known) but on his writing as a whole, and on its potential for writers to come. (It has already borne fruit in works of writers of the Oulipian group, most notably in major novels by Italo Calvino, Georges Perec and Harry Mathews.) Perhaps it's necessary only to add that readers proceed with caution: Cocteau was correct in noting something 'dangerous' in Roussel's writing, a 'charm' against which he had to build 'defenses'. Pierre Loti's writing was like a drug for Roussel, of which, he said, he had to have his daily dose. But Roussel's is far more addictive. Caveat lector.

# Acknowledgements

I would like to thank the Society of Authors for a grant from the Authors' Foundation, which materially assisted the completion of this book.

I am grateful also to Annie Angrémy for permission to consult the Roussel archive in the Bibliothèque Nationale in Paris, and to the staff of the library's Manuscript Department for their unfailing helpfulness and courtesy.

I received a great deal of encouragement and many useful suggestions from my editor at Faber, Julian Loose.

I would also like to thank John Ashbery, Kasia Boddy, Steve Clark, Harry Matthews, Neil Rennie, David Trotter and Trevor Winkfield for their support of this project, and their extremely useful comments on individual chapters.

All quotations from the writings of Raymond Roussel are reproduced by kind permission of Fayard/Pauvert, except for those from *Locus Solus*, which are reproduced by kind permission of Gallimard. Extracts from *Opium* by Jean Cocteau reproduced by kind permission of Peter Owen Ltd, London. Extracts from writings by George Perec: from *Life, A User's Manual*, first published in Great Britain in 1987 by The Harvill Press, copyright © Hachette, 1978, copyright © in the English translation David Bellos, 1987, reproduced by permission of The Harvill Press; from *W or the Memory of Childhood*, first published in France by Editions Denoël, in 1975, first published in Great Britain in 1988 by Harvill, © Editions Denoël, 1975, English translation © Harvill and David Godine, 1988, reproduced by permission of The Harvill Press.

# A Note on Conventions

For the sake of consistency, all translations from the French are my own, except where clearly stated.* Roussel's poetry is quoted in French and followed by a literal translation. His prose is, for the most part, given in English only. Citations are from the recent Pauvert/Fayard edition for works up to *Les Noces* (i.e., volume VI of the *3uvres*); references to later works are to the Jean-Jacques Pauvert edition that began appearing in 1963, except for *Locus Solus*, which is keyed to the 1963 Gallimard edition.

For quotations from works of Roussel that have been translated into English, source notes refer to both the page number of the French text and the page on which the passage cited appears in the English translation: for example, 'IA, p. 240/EIA, p. 245' indicates that the passage quoted is to be found on page 240 of the Pauvert edition of *Impressions d'Afrique* and page 245 of Foord and Heppenstall's translation, *Impressions of Africa*.

References to material in the Fonds Roussel include the archive category number and the folio page number (f). Recto and verso of pages are indicated, when used, by r and v. A list of the archive's contents is to be found in Appendix 1. References to material in the Fonds Rondel are cited by archive category number only, since the pagination of these albums of cuttings is too erratic to be worth giving. Details of this archive's contents are also given in Appendix 1.

Titles and the names of characters are throughout left in the original. Since there seem to be no fixed rules governing capitalization within French titles, I have used what seemed to me to be the most common forms of the titles cited. English

---

* The exceptions are quotations from texts readily available in English translation by authors such as Jules Verne, Georges Perec and Jean Cocteau.

versions of the titles of all Roussel texts to which I refer are given in the Index.

I would like here to express my debt to previous translators of Roussel, and in particular to John Ashbery, Rupert Copeland Cunningham, Lindy Foord and Rayner Heppenstall, Kenneth Koch, Harry Mathews, Antony Melville, Ron Padgett, Martin Sorrell and Trevor Winkfield.

# Abbreviations

## Works by Roussel

| | |
|---|---|
| CJ | *Comment j'ai écrit certains de mes livres* |
| EF | *L'Étoile au front* |
| EP | *Épaves* |
| IA | *Impressions d'Afrique* |
| LS | *Locus Solus* |
| NIA | *Nouvelles Impressions d'Afrique* |
| ŒI-VI | *3uvres* vols. I-VI |
| PS | *La Poussière de soleils* |
| FR | The Fonds Roussel in the Bibliothèque Nationale |
| FRD | The Fonds Rondel in the Bibliothèque Nationale de l'Arsenal |

## Translations of Roussel

| | |
|---|---|
| AB | *Among the Blacks* (trans. Ron Padgett) |
| AT7 | *Selections From Certain of His Books. Atlas Anthology 7* (ed. Alastair Brotchie) |
| EIA | *Impressions of Africa* (trans. Rayner Heppenstall and Lindy Foord) |
| ELS | *Locus Solus* (trans. Rupert Copeland Cunningham) |
| HIW | *How I Wrote Certain of My Books* (1995, ed. Trevor Winkfield) |
| HIW 77 | *How I Wrote Certain of My Books* (1977, ed. Trevor Winkfield) |

## Works by other writers

| | |
|---|---|
| AE | *De l'angoisse à l'extase* (Pierre Janet) |
| AT4 | *Raymond Roussel: Life, Death and Works. Atlas Anthology 4* (ed. Alastair Brotchie et al.) |

# ABBREVIATIONS

| | |
|---|---|
| BN | *Revue de la Bibliothèque Nationale* (Roussel special issue) |
| BZ | *Bizarre* (Roussel special issue) |
| CL | *Comment Lire Raymond Roussel* (Philippe Kerbellec) |
| DG | *Digraphe* (Roussel special issue) |
| DMD | *Dialogues with Marcel Duchamp* (Pierre Cabanne, trans. Ron Padgett) |
| FC | *Raymond Roussel* (François Caradec) |
| FRN | *Free Rein* (André Breton, trans. Michel Parmentier and Jacqueline d'Amboise) |
| MD | *The Essential Writings of Marcel Duchamp* (ed. Michel Sanouillet and Elmer Peterson) |
| MF | *Raymond Roussel* (Michel Foucault, trans. Charles Ruas) |
| O | *Opium* (Jean Cocteau, trans. Margaret Crosland) |
| OU | *Oulipo: A Primer of Potential Literature* (ed. and trans. Warren F. Motte Jr) |
| R & CO | *Roussel & Co.* (Michel Leiris) |
| RG | 'Énigmes et transparence chez Raymond Roussel' (Alain Robbe-Grillet) |
| SD | 'Raymond Roussel: *Nouvelles Impressions d'Afrique*' (Salvador Dalí) |
| SFL | *Sade/Fourier/Loyola* (Roland Barthes) |
| UE | *Une étude sur Raymond Roussel* (Jean Ferry) |
| VH | *Œuvres poétiques* (Victor Hugo) |
| VM | *Vingt mille lieues sous les mots, Raymond Roussel* (Annie Le Brun) |

# Introduction

While in Paris in the course of researching this book, I visited
a bookshop called the Librairie Colbert, which stocks the official
publications of the Bibliothèque Nationale. I wanted to buy a
copy of the 1992 issue of the *Revue de la Bibliothèque Nationale*
that contains an account of the discovery of Roussel's long-
lost manuscripts and essays by various Roussel scholars on the
literary significance of the find. I approached the young man on
duty that afternoon, whose somewhat supercilious appearance
conformed to my notion of a Parisian postgraduate eking out
his grant while completing his doctoral assault on the philosophy
of Derrida or Deleuze. I asked if he thought he might be able
to find me a copy of issue 42 of the *Revue de la Bibliothèque
Nationale*. 'Je suppose,' he answered with a shrug, and I followed him upstairs to the periodicals section. He extracted
number 42 from shelves of the *Revue* in question, and handed
it over with an expression of slightly disdainful puzzlement, as
if to say, 'What could anyone, let alone a non-French person,
want with such a dull publication?' It was the wrong number. I
checked my notes and asked for the following issue. As he
glanced at the photograph of the withdrawn, immaculately
dressed young man (inscribed 'ma photo à 18 ans') adorning
the cover of number 43, his face momentarily relaxed into
understanding. 'Ah . . . Roussel,' he murmured, almost conspira-
torially, and I felt like a neophyte who has just made his first
successful contact with another member of a secret order he has
recently joined.

'Ah . . . Roussel.' In many ways, that can seem the only appropriate response to this most peculiar of writers. Confronted with
a bottle-imp containing miniature figurines dramatizing a large
bird's attempt to strangle Alexander the Great with a golden
thread, or a bas-relief of a girl extracting from a cushion the
doll of a one-eyed dwarf dressed entirely in pink, or a skull

engraved with Old Norse runes sporting a lady barrister's cap made out of pages (themselves printed with runes) from *The Times*, it is difficult, at least initially, not to feel lost for words, in all senses of the phrase. For Roussel's own words are entirely self-sufficient, and require no gloss or explication. Although his vocabulary is at times dauntingly arcane, featuring sistrums and reiters and strange substances like erganasium or iradol, stylistically his work is lucidity itself. It contains no symbols, obscurities or metaphors that need to be explained. His French, as one of the actors who performed in *La Poussière de soleils* commented, is 'irréprochable'. Nor are his narratives fissured by telling gaps or ellipses, or complicated by suppressed details: on the contrary, all aspects of the given situation are presented with exemplary thoroughness. In his poetry we learn everything conceivable about an individual's dress, features, class, current activity and self-image, and in his prose we can rest assured that every element mentioned in the exposition will be shown to have a necessary function in the workings of the narrative. As Alain Robbe-Grillet noted in his 1963 essay on Roussel, his works are characterized by a 'total transparency, which leaves neither shadow nor reflection behind it'.

Roussel's 'transparency', however, as Robbe-Grillet goes on to argue, is of the sort that does not resolve mystery, but creates it. While Roussel's writings make perfect, irrefutable sense on their own distinctive terms, viewed as a whole they end up posing questions one hardly knows how to formulate. 'What he leaves us with', John Ashbery has suggested, 'is a work that is like the perfectly preserved temple of a cult which has disappeared without a trace, or a complicated set of tools whose use cannot be discovered.' Conversely, one can make – as critics such as Michel Foucault, Julia Kristeva, Maurice Blanchot and André Breton have – virtually whatever one likes of works that are at once rigorously self-explanatory and yet utterly reticent as to their ultimate motivation or *raison d'être*.

Until near the end of his life, Roussel himself expressed no doubts regarding the purpose and destiny of his poems, novels and plays: they were to win him fame of the sort enjoyed by Jules Verne and Pierre Loti, by Shakespeare, Victor Hugo, Wagner, Dante and Napoleon. Even his most fervent admirers accept that such predictions are unlikely to be fulfilled: Roussel's experience of *la gloire* pervades his entire *œuvre*, however, and is one of the main factors that make it difficult for critics comfortably to categorize his achievement in relation to the canons of European literature. 'N'est-ce rien? Est-ce tout?' inquired a bewildered contemporary critic: Is his work nothing? Is his work everything? What is clear is that it never accedes to a position between such poles: it acknowledges no relationship with the avant-garde movements with which it has been classified – indeed, seems to appeal to no literary criteria other than its own enigmatic but logical inner imperatives. In replying to Benjamin Péret's request for a dialogue on the subject of Surrealism, Roussel instructed his business manager to explain that 'il ne se classe lui-même dans aucune école' – he does not class himself in any school. Convinced that the exaltation he experienced while writing *La Doublure* constituted an overwhelming proof of his transcendent genius, Roussel could not countenance the thought of belonging to some movement, or even one historical moment.

Roussel's sense of election and singularity was a precondition of his writing. He turned to the Surrealists for support only after he had renounced his literary career and hoped merely for a little posthumous fame. Almost seventy years on, his reputation is still, in many ways, in the balance: although, as I show in my final chapter, Roussel's work had a decisive influence on a number of the twentieth century's most significant artists – Marcel Duchamp, John Ashbery, Georges Perec – he is still not much known outside France, and even there he has only relatively recently received the kind of attention and publication associated with canonical authors.

In this account of his life and writings I have set out to make as clear as possible the aesthetic appeal and implications of the *esprit rousselien*. The unearthing of Roussel's manuscripts has allowed me to explore the genesis of his most famous texts, *Impressions d'Afrique* (1910) and *Locus Solus* (1914), and to establish the scope and nature of the 'prospecting' which preceded the discovery of his unique compositional methods. These manuscripts have also enabled me to trace in greater detail the evolution of various crucial antitheses – poetry/prose, black/

white, male/female – which I suggest structure the development of Roussel's *œuvre*. Although this book does not attempt to be a 'comprehensive biography', where appropriate I have established connections between Roussel's attitudes to writing and to living: Roussel himself discusses the relationship – or rather absence of one – between his work and his travels in his only autobiographical text, 'Comment j'ai écrit certains de mes livres'. 'His life was constructed like his books,' Roussel's psychiatrist Pierre Janet told Michel Leiris soon after Roussel's death: it is my hope that this book manages to delineate the dominant patterns of Roussel's imagination in both spheres. Those interested in a more comprehensive account of Roussel's day-to-day existence, his travels and his family's social milieux should turn to François Caradec's superb biography *Raymond Roussel*, first published in 1972, updated and reissued in 1997. Caradec's book is something of a bible for enthusiasts, and my conception and presentation of Roussel are both greatly influenced by his pioneering researches. When we met in June 1999 he told me of various fresh trails he was exploring: these included a recently unfrozen Swiss bank account held in the name of Raymond Roussel, a projected limited edition of Roussel's brother Georges's poetry, and a mysterious uncle who appears to have been banished from the family after some unknown scandal but who, he conjectured, greatly influenced Raymond during his childhood.

Mine is only the second book ever written on Roussel in English. The first was by the novelist Rayner Heppenstall and was published in 1966. Although useful as far as it goes – it is less than 100 pages long – the book offers only a cursory introduction to the work. For reasons that remain unclear Heppenstall does not, as he acknowledges, 'feel bound to attempt any large critical assessment' of Roussel, who emerges as an engaging curiosity rather than an interesting writer. While it is difficult to calibrate the exact nature of the 'interest' possessed by Roussel's work, I have tried to explain why I and certain others have come to see him as one of the most exhilarating, entertaining and inspiring writers of the century.

In France, on the other hand, Roussel has been the subject of several book-length critical studies: the most important of these are Jean Ferry's *Une étude sur Raymond Roussel* (1953) and *L'Afrique des impressions* (1967), Michel Foucault's *Raymond Roussel* (1963), Sjef Houppermans's *Raymond Roussel: Écriture et désir* (1985), Philippe G. Kerbellec's *Comment Lire Raymond Roussel* (1988) and *Raymond Roussel: au cannibale affable* (1994) and Annie Le Brun's *Vingt mille lieues sous les mots, Raymond Roussel* (1994). Over the last thirty years there have been numerous special issues of magazines devoted to his work, a number of conferences and several collections of essays published by academic presses. When I visited the writer and Rousselian enthusiast Pierre Martory in Paris in 1996, he talked, not wholly approvingly, of the 'Roussel industry', an industry greatly boosted by the unsuspected appearance in 1989 of what became known as *la malle de Roussel* (Roussel's trunk), which included not only drafts of work in progress, fair copies and typescripts, but also a number of wholly new texts.

It was the emergence of this material which prompted Pauvert/Fayard to undertake their ongoing edition of Roussel's complete works; this will run to at least twelve volumes, and possibly many more. Here Roussel appears in full academic dress, re-edited, introduced, annotated, and with all significant textual variants noted in appendices. It is as yet unclear, however, to what extent this enterprise will help to create for Roussel a genuinely secure position in the canon; John Sturrock, for instance, in a recent essay on Roussel, argues it will merely 'ensure that his next relapse into obscurity is some years off'.

My own interest was first kindled by the American poet John Ashbery's two wonderful essays, 'Re-establishing Raymond Roussel' (1962) and 'In Darkest Language' (1967). Ashbery originally intended to write a doctoral thesis on Roussel, and in the early 1960s he assembled all the evidence then available on Roussel's life, publishing career and theatrical extravaganzas. This project was never completed, but Ashbery's miscellaneous writings on Roussel (see bibliography for full details) undoubtedly constitute the best introduction to his work in English. His enthusiasm, furthermore, inspired others associated with the New York School, such as Harry Mathews, Ron Padgett and Trevor Winkfield, to explore and translate Roussel's work. In 1977 Winkfield edited a compilation of extracts from Roussel's writings, *How I Wrote Certain of My Books*, which reprinted both of Ashbery's essays and included translations by himself, Kenneth Koch, Mathews and Ashbery. Eighteen years later he published an expanded version of this which contains additional translations by Ashbery and Mathews (but not Ashbery's second critical essay); it is with this quite widely available anthology that any Anglophone reader looking to initiate him or herself into the mysteries of the Rousselian should begin.

Despite the lucidity or transparency of Roussel's writing, his work does pose very particular problems for the translator. Versions in English tend to dilute the radical compression of his prose style, and inevitably cannot capture the 'poetic' effects of the puns underlying each episode. The first full-length Roussel text to appear in English was *Impressions d'Afrique* (as *Impressions of Africa*) in 1966, translated by Lindy Foord and Rayner Heppenstall; *Locus Solus* followed in 1970, in a superb version by Rupert Copeland Cunningham, and in 1987 Atlas Press issued a volume entitled *Selections from Certain of His Books* that included translations of his two plays, of his early long poem 'La Vue' and of his final, unfinished prose text *Documents pour servir de canevas* (1935).

Both Roussel's novels were published in Britain as part of a John Calder series called *French Surrealism*. As I hope I make clear in my discussion of Roussel's 'little posthumous fame', Surrealism was only one of a series of artistic movements eager to consider Roussel a significant precursor of its own innovations: nouveaux romanciers, pataphysicians, literary theorists and Oulipians have all claimed him as one of their own. Without question the single most influential and rewarding commentator on Roussel's work in French has been Michel Leiris, whose essays were collected first in *Roussel l'ingénu* (1987) and then in the expanded *Roussel & Co.* (1998), which contains, in addition to the five essays and interview that make up *Roussel l'ingénu*, a transcript of a notebook in which Leiris composed rough drafts of his articles on Roussel. Like Ashbery, Leiris planned to write a full-length study that was never completed, and his 'Cahier Raymond Roussel' contains many new facts and provocative lines of inquiry. I have, throughout this book, relied heavily on Leiris's anecdotes of his friend's habits and behaviour, and also on his analyses of Roussel's work. In my 'Coda' I briefly outline some of the ways in which his writings seem to have influenced Leiris's own.

Perhaps the major difficulty faced by all who have undertaken critical considerations of Roussel's work is its seemingly unassailable self-referentiality: to describe one of his novels, plays or poems, Ashbery once noted, 'is like trying to summarize the Manhattan telephone book'. I have assumed that most readers of this study will have little or no acquaintance with Roussel's *œuvre*, and I here apologize to *roussellâtres* who will find my expositions of various episodes from his fiction and drama redundant. However, I could find no way of conveying the extraordinary nature of Roussel's vision without presenting his inventions in some kind of detail. Ashbery is probably right to declare that the power of Roussel's writing is 'something that can be felt but not communicated'. Nevertheless, in the hope of rallying as many new faces to his cause as possible, I have at least tried to evoke the pleasures of immersion in his world: 'Then instantly, I abandoned myself, out of my depth, in the Gulf Stream of your fantasy,' wrote André Gide to Roussel on receiving *Pages choisies* (1918), a selection of extracts from his fiction. It is my hope that this book will induce readers in the twenty-first century to undertake this miraculous plunge.

However, and without intending to compromise his self-evident uniqueness, I have on occasions pointed up analogies between Roussel and other French writers such as Proust and the Marquis de Sade, particularly as presented by Roland Barthes in the essay collected in *Sade/Loyola/Fourrier* (1971). And while my focus has been principally on the patterning and symmetries created by Roussel's works, these are, where appropriate, located in a variety of social and cultural contexts: the Belle Époque and its collapse, the tradition of the dandy, the double life of the fin-de-siècle homosexual, the idealization of artistic genius as a form of displaced religion, the birth of Modernism, and the overwhelming fragmentations of the First World War.

My ambition above all, though, has been to make Roussel available to English readers: I determined to try to make him appear as a writer who is worth reading, rather than as an engaging exotic or an intriguing case history. I myself find the narrative of his career simultaneously sublime and ludicrous, heart-breaking and bewildering, outrageous in its innocence and logic. Yet there is also something dangerous about Roussel: Cocteau feared that over-exposure to his writings would place him 'under a spell from which I could see no escape', while Ashbery has argued that 'there is hidden in Roussel something so strong, so ominous and so pregnant with the darkness of the "infinite spaces" that frightened Pascal, that one feels the need for some sort of protective equipment when one reads him.' However well one knows *Locus Solus* or *Impressions d'Afrique*, they never lose their capacity to unnerve, never come to seem familiar: as I hope this study makes clear, it is in the uncanny distance the work establishes between writer and reader that the peculiar, addictive fascination of Roussel resides.

# CHAPTER I

# How He Wrote Certain of His Books

On 16 April 1932 Raymond Roussel delivered to his publishers
a short autobiographical essay entitled 'Comment j'ai écrit certains de mes livres'. An accompanying letter stipulated that this
text should be kept 'secret' until after the author's death. The
essay, Roussel's literary will and testament, was composed only
after he had abandoned his final and perhaps most ambitious
undertaking, the cycle of thirty radically compressed narratives
that would have constituted a prose equivalent to the labyrinthine poetics of *Nouvelles Impressions d'Afrique* (1932).
Roussel seems to have realized that he had reached the point of
no return, that the complexity of his methodology had evolved
in such a way as to make any new project he attempted unfin-
ishable. Nevertheless, he remained convinced that his methods
might yet prove valuable to others:

> I have always intended to explain the way in which I wrote
> certain of my books (*Impressions d'Afrique, Locus Solus,
> L'Étoile au front* and *La Poussière de soleils*). It involved a
> very special method [*procédé*]. And it seems to me that it
> is my duty to reveal this method, for I have the sense that
> writers in the future may perhaps be able to exploit it
> fruitfully.

At the heart of the *procédé* lies the pun. The first of Roussel's
writings to make use of his obsession with double meanings were
the stories he wrote in his early twenties such as 'Chiquenaude',
'Nanon' and 'Parmi les Noirs', which begin and end with phrases
that are identical except for a single letter, but where each major
word is used in a different sense. 'Parmi les Noirs', for example,
begins: 'Les lettres du blanc sur les bandes du vieux billard'
(The letters [as of the alphabet] in white [chalk] on the cushions
of the old billiard table), and concludes: 'les lettres du blanc sur
les bandes du vieux pillard' (the letters [i.e. missives] sent by the

white man about the hordes of the old plunderer). 'The two phrases found,' he comments, 'it was a question of writing a story that could begin with the first and end with the second.' 'Parmi les Noirs' opens with the narrator composing a crypto-gram on the cushions of a dilapidated billiard table as part of a country-house parlour game; this cryptogram in turn alludes to a novel by one of the guests concerning a white man held hostage in Africa who manages to send letters home to his wife by carrier pigeon. In these letters he relates the exploits of his aged captor and his plundering hordes.

'Now it was from the resolution of this problem', Roussel confides in 'Comment j'ai écrit . . .', 'that I drew all my materials.' The duplicity of language enacted in these early stories was gradually developed by Roussel into a variety of compositional techniques. Puns, Roussel discovered, enabled him to fuse narrative and language into an indivisible whole. In 'Comment j'ai écrit . . .' he reveals how the dazzling perform-ances and inventions of his novels and plays were generated by a systematic exploitation of linguistic duality:

> I would choose a word and then link it to another by the preposition *à*; and these two words, when considered in relation to meanings other than their initial meaning, supplied me with a further creation . . . I will cite some examples . . . 1st *baleine* (a whale) *à îlot* (a small island); 2nd *baleine* (corset whalebone) *à ilote** (a helot or Spartan slave); 1st *duel* (a combat between two people) *à accolade* (an embrace, as when two adversaries, reconciled after the duel, embrace each other); 2nd *duel* (the dual tense in a Greek verb) *à accolade* (typographical bracket); 1st *mou* (a feeble individual) *à raille* (here I thought of the raillery heaped on a lazy student by his comrades); 2nd *mou* (the culinary dish made from the lungs of a calf) *à rail* (railway line).

This particular set of homonyms resulted in one of Roussel's most notorious constructions: in the opening chapter of

---

* There was occasionally, Roussel informs us in a footnote, a slight difference in the spelling of the words he matched together.

*Impressions d'Afrique* (1910) he describes a life-sized statue of a Spartan slave – a helot – clutching at a sword plunged into his heart. The statue is fashioned out of black corset whalebones and is fixed to a trolley – also of corset whalebones – whose wheels rest on two red, gelatinous rails moulded out of prepared calves' lights; statue, trolley and rails are in turn mounted on a platform bearing the inscription DUAL, followed by a bracket and two forms of an ancient Greek verb. When a carefully trained magpie activates an internal spring with its beak, the platform slowly tilts and trolley and statue are set gently in motion.

This sculpture, we later learn, is the handiwork of Norbert Montalescot and his sister Louise, who has been imprisoned by the African king Talou VII for having had an affair with his chief enemy; her release depends on the Montalescots' completion of this and a number of other appallingly difficult tasks. We find out as well that the statue of the helot alludes to a story, supposedly to be found in Thucydides, in which a recalcitrant student-slave is required to learn, on pain of death, the conjugation of various auxiliary verbs. Called to the front of the class, he soon makes a gross mistake in the dual of the aorist and instantly suffers the threatened punishment.

This second order of word-play, making use of the linking properties of *à*, furnished the constituent elements of many of the episodes presented in *Impressions d'Afrique*, but a few originated in a third form of punning, based on the breakdown of haphazardly chosen scraps of language into assonantally related words:

> The *procédé* developed, and I was led to take a random
> phrase from which I would derive images by distorting it,
> a little as one might develop images while devising a rebus.

From 'Napoléon premier empereur', for instance, Roussel harvested the words *nappe ollé ombre miettes hampe air heure* (tablecloth olé shadow crumbs pole wind time). For the first four elements he devised a scene in which castanet-clicking dancers perform a lively flamenco on a fully laden table. This tableau is the work of the sculptor Fuxier, the inventor of certain chemical pastilles capable of shaping water into momentary reliefs; his liquid drawing is so detailed one can even discern the shadows cast by breadcrumbs on the tablecloth. The other three *objets trouvés* Roussel combined to form the wind-clock employed in the land of Cockaigne, where the orientation and strength of the prevailing breeze always matches the hours of the day; accordingly, a pennant attached to a flagpole allows inhabitants to tell the time by indicating the force and direction of the wind. This scene is also sculpted in water-relief by one of Fuxier's miraculous pastilles.

It is this more highly evolved form of the *procédé*, Roussel informs us in 'Comment j'ai écrit . . .', that generated the experiments and acquisitions displayed by Martial Canterel in *Locus Solus* (1914). Roussel claims to have forgotten the fragments underlying most of the novel's characters and events, but does reveal that he denatured phrases drawn from his own earlier writings. The examples he gives are all taken, appropriately enough, from a long early poem called 'La Source' (1904). He also makes clear how important it was for him that the reader should not guess that a method existed beneath the seeming madness. In the final chapter of *Locus Solus* the young fortune-teller Noel spins a die inscribed with three phrases: *l'ai-je eu?* (did I have it?), *l'ai-je* (do I have it?), and *l'aurai-je* (will I have it?). This prophetic die originated in the word *déluge*, which Roussel fragmented into *dé* (die) *l'eus-je* (did I have it?). In 'Comment j'ai écrit . . .' he explains how he deliberately exchanged the *passé simple* for the *passé composé*, fearing that *dé l'eus-je* might leave his secret too exposed to prying eyes.

Roussel developed the *procédé* only after many agonizing years of what he calls prospecting. 'This prospecting did not proceed without causing me torments,' he writes, 'and at times I used to roll on the floor in paroxysms of rage, feeling I would never attain the sensations of art for which I was striving.' The *procédé* appears to have satisfied Roussel's need for his writing to be linguistically self-fulfilling, like a solvable puzzle, and yet to disclose nothing of its purpose or origins; it allows a private compulsion to be gratified without having openly to declare itself. As Robbe-Grillet noted in his essay 'Énigmes et transparence chez Raymond Roussel', Roussel's inventions – like the *procédé* itself – lead nowhere beyond themselves: 'After the riddle always comes the explanation, and everything returns to its original order.' And yet – indeed, probably for precisely these reasons – for Roussel the discovery of the *procédé* was a decisive aesthetic and psychological triumph. 'At last,' he writes, 'when I was nearly thirty, I felt as though I had found my way.'

The *nouveau romancier* Michel Butor has argued that all of Roussel's writing 'is like Proust's, a search for lost time', and certainly the narratives generated by Roussel's linguistic distortions can be seen as fulfilling, on their much smaller scale, an analogous process of recovering what has been fragmented and dispersed. But whereas Proust's novel suggests such recoveries occur only at the whim of involuntary memory, Roussel's methods enact a more deliberate, though buried, programme of disruption and reintegration. Like an all-powerful catalyst, the *procédé* destabilizes language at the level of the word, while simultaneously requiring it to mobilize all available forces to accommodate the new combinations thrown up by the double entendres it exploits. A simple phrase, *maison à espagnolettes* (house with window fasteners), passed through the *procédé* becomes *maison* (royal dynasty) *à espagnolettes* (little Spanish girls), which in turn requires a complex narrative to unite the perilously distant elements – in this case involving identical Spanish twins shipwrecked on the coast of Africa, where they are each made pregnant by the local ruler, give birth simultaneously and thus both initiate a royal dynasty. A line of Victor Hugo's 'Napoléon II':

Eut reçu pour hochet la couronne de Rome

denatured by the more sophisticated version of the *procédé* yields *Ursule brochet lac Huronne drome (hippodrome)* (Ursula pike lake Huron drome (hippodrome)), and some of the characters and events of a tableau based on a fairy tale that includes a girl called Ursula and a pike that swims around Lake Huron 'like a horse loosed in a gigantic hippodrome'. While on one level the *procédé* reveals all words – or fragments of words – to have potential double meanings, on another it imposes on them the strictest possible laws of connection. In the texts themselves, the different levels never acknowledge each other, though they can be seen as engaged in a mutually beneficial, if eccentric, bargain: an anterior series of puns provides the contents of all Roussel's prose narratives, and as if in recompense the pun-words find within those narratives a perfectly impenetrable camouflage. While alive, Roussel consistently refused to expose the precise nature of the literary equation his *procédé*-inspired writings seek to resolve; only posthumously could he reveal the secret dislocations and restitutions that allowed him to experience the 'sensations of art' he so craved.

Although Roussel was willing to divulge how he wrote certain of his books, he drops only oblique hints as to why he developed such singular methods. He defines the *procédé* as 'essentially a poetic method' analogous to that of rhyme: 'In both cases there is unforeseen creation due to phonic combinations.' Like rhyme, the *procédé* is merely a compositional technique, and in itself no guarantee of artistic worth: 'For just as one can employ rhymes to compose good or bad verses, so one can use this method to produce good or bad works.' Nowhere in 'Comment j'ai écrit . . .' does he present the *procédé* to the reader as either a justification of his work or as a key to decoding symbolic truths deliberately hidden within the layers of his writing. Indeed, wholly characteristically, although the essay appears initially to explain everything, one eventually comes to realize that the revelations offered in it make Roussel's writing seem more rather than less problematic.

———

Roussel alludes in 'Comment j'ai écrit . . .' to some worksheets filed among his papers containing detailed explanations of the linguistic distortions from which he derived source material for his two plays, *L'Étoile au front* (first performed in 1924, published in 1925) and *La Poussière de soleils* (first performed in 1926, published in 1927); he also mentions a prose fragment 'written immediately after *Locus Solus* and interrupted by mobilization in 1914 which is mainly concerned with Voltaire and a site filled with fireflies; perhaps', he adds diffidently, 'this manuscript would be worth publishing.' Further, in referring to the first version of his final poem, *Nouvelles Impressions d'Afrique*, he suggests that 'if the manuscript could be retrieved from among my papers it might perhaps prove interesting, such as it is, at least to certain of my readers.' Yet although Roussel clearly signalled in this essay a wish that his draft papers and unfinished or rejected works be preserved and possibly published at some later date, by the time he came to leave Paris for Palermo on 1 June 1933, it seems he had lost interest in the fate of his vast store of manuscripts. On a number of earlier occasions Roussel had shown himself extremely solicitous about work in progress, depositing typescripts in various stages of completion with his financial adviser Eugène Leiris – father of the writer Michel Leiris – for safekeeping. Before his final departure Roussel tidied up many personal affairs and even drew up a new will, but he left no instructions relating to the thousands of pages of rough drafts, fair copies and proofs left behind in the apartment he occupied in the family house on the rue Quentin-Bauchart. Boxed up and placed in storage in a furniture warehouse, these papers were only disinterred when the removal company itself moved premises in 1989.

A few miscellaneous items had in the intervening years trickled into the public domain. John Ashbery tracked down an episode entitled 'À la Havane' intended to introduce the thirty stories which were to make up Roussel's final novel. In the event Roussel completed – or partially completed – only six of these, which he included in the posthumous collection of writings (*Comment j'ai écrit certains de mes livres* (1935)) that he arranged to have published after his death. To make clear to the reader that these stories are unfinished, he allotted them the general title *Documents pour servir de canevas*. 'À la Havane' appeared in the magazine *L'Arc* in 1962, and two years later a special issue of *Bizarre* featured another short, unfinished prose work entitled *Flio*, written in 1914. *Flio* was discovered by Michel Leiris in his father's archives, where he also came across four typed pages of a version of the first canto of *Nouvelles Impressions d'Afrique*, entrusted by Roussel to his father on 6 March 1917; this was published in facsimile in 1968. These discoveries were gathered in a 1972 anthology called *Épaves*, which also collected Roussel's instructions for the fifty-nine illustrations that interleave the text of *Nouvelles Impressions d'Afrique*, several versions of Pierre Frondaie's theatrical adaptation of *Locus Solus*, and the role of one of the actors who performed in the 1912 stage play of *Impressions d'Afrique*.

The nine cartons discovered in the warehouse of the Société Bedel contained a heterogeneous mass of material: hundreds of photographs of the Roussel family at home and abroad; letters received from over 250 correspondents, ranging from illustrious admirers such as Robert Desnos and André Gide to impoverished supplicants eager to enjoy Roussel's legendary largesse; quantities of documents concerning his properties, his expenses, his travels and his ruinously costly theatrical ventures; the diary of a trip Roussel made to Egypt in 1906; a notebook recording the exact wording of the dedications inscribed in the hundreds of complimentary volumes that he sent to his entire acquaintance, or anyone he thought might be prevailed upon to read his work; press clippings, self-promoting publicity handouts, sumptuously bound copies of his own books. Before this sudden windfall, much of Roussel's life had been shrouded in mystery or myth; there now exists a vast archive of evidence pertaining to his financial affairs, his social activities and his extensive travels.

As I began to sift through this vast collection, which has recently become available on microfilm, I felt curiously divided: surely somewhere here there lurks, I found myself thinking, a decisive clue to the Rousselian enigma, the equivalent of *Citizen Kane*'s Rosebud; yet equally I feared that if there were, it might possibly strip him of the intriguing power of his reticence. Having engineered one posthumous revelation that had conclusively altered the way his fiction and plays are read, perhaps somewhere within these pages he had secreted another that would complicate his texts yet further, and translate the experience of reading them on to some hitherto wholly unsuspected plane. Would there be anguished marginalia, memos in which he questioned his entire enterprise, mutilated drafts testifying to the agony of prospecting? Would he emerge as less peculiar, or as racked by self-doubt? Would there be details of intimacies, or perhaps evidence of his having fallen in love with one of the sailors or stable boys or chauffeurs who found him so easy to blackmail?

No, I soon discovered, was the answer to all such questions.

If Roussel ever confided his feelings or details of his private life to paper, then he took care such evidence should not survive. Even the most seemingly promising items found in the nine cartons proved stubbornly unilluminating: one might have presumed, for instance, that the journal of his travels in Egypt would provide some insights into Roussel's inner consciousness, his subjectivity. It consists, however, merely of factual jottings and itineraries, even though, as I will argue in a later chapter, this trip was of paramount significance to his imaginative development.

But while the discovery of these papers could not be said to have expanded in any crucial way our understanding of Roussel as a person, it has decisively altered the configurations of his *œuvre*: the majority of the thousands of pages that now make up the Fonds Roussel are drafts, manuscripts, typescripts and proofs dating from nearly all periods of his literary career. They include a version of *Locus Solus* twice as long as the one Roussel eventually chose to publish, a number of very different drafts of *Impressions d'Afrique* and Roussel's own adaptation of the novel for the stage. As promised in 'Comment j'ai écrit...', the prose fragment 'mainly concerned with Voltaire and a site filled with fireflies' was indeed preserved among his papers, under the title *L'Allée aux lucioles*, but not the first version of *Nouvelles Impressions d'Afrique* also mentioned in the essay, nor the worksheets relating to the composition of his two plays. In fact, very few worksheets of this kind survive, and it is undoubtedly the early part of Roussel's career, before he 'found his way' around the age of thirty, that has been most radically reshaped by the recovery of his working papers.

The two most startling additions to the Roussel canon derive from his years of 'prospecting'. The first, *La Seine*, composed between 1900 and 1903, is a huge, sprawling verse play almost 7,000 lines long and offering some 500 speaking parts. The second, *Les Noces*, also written during Roussel's twenties, is even more ambitious, a tripartite poem that runs to over 20,000 lines and even so is still very far from finished. It is odd that Roussel mentions neither of these Herculean feats of composition in 'Comment j'ai écrit...', nor a number of other incomplete poems, especially one begun in 1906 and set in the bazaar at Minieh that clearly anticipates the Egyptian settings of *Nouvelles Impressions d'Afrique*.

These early manuscripts offer particularly interesting insights into Roussel's methods of writing verse. Many drafts consist of merely a few scattered words per line which form a sort of skeleton for the poem, to be fleshed out at a later stage. Pages and pages of *Les Noces* offer simply a list of rhyme words jotted down the right hand margin. It is difficult to tell to what extent these rhyme words may have functioned as a means of determining the poem's contents, as the *procédé* determined the given elements of his prose narratives. Michel Leiris has argued that 'rhyme never played for Roussel the role of a catalyst the way puns did; for, if one examines the texture of his works in verse, it's impossible to see how rhyme could have served him as a driving force.' On the other hand, the manuscripts do conclusively show that Roussel used rhyme as the crucial first stage in originating his poetry.

What does emerge with absolute clarity from a general consideration of Roussel's manuscripts is the single-minded, almost fanatical nature of his quest for those 'sensations of art' that were the goal of his prospecting. The surviving manuscripts of *Nouvelles Impressions d'Afrique*, for example, present an almost illegible morass of erasures and revisions. 'It is, truly, difficult to grasp the immense amount of time demanded by composition of this kind of verse,' he informs us in 'Comment j'ai écrit . . .'; he even went so far as to calculate that each line cost him fifteen hours of hard labour and the poem as a whole seven years of intensive work. Roussel's manuscripts reveal as dramatically as those of, say, Proust or Joyce or Flaubert his obsessive drive for perfection, although the criteria by which Roussel judged the difference between his 'good and bad works' remain, despite so much primary evidence, difficult to gauge. One wonders, for instance, exactly why the business of perfecting the first version of *Nouvelles Impressions d'Afrique* proved as impossible as he describes it in 'Comment j'ai écrit . . .': 'The initial work completed, I returned to the beginning to polish up the verses. But after a certain time I realized that an entire lifetime would not be sufficient for this polishing, and I abandoned my task. In all it had cost me five years' labour.' The manuscripts of *La*

*Seine* and *Les Noces* offer no indications as to why they too were abandoned after so much effort. The case of *L'Allée aux lucioles* is equally puzzling: Roussel tells us that his work on it was interrupted by his call-up for the First World War, but he also makes clear later in the essay that he was writing again by the winter of the following year, only this time poetry rather than prose.

———

Roussel's extensively illustrated explanations of the *procédé* take up well over half of the essay 'Comment j'ai écrit certains de mes livres'. There follow six much shorter sections in which he briefly discusses what he felt to be the most significant aspects of his personal, social and literary life. The first of these concerns Roussel's sudden recognition of his destiny:

> I would like to draw your attention to a curious crisis which I underwent when I was nineteen, while I was writing *La Doublure*. For several months I experienced an extraordinarily intense sensation of universal glory. Doctor Pierre Janet, who has attended me for many years, has described this crisis in the first volume of his work *De l'angoisse à l'extase* (page 132 and following); there I am designated by the name Martial, chosen because of Martial Canterel in *Locus Solus*.

It is not clear exactly when Roussel began visiting the psychologist Pierre Janet,* but it was almost certainly not at the time of this crisis. It seems more likely that their consultations began in the years immediately preceding the First World War. In his diagnosis of Roussel's case in *De l'angoisse à l'extase* (1926), Janet has no doubts that this crisis was the decisive

* Janet (1859–1947) was a highly respected psychologist. He published a number of books on nervous disorders, and his work was referred to on several occasions by Freud. Interestingly, neither Janet nor Freud could take the work of the Surrealists seriously. Janet considered them self-indulgent obsessives, while Breton found himself wholly unable to convince Freud of the value of the movement's productions. For an account of Breton's abortive meeting with Freud, see Mark Polizzotti's *Revolution of the Mind: The Life of André Breton* (New York: Farrar Straus & Giroux, 1995), pp. 161–3.

event in Roussel's psychological history: it was the 'disorder' in which all his later depressions and obsessions had their origin. Janet's case history of Roussel attempts to prove that he suffered, like the other patients discussed in his book, a displaced form of religious mania. Janet argues that Roussel's misguided conviction of his literary genius can be seen as analogous to the holy ecstasies of the saints:

> Martial, a young neuropath who is timid, scrupulous and easily depressed, suffered, for five or six months when he was nineteen, from a mental condition that even he considers extraordinary. Taking up literature, which he preferred to the other studies he had pursued up to that point, he undertook to write a great work in verse which he wanted to complete before he reached the age of twenty. Since this poem was to consist of several thousand verses, he worked assiduously, in fact almost without stopping, by day and by night, and without feeling the least symptoms of tiredness. He realized he was being gradually overwhelmed by a strange rapture: 'One understands by some peculiar means that one is creating a masterpiece, that one is a prodigy; there are child prodigies who have revealed their genius at the age of eight – I was revealing mine at the age of nineteen. I was the equal of Dante and of Shakespeare, I was feeling what Victor Hugo had felt when he was seventy, what Napoleon had felt in 1811 and what Tannhäuser had felt while musing on Venusberg:* I experienced *la gloire* . . . No, *la gloire* is not an idea, or something one derives from hearing one's name constantly on the lips of strangers. No, it is not a question of knowing the value of your work, or of knowing that you deserve glory. I was not experiencing the need or the desire for glory, since I had never even considered such

---

* In Wagner's opera *Tannhäuser* (1845), the knightly minstrel Tannhäuser spends a year with Venus, the goddess of love, in Venusberg. In Act II he returns to earth, but under Venus's influence, extols the wonders of his sojourn with her, to the annoyance of all present except the heroine, the faithful Elizabeth. In the course of describing his loss of the sensation of *la gloire*, Roussel again compares himself with Wagner's hero: 'I am Tannhäuser looking back on Venusberg' (cj, p. 131/AT4, p. 41).

matters before. This glory was a fact, an established fact, a sensation, *j'avais la gloire* . . . Whatever I wrote was surrounded by rays of light; I used to close the curtains, for I was afraid that the shining rays emanating from my pen might escape into the outside world through even the smallest chink; I wanted suddenly to throw back the screen and light up the world. To leave these papers lying about would have sent out rays of light as far as China, and the desperate crowd would have flung themselves upon my house. But it was in vain I took such precautions, for rays of light were streaming from me and through the walls, I was carrying the sun within myself and could do nothing to impede the tremendous light I was radiating. Each line was repeated in thousands of copies, and I wrote with a thousand flaming pen-nibs. Without a doubt, when the volume appeared, this blinding furnace would be revealed and would illuminate the entire universe, but what no one would believe was that I was carrying it all along within myself . . . I was at that moment in a state of unheard-of bliss, a single blow of the pickaxe had opened up an entire seam of marvels, I had won the most dazzling first prize. I lived more during that time than in any other period of my existence.'

It is perhaps the naïvety of Roussel's vision which is most striking. He never seems to have considered his ecstasy as symptomatic of inner anxieties or as a phase in his personal or literary development; indeed, a phase of a sort not wholly uncommon in nineteenth- and twentieth-century French literature – one thinks of Flaubert's *Saint Antoine* or Georges Bataille's post-war religious mania. 'He was a positivist,' Michel Leiris commented in an interview in 1986, 'and he suffered for it.' The literalness of Roussel's revelation meant he could never be content with a merely conceptual ideal, or a mere figure of power such as Nietschze's Übermensch or Wallace Stevens's Major Man. 'This glory bursts forth,' he told Janet, 'rays of light stream from one's pen, one's paper, from one's whole person.' It was as self-fulfilling physical facts that he experienced his glory and his genius, and it was in physical terms that he experienced his disappointment at the book's failure.

> When *La Doublure* appeared on 10 June 1897, its lack of success shattered me. I felt as though I had plummeted to earth from the prodigious heights of glory. The shock brought me out in a kind of skin disease, which took the form of a rash covering my entire body; my mother, who believed I had measles, had me examined by our doctor. This shock resulted, most crucially, in my developing a dreadful nervous illness, from which I suffered for many years.

Roussel's exalted vision of the all-conquering glory of the elect permeates many of his writings. The title of his first prose play, for instance, *L'Étoile au front* refers to an apocryphal book called *The Predestined* by one Boissenin, a psychographer, whose central poetic image, as the collector Joussac explains, is that of 'the star on the forehead'. According to Boissenin, this sign of genius 'cannot be acquired' during life; only a rare few are born with it. This star on the forehead is

> the sublime mark of the great creators in all the various branches of the arts. Unwavering in his belief that divine and all-powerful innate gifts are distributed randomly, he shows the odd manner in which, throughout the ages and from top to bottom of the social scale, these stars have been allocated. He compares numerous wonderful careers accomplished against the odds with the wretched achievements of mediocrities who happen to have the wind in their sails! Here, one of the elect, misunderstood by all around him – who try to defeat him by starving him – defies misery to attain his goal; there, another, who could have lived an idle life, gives to the world a strange example of relentless hard work and manly fortitude.

The immensely wealthy, furiously industrious Roussel seems to be rather pointedly referring to the circumstances of his own quest for renown in this final example. It is the same thirst for glory that motivates the exceptionally gifted virtuosi of *Impressions d'Afrique*, who form a club called the Incomparables and adopt for their symbol the image of an effulgent sun radiating golden beams in all directions. In *Locus Solus* Roussel creates a more literal embodiment of pure incandescence, a vast diamond-shaped receptacle (two metres high by three metres wide) which, when filled with the diversely-propertied *aqua micans*, emits 'an almost unbearable brightness, flashing like lightning in all directions.' Oddly, *La Doublure* (1897) itself, during the composition of which he experienced his overwhelmingly intense epiphany, is a minutely realist account of a series of professional and amorous failures suffered by a talentless theatrical understudy; like a number of his unfinished early poems, it tells a seedy story of desertion and betrayal. At no point does it reflect the blinding revelations that dazzled its young author, indeed proved the apogee of his existence. 'Ah!' Janet records Roussel brooding, 'that sensation of moral sunlight, I have never been able to recover it. I seek it always and I will seek it for ever. I would give all my remaining years of life to relive one instant of that glory.'

*De l'angoisse à l'extase* contains a number of discussions and illustrations of Roussel's psychopathology. There is no indication of exactly when Janet recorded the statements he attributes to Roussel. In Volume I he presents his 'poor little invalid' as forty-five, while in Volume II – in which he describes Roussel's obsession with the laxity of modern dress codes – the patient is five years younger. However, Roussel's decision to reprint the pages Janet devotes to his condition in Volume I of his book in the *Citations documentaires* section of his final collection of miscellaneous writings suggests that he remained to the end unembarrassed by the extravagant predictions he made to Janet about his literary career:

I shall reach immense heights and I am destined for blazing
glory. It may take a long time, but I shall enjoy greater
glory than Victor Hugo or Napoleon. Wagner died twenty-
five years too soon and never knew his own glory, but I
hope to live long enough to contemplate my own . . . There
lies within me a glory of immense force, as in a powerful
shell that has not yet exploded . . . This glory will be evident
in every one of my works, and will reflect on all the acts

of my life; people will research all the acts of my childhood and admire the way I played prisoners' base. No author has been, or can ever be greater than I, although no one is aware of this yet today. Well, what can one expect – there are some shells which explode with great difficulty, but when they do explode! . . . Whatever you may think, there are some who are predestined! As the poet says: *et voilà qu'on se sent une brûlure au front . . . L'étoile que l'on porte au front resplendissante*. (And there are those who feel a burning on their forehead . . . The star which they carry on their shining brow.) Yes, I have felt that I too carry a star on my forehead, and I will never forget it.

———

Roussel lavished on a number of authors whom he believed to be similarly 'predestined' exactly the sort of fervent, unconditional admiration he was convinced that he would one day receive himself. The two writers he worshipped most passionately were Pierre Loti and Jules Verne. The dedications inscribed in the volumes of his own work that he dispatched as humble offerings to the godlike Loti fully testify to his veneration. According to the catalogue he kept of these inscriptions, in *Locus Solus* he wrote: 'To Pierre Loti, to the superman whose name one should not even pronounce except on one's knees, immeasurably fanatical homage.' In a postscript Roussel adds: 'I am as addicted to the pages of Loti as a morphine addict to morphine, I *must* have my ration of Loti each day.' On the title page of his 1918 selection of writings, *Pages choisies*, he records having written: 'Offered, on bended knee, to Mata Reva' (Loti's Tahitian name in *Le Mariage de Loti* (1880)). But Roussel also sensed that he shared with Loti a deeper affinity. After his return from the pilgrimage, as he liked to call it, that he made to Tahiti in 1920 Roussel wrote to Loti's secretary, Gaston Mauberger, with a very special request:

You who have the great happiness of being able to approach the Master, would it be possible for you to ask Him a question to which I attach enormous psychological significance? What I would like to know is if Monsieur

Pierre Loti, towards the age of nineteen or twenty, when he began to write and discovered that he was endowed with genius, if he did not experience, during a short period of several months, a sensation of universal radiant glory as intense as that he perhaps experiences today, when he has reached such a prodigious peak. It would have been a purely interior sensation and one doubtless followed by a terrible disappointment when, on the publication of his first writings, the public did not immediately realize that he had been born a great poet. I think that the Master will be able to respond very categorically, for, if the answer is in the affirmative, this sensation must have left immeasurably profound traces in his memory.

Mauberger's reply does not survive, but it seems unlikely he was able to confirm that the *maître* had experienced a delirium exactly equivalent to Roussel's own.

Despite the gifts he showered on Loti and his family, Roussel never managed to meet his idol in person. He did, however, seize the opportunity when it was offered to pay court to the writer he adored above all others. During his military service, which began in 1898, Roussel was posted to an infantry regiment based in Amiens, where, as he records in the short section of 'Comment j'ai écrit . . .' devoted to Jules Verne, he was able to visit his hero and 'shake the hand that had written so many immortal works.' Verne, he here asserts, 'raised himself to the highest peaks that can be attained by human language . . . O incomparable master, may you be blessed for the sublime hours which I have spent throughout my life endlessly reading and rereading your works.' Roussel was undoubtedly aware of the linguistic games secreted within Verne's fictions,* and which in turn surely influenced his development of the *procédé*. His passion for Verne was such that he could not bear to hear his name mentioned in public. In 1921 Eugène Leiris – who died later in the year – underwent a serious operation, and asked

---

* For discussion of Verne's cryptograms and language machines, see Marcel Moré, *Le Très Curieux Jules Verne* (Paris: Gallimard, 1960) and Andrew Martin's *The Mask of the Prophet: The Extraordinary Fictions of Jules Verne* (Oxford: Oxford University Press, 1990).

Roussel if he could borrow a Jules Verne novel to read during his convalescence. Roussel replied:

> Ask of me my life, but do not ask me to lend you a Jules Verne! I have such enthusiasm for his works that I am 'jealous' of them. If you reread them, I beg you never to speak of them, never even to pronounce his name in front of me, for it seems to me a sacrilege to pronounce his name except on one's knees. It is He who is, and by a long way, *the greatest literary genius of all time*; he will 'remain' when all the other authors of our time will be long forgotten. It is, furthermore, as monstrous to make children read him as to make them learn the Fables of Fontaine; they are so profound that very few adults are yet fit to appreciate them.

The jealous nature of Roussel's love for his preferred authors was reflected in his idiosyncratic reading habits: he liked to tear out the pages of a favourite book, so that no one could tell what he was reading, and then have his chauffeur drive him through the countryside while he pored over a specially chosen episode of Verne or Loti or Victor Hugo in the back seat.

━━━━━

In his discussion of Roussel's case, Pierre Janet pays little attention to Roussel's writings, which he appears to have considered important only as a symptom of his patient's monomania. 'These literary works,' he remarks, 'whose worth I am not qualified to investigate, have so far had virtually no success; if one sets aside certain initiates [i.e. the Surrealists, much despised by Janet] who are interested in them, they are unread, and considered insignificant.' Janet does, however, refer on a couple of occasions to the peculiarity of Roussel's aesthetic theories. 'Martial has a very interesting conception of literary beauty,' he recounts. 'The work must contain nothing real, no observations on the world or the mind, nothing but completely imaginary combinations.' He also quotes, in Volume II of his study, Roussel's own justification of his literary methods: ' "If there was anything real in those descriptions," Martial said, "it would be ugly." '

In the paragraph on his travels that follows his encomium on

Jules Verne, Roussel explicitly directs our attention to the strict separation that he sought to maintain between his life and his writings:

> It is also important that I mention here a rather curious fact. I have travelled a great deal. Notably, in 1920–21, I travelled around the world by way of India, Australia, New Zealand, the Pacific archipelagos, China, Japan and America. (In the course of this voyage I stopped for a while in Tahiti, where I met up with several of the original characters featured in Pierre Loti's wonderful book.) I already knew the principal countries of Europe, Egypt and all of North Africa, and later I visited Constantinople, Asia Minor and Persia. Now, from all these travels I never took a single thing for my books. It seems to me that this is worth pointing out, since it illustrates so clearly how everything in my works derives from the imagination.

The absolute distinction Roussel makes here between imaginative and physical worlds can be seen as informing both his punctiliously regulated behaviour and his meticulously organized *œuvre*. In 'Conception et réalité chez Raymond Roussel' Michel Leiris detailed some of the strategies with which this late and extreme embodiment of the fastidious dandy attempted to screen out or neutralize the anxieties of living. Convinced that eating would spoil his 'serenity', he fasted for days on end. At social events he became so afraid of causing offence, or of himself being offended, that he would pre-empt all potentially upsetting topics by asking an endless series of factual questions. For a period tunnels caused him extreme anguish, and he avoided travelling at night for fear of entering one unawares. He wore his collars only once, his neckties three times, and a suit, an overcoat and suspenders fifteen times. His writing routines were just as disciplined: Roussel began and ended his daily stints on the hour, like an office worker.

'Everything that is new disturbs me,' he told Janet, and his travels were certainly not undertaken in the anticipation that foreign countries might offer him opportunities for original or unlikely experiences. Roussel seems to have viewed Tahiti, for instance, wholly through the filter of *Le Mariage de Loti*. On arrival in Papeete he dispatched to his hero a bouquet of flowers and a postcard explaining their provenance:

Dear Master,
I send you these flowers picked from the bank of the stream of Fataoua by a pious pilgrim come to this delightful island to kiss the traces left by your footprints here.
Papeete, 1st October 1920.
    Raymond Roussel

As noted in 'Comment j'ai écrit . . .', Roussel at once set about tracking down all surviving originals of the characters featured in Loti's book. He even initiated a friendship with the Tahitian royal family: direct descendants of the Pomare V whom Loti had met over forty years earlier, they held for Roussel a special fascination, and he remained in contact with them for the rest of his life.

Roussel's principled exclusion of his travels from his own writings did not prevent him from responding to the countries he visited very much in terms of his personal literary and artistic interests. 'Here I am in Baghdad,' he announces on a postcard written during his 1927 trip to the Middle East, 'the country of 1001 nights and Ali-Baba, which reminds me of Lecocq [composer of the operetta *Ali-Baba*]; the people wear costumes even more extraordinary than those of the chorus at the Gaîté [a Parisian theatre].' 'Here I am in Constantinople,' he exclaims in another, 'and I have already gathered a plant from the tomb of . . . you know who.' 'You know who' was Aziyadé, the eponymous heroine of Loti's account of his adventures in Turkey. As Michel Leiris points out in an essay on Roussel entitled 'Le voyageur et son ombre,' published in 1935:

Roussel never really travelled . . . It seems likely that the outside world never broke through into the universe he carried within him, and that, in all the countries he visited, he saw only what he had put there in advance, elements which corresponded absolutely with that universe that was peculiar to him . . . He valued the imaginary above all else, and seems to have experienced a much stronger attraction for everything that was theatrical, trompe-l'oeil, illusionary, than for Reality.

———

Despite his insistence on the unbridgeable gulf between his life and his work, Roussel decided to include in 'Comment j'ai écrit...' some 'brief biographical notes' that are perhaps best treated as a sort of enigmatic grid – like those one so often finds in his novels and plays – designed to provide the initial clue to the complex lineaments of the Rousselian. Though he chronicles an almost unbroken sequence of failures and disappointments, reading between the lines of his clipped, elliptical prose one realizes that Roussel is here staking one final claim to the glory his contemporaries so unaccountably refused him.

Roussel first draws our attention to the brilliance of his family connections: his sister Germaine made two noble marriages, firstly to Charles le Tonnelier, Count of Breteuil, and then, after his death, to Charles Ney, Duke of Elchingen and later Prince of Moscow. In the event, Germaine's second marriage proved an unhappy one, and the couple separated, though not before Germaine had given birth to a son, Michel Ney, Roussel's nephew and sole heir. Roussel was immensely proud of his links to Germaine's estranged husband, and once told Michel Leiris that he wished to be buried under a plain marble slab covering ten normal-sized plots and bearing the simple inscription: Raymond Roussel, Brother-in-law of the Prince of Moscow. In 'Comment j'ai écrit...' – written several years after Germaine's death – Roussel dilates at length on Ney's links with the main families of the Empire. The respect was not mutual: Roussel had long been something of an embarrassment to his relatives, who seem never to have taken his literary ambitions seriously. According to Michel Ney, the family deeply resented the loss of face caused by his literary and theatrical disasters. Ney himself, who inherited the rights to all Roussel's publications, made no effort to further his uncle's reputation after his death, indeed for a time refused to allow his work to be reprinted. Ney agreed to Pauvert's plans for a complete edition in the early 1960s only after he had been persuaded that he might thereby recoup a slice of his squandered inheritance. While discussing this new edition with John Ashbery, he asked if it were possible Roussel might become as popular as Françoise Sagan. 'Pourquoi pas?' Ashbery deftly responded.

From *L'Étoile au front* on, Roussel had printed in the front of each of his new books a *cahier de citations* that included every scrap of praise, however lukewarm or ambiguous, garnered by his previous works. It is only in 'Comment j'ai écrit . . .' that he finally abandons the fiction that his books might achieve for him during his lifetime the universal glory for which he yearned. Instead, he presents himself as a neglected, misunderstood genius. Of his first novel he observes: '*Impressions d'Afrique* appeared as a serial in the *Gaulois du Dimanche* and went completely unnoticed. Likewise, when this work appeared in the bookshops, no one paid any attention to it.' *Locus Solus* fared, according to Roussel, no better: the serial passed 'completely unremarked', while of its sales as a novel he tersely pronounces in an isolated paragraph: 'In the bookshops, nothing.' Now in fact both *Impressions d'Afrique* and *Locus Solus* eventually received quite extensive and favourable coverage, as Roussel's own compilations of reviews abundantly testify: they range from comments by leading literary figures, such as André Gide, Edmond Rostand, Robert Desnos, André Breton, Robert de Montesquiou and Édouard Dujardin, to the intrigued, if somewhat baffled, responses of many of the leading reviewers of the day. Not everyone greeted Roussel's gifts in the exalted terms in which he hailed those of Loti and Verne, but his two novels by no means 'passed unremarked.'

Roussel's idea of success, however, greatly differed from that of writers such as Gide, Breton or Desnos. He had no interest in being a *succès d'estime*, or belonging to an artistic avant-garde. 'Why aren't I as famous as Loti?' he lamented in 1928 to Jean Cocteau, whom he met in the Saint-Cloud clinic, where both were undergoing detoxification. He tried to measure the impact of even his most rebarbative texts on the boulevards and in the music halls. His early poem, 'La Vue', for instance, consists of a sixty-page description of a tiny picture of a beach-scene set into the lens of a pen-holder, and eventually proved a crucial influence on the development of the nouveau roman –

indeed, Alain Robbe-Grillet initially intended to call his early novel, *Le Voyeur* (1955) by the title *La Vue*, in homage to Roussel.

In 'Comment j'ai écrit . . .' Roussel greatly prides himself on a possible reference to his poem in the *Sire de Vergy*, 'an operetta then playing at the Variétés; one of the characters, I forget which, studied, in a penholder which Eve La Vallière [a well-known actress of the time] was using, a view depicting the Battle of Tolbiac.' Though battered by the storms of derision provoked by the theatrical version of *Locus Solus*, Roussel was at least guaranteed his fifteen minutes of fame, even if only as the butt of vaudeville jokes:

> The affair created an immense stir, and overnight I became famous. But, far from being a success, it became a scandal. For apart from the small group of supporters [the Surrealists] whom I have mentioned, everyone else was united against me . . . I was once again called a lunatic and a hoaxer; all the critics expostulated indignantly. But at least one goal had been achieved: the title of one of my works became celebrated. Every variety show that year included a *Locus Solus* sketch, and the titles of two shows took their inspiration from mine: *Cocus Solus* (which, more successful than my play, its precursor, ran for more than a hundred performances) and *Blocus Solus ou les bâtons dans les Ruhrs*.

How much comfort Roussel drew from the vociferous support of the Surrealists is less easy to judge. 'People say I'm a Dadaist,' he remarked to Michel Leiris, 'but I don't even know what Dadaism is!' In 1927 Philippe Soupault wrote to Roussel offering to publish his next work at Kra, the small radical publishing house of which he was a literary editor. 'I feel that your work', Soupault wrote, 'ought to be on the list of a modern house that publishes real literature, of the kind I am trying to create. Are you absolutely committed to Lemerre as your editor? It seems to me that by publishing with a young and lively editor you would find a new public, closer to you and your work.' Roussel was not tempted, even though Lemerre did nothing to publicize his books and charged him exorbitant sums to cover production and distribution costs. His rejection of Soupault's offer suggests Roussel had no wish, at least at this stage, to be associated with the writers to whom his posthumous reputation is most decisively indebted.

Nevertheless, Roussel appears to have accepted towards the end of his life that what chances his work had of survival lay in their hands. In his final will, made on 20 January 1933, four months prior to his departure from Paris, Roussel carefully stipulated that a copy of 'Comment j'ai écrit certains de mes livres' be sent to nearly all the leading Surrealists. His list of twenty-two names includes Robert Desnos, Paul Éluard, Tristan Tzara, Michel Leiris, André Breton, René Char, Salvador Dalí, Philippe Soupault and Louis Aragon. And in a letter apparently never sent, but found among his papers, Roussel more or less asks his 'chers confrères' to be his literary trustees:

> Thinking of the good will you have always shown towards my books, it occurred to me that you might be interested to know by what very special method I wrote certain of them – a method explained in the manuscript here enclosed. An identical manuscript has been deposited with my lawyer, Monsieur Constantin, at 9 rue Boissy-d'Anglas, and I have left with the publishing house Lemerre, 23–33 passage Choiseul, the money required to publish it. But a manuscript can go astray, wholly or in part. If this happens to the manuscript which is deposited with my lawyer, I count on your kindness to lend the publisher this one so that the work may appear all the same.
> Very confraternally yours,
> Raymond Roussel

Roussel was undoubtedly grateful to the Surrealists for defending him against the abusive barrackers who attended his plays, as he notes in 'Comment j'ai écrit ...', 'only for the pleasure of being present at a stormy gathering'. It was clearly never, on the other hand, his intention to provoke theatregoers in the manner of events staged by such as Breton or Tzara. In an essay published in 1928 Roger Vitrac recalls going backstage after an especially turbulent performance of *Locus Solus* during which the actors were continually heckled and booed. ' "There's a bit of a row, isn't there?" acknowledged the puzzled author; "We must cut it a bit and it will go all right." ' Roussel longed to enchant rather than outrage his audiences; while the Surrealists enthusiastically engaged in pitched battles with their riotous adversaries, Roussel sat, teeth clenched, in the front row. He ends his portrayal of his theatrical career in 'Comment j'ai écrit . . .' as if on the verge of a triumphant breakthrough. He is discussing the reception accorded his final play, *La Poussière de soleils*:

> The play was wholly misunderstood; and with a few exceptions the reviews were appalling.
>
> A series of performances at the Renaissance a short while later were no more successful.
>
> While the curtain was falling, people shouted sarcastically, 'Author! . . . Author! . . .' And yet, at each of my shows, I saw new faces rallying to my cause.

Michel Leiris remembers events rather differently:

> Despite his constant disappointments, he never missed a performance of his plays. However, in the course of a stormy evening at the Renaissance, during the run of *La Poussière de soleils*, he left before the end of the show, declaring that he could positively take no more; and he never attended a single further performance.

———

It is to the suffering caused by his failures, rather than the golden triumph promised by the new faces hailing his genius, that Roussel returns in the final section of 'Comment j'ai écrit . . .':

> In bringing this essay to a close, I must refer again to the pain I have suffered at seeing my works run up against an almost totally hostile incomprehension.

Two thoughts console Roussel as he bids farewell to a literary career that, far from fulfilling his early vision of universal fame, he now views as a bitter series of rejections. Firstly, he recalls his prowess as a drawing-room singer and mimic of actors and acquaintances. Roussel spent months preparing each act, often visiting the same show dozens of times, and he carried around a list of the friends whose mannerisms he could accurately reproduce. In *Impressions d'Afrique* the youngest of the Boucharessas brothers, Bob (who is only four) performs a variety of imitations – a train getting up speed, the cries of domestic animals, hunting horns, a violin solo, the plaintive notes of a cello – that are so lifelike they afford 'a complete illusion of reality'. By most accounts Roussel was similarly gifted, and his turns were as well received as he claims in the penultimate paragraph of 'Comment j'ai écrit . . .':

> The only kind of success I have ever really experienced was while performing songs to my own piano accompaniments, and above all from my numerous impersonations of actors and a variety of ordinary people. But there at least my success was enormous and complete.

His other appeal is to posterity. Denied in his lifetime the honours he felt were his due, Roussel peers cautiously into the future awaiting his literary corpus after his death:

> And so I seek comfort, for want of anything better, in the hope that perhaps I will enjoy a little posthumous fame on account of my books.

# CHAPTER 2

# Many Years of Perfect Bliss

Roussel writes of his early life in 'Comment j'ai écrit . . .':

> I have preserved of my childhood a delightful memory. I can claim to have known at that time many years of perfect bliss.

Roussel was born on 20 January 1877, the third child of Eugène and Marguerite Roussel. The family belonged to the Parisian haute bourgeoisie. Eugène Roussel was a stockbroker and an extremely successful speculator in the capital's property market. At the time of Roussel's birth the family lived at 25 boulevard Malesherbes, near-neighbours of the Prousts, who occupied number 9.

On the death of Marguerite Roussel's mother the previous year, the Roussels had also inherited a large estate at 25 boulevard Richard-Wallace in Neuilly, just west of the bois de Boulogne. In 1883 the family moved from boulevard Malesherbes to a large hôtel at 50 rue de Chaillot, just off the Champs-Elysées.

Roussel does not specify in 'Comment j'ai écrit . . .' the sources of his childhood happiness. He was undoubtedly closer to his mother and sister than to his brother and father. 'I was brought up with my sister Germaine,' he tells us. 'Our elder brother Georges, who died in 1901, was already almost a young man while we were still children.' Roussel's writings often feature passionate friendships between siblings, such as the twins A . . . L . . . and M . . . in 'À la Havane', or Zéoug and Leidjé in *L'Étoile au front*; he also frequently describes intense relationships between children of different parents brought up as brother and sister. In the short story 'Nanon', for instance, Nanon is adopted into the Pennanhoat family when she is two and Sylvestre Pennanhoat five. As they grow up they become increasingly fond of each other:

Sylvestre was madly in love with Nanon and Nanon
adored Sylvestre. Like Paul and Virginie, they had always
been everything to each other, and they would not have been
able to live apart. Sylvestre went along with Nanon's caprices
and anticipated her every desire; he shared his games with
the little girl, making her jump on his knees, and would
deliberately allow himself to be caught during frantic games
of hide-and-seek.

Alas, when she is fourteen Nanon is stricken with a terrible
fever after attending a church service on Christmas Eve, and she
dies having confessed her love and enjoyed a first and final
ecstatic kiss with her foster-brother.

Roussel's novels also feature several passionate, abruptly ter-
minated relationships between foster-siblings. In *Impressions
d'Afrique* we learn the history of Séil-Kor – a west African boy
adopted by a French explorer at the age of ten – and Nina (also
ten). Like Nanon, Nina dies of a fever, an event that leaves Séil-
Kor 'crazed with despair':

> he came to loathe the places till then divinely illuminated by
> his friend's presence. The sight of the scenes he had so often
> contemplated with Nina created a horrible contrast between
> his present grief and his lost happiness.

The idyllic childhood romance of François-Charles Cortier and
Andrée Aparicio in *Locus Solus* ends equally tragically: the very
night Andrée informs her foster-father François-Jules Cortier of
her love for his son, François-Jules – who is in love with her
himself – strangles her in a fit of passion, and then violates
her corpse. This appalling crime comes to light only as the
result of the scientific researches of the novel's presiding genius,
Martial Canterel.

I mention these stories because the rupture they enact seems
mimetic of the division Roussel established between his adult
self and his childhood experiences. In 'Le voyageur et son ombre'
Michel Leiris recalls:

> Certain towns which evoked particularly happy memories
> of his childhood were taboo for him: for example, Aix-les-
> Bains (which he would not even pass through by train),

Luchon and Saint-Moritz were towns to which he wished never to return, for fear of spoiling his memories.

On the other hand Roussel obviously considered his formative years crucial to an understanding of his achievement; in his discussions with Janet he vehemently insisted that 'People will research the acts of my childhood and admire the way I played "prisoner's base".' We are unlikely to discover evidence of Roussel's prowess in children's games, but the numerous photographs recently discovered among his papers reveal something of the Roussel family's favourite amusements. They appear to have enjoyed dressing up as much as the Incomparables: young Raymond is pictured sporting a variety of fancy costumes, by turns a chambermaid, a farmer's wife, a comic-opera soldier, a court abbé, a Neapolitan brigand, a young marquis, all frills and braid (see plates 2, 3 and 4). Madame Roussel appears in the guise of a Roman tragic heroine, leaning pensively on a fake classical plinth. On the back of the picture she has noted 'en moineau de Lesbie' to indicate she is aping Catullus's mistress mourning her lost sparrow. Another photo reveals her in front of a mirror modelling the effect of a string of pearls against a newly acquired creation of the *grand couturier* Charles Worth.

If Roussel, from one perspective, can seem an outlandish version of the fin-de-siècle dandy, his mother, analogously, registers as almost a parody of the Belle Époque *grande dame*. Her surviving appointment diaries reveal a more or less unceasing whirl of entertaining, travelling and spending, spending, spending: she collected Old Masters and modern painters, sculptures and miniatures, glassware and fans, old Chinese and old European porcelain, gems and tiny lapdogs, old carpets and Louis XIV tables and chairs. The jewel in her costly crown, however, was her collection of Dresden figurines, which was reckoned the most significant of the era: seventy-eight of these are listed in the catalogue of the sale of her effects after her death.

To enjoy a life of absolute luxury, Roussel had no need, then, to discover with the first blow of his pickaxe a seam of marvellous riches. And he was never overtly to rebel against his mother's principles, lifestyle or extremely conventional tastes in art and music. Roussel's love of Jules Verne, for instance, may have originated in a tradition described by Louis Aragon in his autobiography:

> Each evening the servants would gather in the salon, and there they would listen with Madame Roussel to her son read out loud from Verne's *Voyages extraordinaires*, novel after novel; on reaching the end of the cycle, he would return to the first one, and begin all over again.

Roussel's refusal to discuss in detail, either in his writings or during his life, his 'many years of perfect bliss' suggests that memories of this sort were too precious ever to be broached, and contrasts absolutely with the elaborate excavations of the events of his childhood undertaken by his early neighbour, Proust. Roussel has been figured by a number of those who have written on him as some kind of inverted antithesis to Proust: his 'dark and distorted reflection,' as Ashbery puts it, 'the Proust of dreams' in Cocteau's phrase. In his Roussel notebook, Leiris ponders at length on the similarities between the two:

> They were from the same epoch, and both were rich bourgeois and homosexual. Both shared the same taste for 'imitation'. Same way of looking at things as if through a microscope. Same cult of childhood memories. Haunted by the passing of time and by death. Sought refuge, not in God, but in a universe unique to each, but which was created from all sorts of bits and pieces. Both escaped into vaudeville, into trivial, even scatological comedy. Had comparable ways of insulating themselves: one in his cork-lined bedroom, the other, when travelling by boat, in his cabin.* Same absence of conformism under 'orthodox' exteriors. Similar way in which each was captivated by the names of the nobility (feudal hierarchies for Proust, First Empire for Roussel).

---

* Leiris is referring to Roussel's indifference to his surroundings during his world tour: when asked about tropical sunsets, he responded he had not had time to notice them, since he was busy working in his cabin (R & Co, p. 211).

And, one might add, both were exceptionally attached to their mothers. Madame Roussel was thirty at the time of Raymond's birth, and died thirty-four years later in 1911, addicted, according to Leiris – who describes her in his journal as 'a shrewish character, who caused RR much suffering' – to morphine. During this period they were hardly ever apart. Roussel was so grief-stricken by her death he had a pane of glass inserted into the lid of her coffin so he could gaze on her features up to the last possible moment. The nature of their relationship is perhaps best suggested by a letter Marguerite sent her son in 1902, when Roussel was twenty-five. He had cut out and dispatched to her a series of comic drawings of monkeys, one of which, he jokily pointed out, resembled himself. Madame Roussel was not amused:

> All the world agrees that I have created a physical and moral masterpiece (apart from a few distorted ideas, but these are almost already in the past). So, no more bad jokes against my dearest darling, to whom I have raised an altar in my heart from which no one will dislodge him.

It seems probable that her cryptic allusion to Roussel's 'distorted ideas' refers to the crisis he suffered five years earlier after the publication of *La Doublure*. Though not prepared to take his writing seriously, Madame Roussel clearly adored her youngest child, and even in his adult years Roussel was rarely separated from her for more than a few weeks at a time.

While writers such as Paul Bourget occasionally attended Madame Roussel's *soirées*, she was more interested in composers and singers.* She had a season ticket to the Opéra, and enjoyed close friendships with a number of prominent performers. Her passion for music is the only information about his mother divulged in 'Comment j'ai écrit . . .':

> My mother adored music and, on discovering I had a certain talent, transferred me, when I was thirteen, from school to

---

* For a full account of Madame Roussel's salon and its habitués, see Philippe G. Kerbellec's 'Who's Who' in DG, pp. 186–203.

the Conservatory, having prevailed over my father's not particularly serious objections.

Roussel's interest in music registers in his writing in a variety of ways. A large proportion of the performances described in *Impressions d'Afrique*, for instance, involve unlikely ways of creating or generating music. The chemist Bex demonstrates the amazing powers of his thermo-orchestra, which utilizes *bexium*, a metal endowed with prodigious thermal sensitivity: by varying the temperature within a specially encased set of instruments (horns, strings, keyboards and percussion), Bex is able to create any number of musical effects – a slow cantilena, an adagio, a scherzo, dances, overtures, medleys and variations. The carefully trained worm of the Hungarian Skarioffszky reveals an equally extraordinary repertoire. This worm is able to play Hungarian melodies, czardas and waltzes on a zither through the most ingenious of means. The worm is placed by Skarioffszky in a large transparent trough full of a strange water that is as heavy as mercury. A narrow slit runs the length of the bottom of this V-shaped container. Underneath this slit is placed a zither. By arching his body the worm is able to regulate the flow of drops of heavy water on to the strings of the zither; he becomes so adept at this that he faultlessly executes wondrously complex Hungarian rhapsodies with a 'savagely dramatic range of expression'. Other notable musical performers in *Impressions d'Afrique* include Tancrède Boucharessas, a cripple without legs or arms, who still manages to perform as a one-man band on a set of pan-pipes, an accordion, a triangle, drum and cymbals; the colossally-mouthed Ludovic who sings all four parts of 'Frère Jacques' simultaneously; the one-legged Lelgoualch who charms his audiences with haunting Breton airs played on a flute carved from his own tibia; and the emaciated Alcott brothers, whose bodies, when carefully dispersed across a field at the correct angles to each other, reverberate arpeggios sung by their father, thereby 'creating the effect of a choir, faultlessly in harmony, by means of the rich, sustained polyphony produced by the combined echoes'.

These novel methods of composition and performance are not only the product of the *procédé*, but are also analogous to it;

just as Roussel combined the unlikely elements thrown up by his system of punning by adapting traditional, often fairy-tale, narratives, so his musicians devote all their ingenuity to finding fabulous ways of performing conventional styles of music. His final poem, *Nouvelles Impressions d'Afrique*, offers a more extreme example even than his *procédé*-inspired prose works of Roussel's compulsion to fuse the banal and the *outré*. The poem merely illustrates a few obvious maxims (we all occasionally need help, all things grow old), but Roussel's elaborate symphonic arrangement and development of these trite themes through continually expanding parentheses and footnotes makes the poem as unpredictable and tumultuous as the 'majestic' combinations generated by Bex's thermo-orchestra or the 'rich sustained polyphony' created by the echoing bodies of the Alcott family.

Performances of the kind featured in his novels are a far cry from Roussel's personal musical enthusiasms, which, like those of his mother, were conventional: Gounod, Wagner and Jules Massenet, whom he revered so intensely he once abruptly abandoned a dining partner who happened to dismiss Massenet's music as 'good only for concierges'.

Madame Roussel's peremptory overriding of her husband's 'not particularly serious objections' to their youngest son's transfer from the Lycée Janson-de-Sailly to the Conservatory was probably typical of their marital relations. Michel Leiris learned from Roussel's companion Charlotte Dufrène that Roussel had once declared his father 'had never counted for much in the family'. Roussel's older brother Georges had already opted for art rather than finance, and embarked on a career as a sculptor that was cut short by his early death from tuberculosis at the age of thirty-two. Money plays an important role in the economy of Roussel's narratives, but his treatment of fiscal matters does not incline one to believe he would have been successful in the stockbroking circles in which his father moved. The quest for wealth in Roussel is normally some kind of bizarre treasure-hunt like that pursued through the five acts and twenty-four tableaux of *La Poussière de soleils*: the trail leads Julien Blache, sole heir to his misanthropic uncle's cunningly hidden fortune, from a bookplate affixed to the inside cover of an Aesop in green binding to a sonnet engraved on the skull of an Italian poet, to a sepia drawing that depicts a stone imprinted with the skeleton of a pterodactyl, to a freak who never stops grinning, to a volume containing accounts of black masses interspersed with lewd engravings, to a stuffed swallow, and so on and so on, through clue after clue, until the chase culminates in the discovery of a casket of gems secreted in a well. Armand Vage in the fifth document of *Documents pour servir de canevas* retrieves his inheritance by similar means – a cipher-stencil that he applies to a number of printed texts collated by his avaricious older sister:

> At the twenty-first attempt, immediately struck by the words 'cube' and 'petrify', perfectly framed in the two holes of the stencil, Armand Vage abstained from further meditative reading: *a cube would petrify him*. Having raised, from the bank of a stream that flowed through his sister's garden, a remarkably cubical mossy stone, he discovered a substantial hoard of money.

One wonders, too, what Eugène Roussel would have made of the frenzied financial transactions that precede the gala of the Incomparables in *Impressions d'Afrique*. It is decided that a prize will be awarded to the act that elicits the most enthusiastic response from the audience, and to generate more excitement still, a hundred shares are issued in the name of each performer, and distributed in lots for two hundred francs each. The architect Chènevillot constructs a miniature version of the Paris Bourse, and for twenty minutes each day the floor is open for speculators to buy and sell their shares. To emphasize the originality of this peculiar financial market it is decreed that orders will only be accepted if delivered in alexandrine couplets, so agents and punters bawl execrable rhyming verse at each other during each day's frenetic twenty minutes of pre-Gala trading. As on any stock exchange, prices fluctuate according to the ebb and flow of information and rumour: Carmichaëls drop nine points when the young singer Carmichaël is reported to be suffering from a sore throat, but next day when the news proves false his stock rebounds by twelve francs. The marksman Balbet intends to demonstrate his skill by shooting away the white of a distantly placed soft-boiled egg while leaving the yolk intact; conflicting assessments of the state of his rifle and cartridges drive his share price wildly up and down.

Eugène Roussel died in 1894 when Roussel was seventeen, the year in which his literary career commenced:

> When I was sixteen I began attempting to compose melodies, writing the lyrics myself. These lyrics always came easily enough, but I had a great deal of difficulty with the music. One day, when I was seventeen, I decided to abandon music altogether and devote myself entirely to verse; my vocation was settled.
>
> From that moment on I was seized by a fever of work. I laboured, so to speak, night and day for months on end.

It is possible the events were on some level connected – or at least the relationship between poetry and death is one that Roussel himself makes in an odd footnote to his discussion of the composition of his final poem in 'Comment j'ai écrit . . .':

> Since I have introduced the subject of the poetic side of my work, I would like to quote four lines which in my early youth it amused me to add to Victor Hugo's poem ['Autre Guitare' from his volume *Les Rayons et les Ombres*] beginning:

> > Comment, disaient-ils,
> > Avec nos nacelles
> > Fuir les alguazils?*
> > – Ramez, disaient-elles.

How, they asked,/ With our skiffs/ Can we flee the alguazils?/ – Row, they said.

Here are those four lines intended to follow the concluding lines of the poem:

> > – Comment, disaient-ils,
> > Nous sentant des ailes

---

* An *alguazil* is a Spanish officer licensed to make arrests. Hugo's poem was composed on 18 July 1838 (VH, p. 1079).

Quitter nos corps vils?
– Mourez, disaient-elles.

– How, they asked,/ Feeling we have wings/ Can we leave our vile
bodies?/ – Die, they said.

Aside from a few standard childhood poems, this bleak quat-
rain is probably the earliest of Roussel's verses to have survived,
and neatly balances the megalomaniac raptures of *Mon Âme*,
which was written in 1894 but not published until after the
appearance of *La Doublure* three years later, and not collected
in book form until 1932, when it was included, in a slightly
modified form and under the title *L'Âme de Victor Hugo*, as a
companion piece to *Nouvelles Impressions d'Afrique*.

The original version of *Mon Âme* was printed in the newspaper
*Le Gaulois* on 12 July 1897, prefaced by a headnote that
informed the reader:

> M. Raymond Roussel is the celebrated author of *La
> Doublure*; we asked him for a contribution and he has given
> us one of his first poems; he wrote it three years ago; he was
> then only just seventeen, and one can judge from that fact
> the sort of promise his precocious and fecund genius holds
> for the future.

The poem is itself about the author's precocious and fecund
genius:

> Mon âme est une étrange usine
> Où se battent le feu, les eaux,
> Dieu sait la fantastique cuisine
> Que font ses immenses fourneaux.
>
> C'est une gigantesque mine
> Où sonnent des coups de marteaux.
> Au centre un brasier l'illumine
> Avec des bords monumentaux;
>
> Un peuple d'ouvriers grimace
> Pour sortir de ce gouffre en feu

Les rimes jaillissant en masse
Des profondeurs de son milieu.

(lines 1–12)

My soul is a strange factory/ Where fire and water seethe,/ Only God knows the incredible things created/ By these immense furnaces.

It is a huge mine/ Where hammer blows ring./ It is illuminated from the centre by a brazier/ With enormous sides;

A multitude of workers grimace/ As they extract from this fiery pit/ Rhymes flying like masses of sparks/ Out of the inner depths.

What is most startling about *Mon Âme* is the relentless fervour with which Roussel expands this standard conceit.* The poem is in three parts. In the first, which runs to 320 lines, Roussel presents his turbulent creative powers generating endless verses that inspire universal admiration. The industrial and mining metaphors are fulsomely developed. Vast quantities of coal are delivered to feed the colossal furnaces; leaping flames sear the air like lightning, and the pit glows red-hot at moments of extreme inspiration. Roussel figures himself as an all-powerful factory owner respectfully worshipped by his army of obedient hands:

Je gouverne
Mon peuple d'ouvriers, en roi,
Entouré dans l'ample caverne
De respect, de gloire et d'effroi;

Quand, à cheval, à l'aube terne,
Je pars pour le gouffre en émoi,
Sur mon passage on se prosterne
De tous les côtés devant moi.

(lines 73–80)

I govern/ My mass of workers, like a king/ Surrounded in my roomy cave/ With respect, glory, and dread;

* The French critic Annie Le Brun has suggested that Roussel probably derived the conceit from a poem entitled 'Sonnet' in François Coppée's 1891 collection *Le Cahier Rouge*. For further discussion of the poem's relationship with Coppée, see her *Vingt mille lieues sous les mots, Raymond Roussel* (Paris: Pauvert/Fayard, 1994), hereafter VM, p. 39.

When, on horseback, in the dim dawn/ I leave excitedly for my pit,/ As I pass people prostrate themselves/ From all my sides at my feet.

He also imagines a huge crowd continually arriving from all over the world to render homage to his literary genius. They disembark at the nearby docks and swarm towards the site of production:

> C'est toute une foule qui paye
> Pour voir cette âme où tout rougit,
> Adeptes dont chacun essaye
> De voir au fond, quand il me lit.

(lines 96–100)

It is an enormous crowd who pay/ To see this soul in which everything is red-hot,/ They are my followers, and each one tries/ To see into my depths when he reads me.

Roussel gracefully conducts the ever-growing cortège towards the divine fires. Arrived at the edge of the fiery gulf, Roussel's countless admirers bow their heads in wonder:

> La foule à voix basse bredouille
> Des prières entre les dents,
> Puis, joignant les mains, s'agenouille
> Tout entière en quelques instants.
>
> Sur mon cheval seul je domine
> Mes fidèles en pamoison
> Dont la foule couvre la mine
> En tous sens jusqu'à l'horizon.
>
> . . .
>
> Pour ne plus voir ces idolâtres
> Je travaille en fermant les yeux,
> Sans souci de ces roussellâtres
> Qui me mettent au rang des dieux.

(lines 213–20, 225–8)

The crowd with a low voice mumbles/ Prayers under the breath,/ Then, clasping their hands, all kneel/ Together for several moments.

On my horse alone I hold sway/ Over my swooning congregation

– / The crowd covers the mine/ In all directions, right to the horizon . . .

So as not to see these worshippers/ I work with my eyes closed/ Without care for these *roussellâtres*/ Who consider me on a plane with the gods.

One of the most arresting features of Roussel's experience of 'la gloire' was this thrilling dread of being martyred by his followers. During this period he wrote only in carefully screened rooms, fearing even a glimpse of his work in progress might prove inflammatory; as he told Janet, 'To leave these papers lying about would have sent out rays of light as far as China, and the desperate crowd would have flung themselves upon my house.' His worshippers in *Mon Âme* are more disciplined, and content themselves with a solemn hymn to his genius:

> Et le pieux cantique monte,
> Dans chaque voix on sent la foi,
> En latin d'église il raconte
> Mes poèmes, ma gloire et moi.

(lines 249–52)

And the pious canticle rises,/ In each voice one can sense the faith,/ In church Latin each tells the story/ Of my poems, of my glory, and of me.

Meanwhile, Roussel yet further stokes his imaginative furnace and offers as an example of his poetic inventiveness the beginnings of a tableau: a young couple lie under some trees by a lake on a beautiful summer evening; the man watches his fresh-faced partner sleeping, and seems to be waiting for her to awake. But even while producing this genre scene the poet is aware of the adoring crowds, quivering with amazement. The section ends as Roussel's inspiration subsides late at night: the mine and factory flames die down and begin to smoke, all grows calm and the poet falls asleep.

Whereas in this first part Roussel reveals himself imperiously in command of the subterranean creative process, as his workmen weld and hammer the pliant, red-hot metal into shape, in section II he explores the dark, passive inverse of this ideal of omnipotent control. Not all the gulf's flames have been extinguished, and in a nightmare the poet is agonizingly forced to conjure up a series of surreally disjointed visions: a large mocking crowd, a strange troop of halberdiers, hunters dressed in green and in full cry, a musical theatre scene that involves a shepherd playing his pipe and a bevy of dancers dressed as hemp-spinners all brandishing their distaffs. Other scenes of this unspooling nightmare seem to express more personal anxieties: Roussel finds himself compulsively writing enormously long works as part of his prospecting, or as he calls it here, his *réflexion*:

> Je me désole et je me lasse
> De ne rien inventer de bon,
> Et par un effort je ramasse
> À terre un morceau de charbon.
>
> Je le jette en bas dans l'espace
> Pour nourrir la combustion,
> Et comme avant, la tête basse,
> Je reprends ma réflexion.
>
> Et sans le vouloir je commence,
> Débutant par 'Notre-Seigneur
> Jésus-Christ' un cantique immense
> Qui m'effraye par sa longueur.
>
> Sans pouvoir m'arrêter j'y pense,
> Et j'écris en vers sans valeur
> Que le bien a sa récompense,
> Que le mal donne la douleur.
>
> Sur le bord du puits je me traîne
> Lourdement et tout de travers,
> Me plaignant que nul ne comprenne
> L'infini dans mon moindre vers.

(lines 377–96)

I grieve and grow tired/ Of not inventing anything good,/ And by an effort, I pick up/ From the ground a bit of charcoal.

I throw it down into space/ To generate some combustion,/ And as before, my head lowered/ I take up again my reflections.

And without wanting to, I begin,/ Starting with an 'Our Lord/ Jesus Christ,' an immense canticle/ Which terrifies me by its length.

Without being able to stop myself, I think about it,/ And I write in worthless verse/ That good has its reward/ And evil brings unhappiness.

On the edge of the pit I crawl/ In a manner weary and all wrong/ Complaining that no one realizes/ The infinite is in my least verse.

These terrible compositional tasks seem to prefigure the unstoppable logorrhea of works such as *La Seine* and *Les Noces*. Equally prescient is the complaint that no one will understand his writings. In section I Roussel confidently figured endless numbers of adept readers plumbing the depths of his imaginative world, but in this negative nightmare realm the misunderstood author is either mocked or ignored; the infinite truths embodied in his least verses meet only the 'hostile incomprehension' lamented a lifetime later in 'Comment j'ai écrit . . .'

The kaleidoscopic confusion of fragmentary, conflicting scenes settles down towards the end of the section into a more stable narrative, again involving, as in part I, a pair of lovers. This time, however, the poet yearns to enter the scene and win the woman himself. As the couple glide along in a gondola, the poet and woman exchange longing glances; but each time he reaches out to touch her, the gondola drifts away on a current. He makes one last desperate effort to take possession of her:

> Mon coeur bat très fort et palpite,
> Car la femme me tend les bras;
> À la fin je me précipite
> Vers elle, mais ne l'atteins pas.
>
> Maintenant dans le puits très vite
> Je m'engloutis sans voir le bas,
> Au milieu du feu je m'agite
> Faisant dans le vide des pas.

(lines 496–504)

My heart beats fast and throbs/ For the woman is holding out her arms;/ Eventually I fling myself/ Towards her, but cannot reach her.

Now down the shaft at great speed/ I plummet, unable to see the

bottom,/ In the middle of the fire I flounder about/ Taking steps
in the void.

In part I the poet proclaimed himself the ineffable centre of
creation; here he is a hapless spectre pathetically excluded from
his own fictions. The poet plunges in free fall through the
bottomless fiery gulf of his vertiginous imaginings, until he
awakes, covered in sweat, with the dawn.

In the eight quatrains of section III Roussel struggles free of
this nightmare vision of frustrated, chaotic creativity and insists
again on his imagination's unlimited powers and absolute value.
By staying up all night working he is able to remain in control
of the powerful energies that a fresh army of workers – the
night shift – now begins to exploit. In the poem's conclusion
Roussel declares himself surer than ever of his glorious destiny;
a new flame is kindled, and

> Regardant fuir au milieu d'elle
> Les vers surgissant sans effort,
> Dans la postérité fidèle
> Je vois plus tard grandir mon sort.
>
> À cette explosion voisine
> De mon génie universel
> Je vois le monde qui s'incline
> Devant ce nom: Raymond Roussel.
>
> Sur la terre que je domine
> Je vois ce feu continuel
> Qui seul et sans frère illumine
> Partout l'univers actuel.

(lines 533–44)

Watching flying from the middle of this flame/ The verses which
rise up without difficulty,/ In faithful posterity/ I see my destiny will
in the future grow even greater.

At this explosion deriving/ From my universal genius/ I see the
world bow/ Before this name: Raymond Roussel.

On the earth which I dominate/ I see the continual fire/ Which
alone and without rival illuminates/ The existing universe
everywhere.

By 1932, however, when Roussel decided to include *Mon Âme* in the volume containing his final poem, *Nouvelles Impressions d'Afrique*, he realized he could not trust even 'faithful posterity' to accord his work the plaudits the poem predicts. Therefore he changed the poem's title to *L'Âme de Victor Hugo*, and introduced it in the following terms:

> One night I dreamed I saw Victor Hugo writing at his desk, and this is what I read as I leaned over his shoulder.

The poem was thus transformed from a hymn to his own genius into an overblown homage to the third member of Roussel's holy trinity. This alteration also necessitated a few changes to the text itself. In lines 227–8 Roussel alludes to the idolatrous *roussellâtres* who adore him like a god. Instead of replacing *roussellâtres* with *hugoâtres*, however, Roussel opted to leave the line with a blank where his name had been, to be filled in by the discerning reader: 'Sans souci de ces　　　lâtres/ Qui me mettent au rang des dieux.' In the poem's penultimate stanza Roussel again left a trace of the poem's original subject:

> À cette explosion voisine
> De mon génie universel
> Je vois le monde qui s'incline
> Devant ce nom: Victor Hugo.

Any reader properly initiated into the mysteries of Roussel's art will know exactly whose name offers the correct rhyme to *universel*.

———

*Mon Âme* was published in *Le Gaulois* with the following endnote celebrating the twenty-year-old Roussel's precocious literary development:

> This poem made up part of a collection entitled *Des Choses*; it was followed by two very long poems: the *Palais* and the *Île déserte*; then a new collection of separate poems: *Sanguines*; finally he began to draw closer to his *véritable roman* with: *Un Somme*, *Jours gras* and above all *Souffre-*

*Douleur*, which was written just before the incredible *Doublure*.

These works must have been written during the 'fever of work' that possessed Roussel following his decision to abandon music and devote himself to literature. None of them survive, though it is possible that drafts of two untitled and unfinished poems may be related to these compositions.

The first and much the longer of these drafts is a lurid slice of low life that anticipates the melodramatic excesses of 'À l'Ambigu', the third section of *Les Noces*. It presents the murder of a rich young aristocrat by a bedraggled *fille de trottoir*. The poem's main interest resides in its unremitting focus on the external details of the scene; this sketch offers the earliest example of the meticulous and seemingly inexhaustible powers of description that so dominate Roussel's early poetry. Like *La Doublure* and the three long poems collected in *La Vue*, much of the draft is devoted to a precise observation of minute particulars. Roussel forensically examines the poor prostitute's lodgings, furniture and clothes, noting, for instance, the zig-zag pattern formed by the stay-laces of her corset (lines 173–5). The characters, on the other hand, are dramatized in the most cursory of ways. The aristocrat forthrightly declares:

> Car il me faut l'amour cynique
> Où le frisson se communique
> Sur de puants grabats,
> L'amour où l'instinct seul s'indique
> Et la volupté spasmodique
> Sur des filles en bas.

(lines 43–8)

For I need a shameless love/ In which thrills are exchanged/ On filthy pallets,/ A love governed wholly by physical instinct/ And the spasms of pleasure/ I get from girls in stockings.

This particular 'fille en bas' stabs him to death in order to steal his money and jewels. She experiences no qualms of conscience once the deed is done:

Tout en admirant sa recette
Et l'éclair de chaque facette
Sur les joyaux, sans repentir
Promptement elle se corsette
de partir.

(lines 376–80)

All the while admiring her takings/ And the light shining from each facet/ Of the jewels, without repenting/ She promptly dons her corset/ [And gets ready] to depart.

The poem peters out after her flight from the scene of the crime through the night streets of Paris. A couple of scattered rhyme words (*costum*/costume) and (*mardi*/as in *mardi gras*) jotted down the right-hand margin at the beginning of the unwritten third section suggest that she, like Gaspard and Roberte in *La Doublure*, or Claude in one of the drafts of *Les Noces*, planned to seek refuge in the world of carnival.

The second unfinished poem dating from this period belongs to a very different genre. It is perhaps a version of the *Palais* or the *Île déserte* mentioned in the biographical note appended to *Mon Âme*, but equally a parenthetical marginal note '(j. gras)' after line 86 suggests a possible link with *Jours gras*. An unnamed traveller wanders through a wood and eventually arrives at a deserted manor house. An irresistible supernatural power forces him to mount the front steps and enter the front door, which promptly closes of its own accord behind him. He drifts through the cavernous house at random until accosted by a horde of phantoms who noiselessly approach and seem poised to menace him in some undefined way (lines 141–2). At this climactic moment the poem breaks off, like a children's story to be continued the next evening. Thus, while the longer of these early drafts can be seen as a harbinger of Roussel's fascination with description for its own sake, this second one looks forward to the world of fairy tales that underlies so many of his later prose narratives – and, like them, also back to the many years of perfect bliss of his childhood.

———

Roussel wrote *La Doublure* over a period of around six months in 1896. Its composition, as he tells us in 'Comment j'ai écrit . . .', 'coincided with the crisis described by Pierre Janet.' During this state of elation Roussel 'lost all interest in anything else and had great difficulty in interrupting his work in order to eat from time to time. He was not entirely motionless; he used to take a few steps and then write a little, but he would also remain immobile for hours on end, pen in hand, absorbed in his reverie and his sensations of glory.' It is hard to reconcile this drab, scrupulously detailed, enormously long poem with the visions of blazing immortality that obsessed its author. To the end of his life Roussel believed that *Mon Âme* and *La Doublure* were his greatest achievements, a conviction that seems never to have wavered. Janet records:

> Martial wrote other volumes, it is true, but not in order to create something superior to the first; there can be no progress in the absolute, and he experienced with his initial attempt the very absolute of glory. These other works will only help the ignorant and behind-the-times public to read and see the radiance of the first.

In one of his final notes to his publishers, written on 30 May 1933, he stipulated that all posthumous printings of his work should use as a frontispiece a photograph taken during this golden era, at Milan in October 1896 (see Plate 5): flawlessly dressed, his right hand hooked into his fob pocket while the other rests lightly on a semi-rustic photographer's prop, Roussel stares implacably into the distance, a model of manly fortitude.

*La Doublure* itself is about irresolution, failure, obscurity and mundane disappointment. The title refers to the central male character's aborted career as an actor. Though convinced of his own talent, he can only ever find work as a theatrical understudy (*doublure*). The poem opens with Gaspard on stage in a period melodrama. In his hand he holds a drawn sword; when the situation which caused him to unsheathe it is defused, he attempts, in a single sweeping gesture, to return his weapon to its scabbard:

> mais il remue et tremble,
> Ses mains ne peuvent pas faire toucher ensemble,

La pointe, avec le haut du fourreau noir en cuir,
Qui tournent tous les deux en paraissant se fuir.
Gaspard, très rouge avec sa fraise qui l'engonce,
Rage et devient nerveux.

                                                    (lines 17–22)

but he fidgets and trembles,/ His hands cannot bring together/ The tip of the sword and the opening of the black leather scabbard,/ Which both twist, as if trying to escape each other./ Gaspard, red-faced and hunched up in his ruff,/ Grows angry and nervous.

The audience begins to mock and barrack him; at length he succeeds in sheathing his sword, but then fluffs his next speech, and is yet again assailed by ironic catcalls.

Gaspard is an unsuccessful replacement lover as well as an unsuccessful replacement actor. He and Roberte – a demi-mondaine – can only be together when her richer beau Paul is away, as he is on the night of this disastrous performance. To console Gaspard, Roberte impulsively suggests they leave the capital together as soon as possible for a holiday in the south of France. They decide to go to Nice, and while there they join in the carnival festivities. Around two-thirds of the poem's almost 5,600 lines are devoted to precise descriptions of the masks, costumes and activities of the swarming crowd of revellers. In a final 700-line section we learn that Gaspard has since been abandoned by Roberte, and having failed to find work in any of the theatres in Paris, is now performing with a travelling fair currently based in Neuilly.

*La Doublure* is prefaced by a short, cryptic note to the reader:

WARNING
As this book is a novel, one must begin on the
first page and finish on the last.
The Author

Perhaps shadowing this instruction in the obvious is the more paradoxical notion that, as this book is a novel, it had to be written in verse. Just as the *procédé* is 'essentially a poetic method', though it produces prose, so the poetry of Roussel's early career longs to be fused with all that pertains to the novel. Only four pages of the original draft of *La Doublure* survive, but these again make clear the decisive role played by rhyme words in the process of composition. A number of lines in this draft consist solely of rhyme words, while most are made up of rhyme words and about half the required syllables. The poem itself, on the other hand, appears determined to disguise as best it can the primacy of rhyme in Roussel's methodology: its flat, unobtrusive alexandrines carefully submerge each couplet's original source as effectively as the *procédé*-generated narratives conceal the homonyms that determine their contents. Only through poetry could Roussel approach 'son véritable roman', and only through prose fulfil his 'procédé poétique'.

The relationship between the uniquely chosen, divinely inspired Roussel and the colourless, unoriginal, frustrated Gaspard can perhaps be seen as embodying an equivalent polarity. Roussel's violent exaltation ('I wrote with a thousand flaming pen-nibs') led not to the expounding of vatic truths but to a remorselessly level depiction of ordinariness: Gaspard's experiences are neither resonant nor paradigmatic; they can be related to no system of meaning beyond the immediate imperatives of time and place. The poem makes scant use of nineteenth-century conventions of motivation and subjectivity, yet appears wholly unaware of the scale and nature of its rejections. More unnerving still, *La Doublure* seems devoid of an ascertainable artistic intention; one searches in vain beneath its painstakingly detailed surfaces for clues to its ulterior purpose.

Alain Robbe-Grillet has perhaps best analysed the peculiar hypnotic power of Roussel's descriptive methods:

> We are in a *flat* and *discontinuous* universe where everything refers only to itself. A universe of fixity, of repetition, of absolute clarity, which enchants and discourages the explorer . . . The clarity, the transparency, exclude the existence of other worlds behind things, and yet we discover that we can no longer get out of *this* world.

Yet equally Roussel's modernity seems purely a matter of chance. He would no more have understood, or responded to, Robbe-Grillet's nouveau roman than he did to the experiments of the Surrealists, whose work, he is reported as saying, he found 'un peu obscur'. Perhaps the most disconcerting aspect of the poem is that not only does it take absolutely for granted the futility of attempting to escape '*this* world,' but its every line communicates an unquestioning certainty that there is no other way in which it might be represented. The all-irradiating *gloire* is transformed within the poem into a compulsion to register every descriptive possibility. Roussel's exhaustive observations, like his beckoning destiny, acknowledge no limits.

The radical effects of this literary technique, as deployed not only in *La Doublure* but *La Seine*, *Les Noces* and *La Vue*, derive from its unremitting fidelity to the wearying uniqueness of any given instant or scene. The poems prove – if proof were needed – that 'really, universally, relations stop nowhere', as Henry James once phrased it. *La Doublure* and his other early long poems might continue for ever, mesmerically in thrall to the world's banality and open-endedness. Obversely, these poems avoid constructing a hierarchy of events or actions: the sexual encounter between Gaspard and Roberte in section II of *La Doublure* is presented with the same deadpan, microscopic accuracy as the carnival masks that occupy the bulk of the poem:

> Puis il écarte sa chemise qu'un lacet
> Étroit, bleu, formant un grand nœud au milieu, fronce;
> Ensuite dans l'espace entr'ouvert il enfonce
> Sa figure, pour la baiser entre les seins;
> Sur sa poitrine à la peau blanche des dessins
> Compliqués sont formés d'un côté par des veines;
> Son corset par devant a ses agrafes pleines
> De reflets sur leur cuivre étincelant, plat . . .

(lines 492–9)

Then he parts her shirt which a lace,/ Narrow, blue, forming a large knot in the middle, gathers;/ Then in the half-open space he inserts/ His face, to kiss her between the breasts;/ On the white skin of her chest complicated designs/ Are formed on one side by veins;/ Her corset has, at the front, hooks played upon/ By reflections caught in their flat, gleaming copper . . .

Roussel's dispassionate lucidity neutralizes the emotive potential of the scene; to quote Robbe-Grillet again, 'Roussel describes, and beyond what he describes, there is nothing.' What unsettles the reader most is his serene unawareness of the personal drama into which he might develop his alienated, all-embracing, all-nullifying vision. It is the absence of this drama which most distinguishes Roussel from all other innovative writers of his period. In the grip of his *gloire*, he proceeds wholly convinced that 'l'infini' is embodied in his 'moindre vers'. The redemption it promises will be comprehensive and undiscriminating; as he told Janet, 'it will be seen in every one of my works, and will reflect on all the acts of my life.' Confident in his election, Roussel had no need to confront or harangue or convert his audience, for his supreme power 'was a fact, an established fact'.

---

We know from his mother's engagement books that Roussel attended the carnival in Nice each winter at least from the age of thirteen onwards. During this period the carnival attracted up to 25,000 visitors: they came to witness or take part in a series of cavalcades, confetti fights, flower battles and processions of floats and *têtes de carton* (huge, grotesque masks that normally embody a mildly subversive pun or visual joke). Roussel was clearly fascinated to the point of obsession by this topsy-turvy world, its exaggerated trompe l'oeil surfaces and walking double meanings. The 4,300 lines of *La Doublure* spent in describing the Mardi Gras parade – the carnival's most anarchic and populist event – by no means constituted his only attempt to convey its attractions: he returned to the subject again in the poems 'L'Inconsolable' and *Têtes de Carton du Carnaval de Nice*, both published in *Le Gaulois du Dimanche* in September 1904, and collected in the 'Citations documentaires' section of *Comment j'ai écrit certains de mes livres*. His unpublished manuscripts include yet more *têtes de carton*: a house painter at work on a restaurant whose placard declares 'Je restaure un restaurant'; an army major embracing a maid as she washes up, the motto reading 'L'Officier à L'Office' (the officer in the pantry/at his duty); a whistling drunkard whose sign declares JE SIFFLE (I whistle/guzzle) followed by, in brackets, '(deux litres par repas)'. Among his papers were found a poster for the Nice carnival of 1896 and an issue of the journal *Courrier des étrangers* of 20 February 1896, containing an illustrated account of the highlights of the festival. Roussel has underlined in blue pencil the direction of the route taken by the procession that year.

The floats and masks described by Roussel do not, however, directly correspond with those parading in the carnival on that or any previous year.* 'Chez moi l'imagination est tout,' he proclaimed in 'Comment j'ai écrit...', and it was obviously crucial to his artistic purposes that even when presenting an actual event his writing should situate itself in the domain of conception rather than reality. The carnival seems to have been for Roussel the thematic equivalent of the rhyming prose of his early verse works, or the poetic methodology of the fiction: it allowed him to unite the wholly imaginary and the hyperrealist into a seamless, invulnerable, never-ending continuum.

Accordingly, Roussel's gaze expansively mediates between the representative signifiers of each mask and the reveller half-concealed beneath. Gaspard finds himself jostled by a group of men dressed as roosters:

> tous les deux pas
> Ils lèvent tour à tour et rebaissent leurs bras,
> De la sorte, faisant battre de grandes ailes
> En plumes de plusieurs couleurs, et sous lesquelles
> On aperçoit parfois, dans des moments subits,
> Quand elles sont en l'air, un peu de leurs habits,
> Mais avec une extrême et vive promptitude.
> Dans l'ensemble, à côté de la similitude
> De coqs mêmes, le seul visage différent
> De chaque homme, qu'on voit sous le gros bec, surprend;
> Le premier a la face assez pleine et rougeaude;
> Le deuxième a des yeux d'expression nigaude...
>
> (lines 1279–90)

every two steps/ By turns they lift and lower their arms,/ And in this way beat their large wings/ In feathers of different colours, and underneath which/ One occasionally catches at unexpected

* For further discussion of the relationship between Roussel's *têtes de carton* and those in the 1896 parade, see Annie Le Brun, VM, pp. 81–4.

moments/ When their wings are raised, glimpses of their clothes/ But only very brief glimpses./ Considered altogether, in comparison with the similarity/ Of the roosters themselves, the different face/ Of each man, which one can see under the huge beak, is surpising:/ The first has a face quite plump and red;/ The second has eyes with a foolish expression . . .

And so on and on. The binary oppositions of the passage are characteristic not just of *La Doublure*, with its doubling understudies, but of Roussel's entire imaginative world; his writing can almost invariably be resolved into neatly balanced antitheses – 'equations of facts', as Robert de Montesquiou called them. Narrative or description expand to fill the gap created between any given word and its punned or rhyming twin; turning language inside out to reveal its lining – another meaning of *doublure* – Roussel confounds the very notion of discriminating purposefully between inner and outer, between the painted papier-mâché rooster and the man inside the *tête de carton*. Both afford contrasted but equal opportunities for exactly similar kinds of description; the more fastidiously Roussel traces the differences between artifice and nature, the more impossible it becomes to tell them apart.

The importance of double meanings to the irrefutable illogic of carnival becomes particularly apparent in the masks Roussel describes that are based on word-play: 'Je soutiens un souteneur,' (line 2336) declares the placard on a mask featuring a policeman lifting up a pimp (un souteneur); 'Je suis chauve, hein!' (line 3919) (*chauvin* meaning chauvinist) proclaims that affixed to the model of a bald (*chauve*) man singing the Marseillaise and brandishing the tricolore; one of a schoolmaster caning a young urchin has *pan* (whack/flap of garment) sewn on to his outsized, flying coat-tails. As Michel Foucault first pointed out, such puns directly prefigure the materialization of language effected by the *procédé*.

*La Doublure* ends, like all Roussel's long early verse works, on a note of isolation and despair. An embittered Gaspard can imagine no possible end to his humiliations. While he waits to perform the role of Méphisto in the travelling fair's pantomime and *la patronne* noisily cries up the forthcoming performance, he reflects on his failure as a lover and an actor. Inevitably he traces his misery back to the terrible night he failed to return his sword to its sheath. In the poem's final, solitary line he contemplates with piercing bleakness the indifferent heavens:

> La patronne, en mettant parfois des différences
> Dans ses phrases, répète: «On commence *Les Transes*
> *De la Marquise*, entrez, mesdames et messieurs.»
>
> Gaspard regarde, en haut, les étoiles aux cieux.

(lines 5583–6)

The patronne, sometimes varying/ Her phrasing, repeats: 'Roll up, *Les Transes/ de la Marquise* is beginning, ladies and gentlemen.'// Gaspard looks up at the stars in the sky above.

---

*La Doublure* is in many ways an extraordinary work, but not one likely to appeal in any age to the vast popular audience of which Roussel dreamed. It was published on 10 June 1897, and received two reviews. A week after it appeared, an anonymous notice in *L'Illustration* reported Roussel's novel in verse to be 'more or less unintelligible'; five months later, in the *Revue Blanche*, Gustave Kahn declared it 'fort ennuyeux' (very boring). Roussel was bewildered by the lack of instant and widespread acclamation. In Janet's words:

> When the volume appeared and the young man, with great
> emotion, went out into the street and realized that no one
> was turning to stare at him as he passed, the sensations of
> glory and luminosity were suddenly extinguished. There then
> began a real crisis of melancholic depression, which took
> the strange form of a kind of persecution mania; he became
> deliriously obsessed by the idea that all men were constantly
> denigrating each other. This depression lasted for a long time
> and healed very slowly; its traces remain even today.

His decision to publish *La Doublure* – and all subsequent books – at his own expense with the publishing house Lemerre* further

---

\* The firm was founded in 1866 and established a reputation as the foremost publisher of the Parnassians. In the 1870s the list included Verlaine and Leconte de Lisle. Lemerre probably became Roussel's publisher on the recommendation diminished the possibility of his work receiving the rapturous adulation he felt it deserved. Lemerre made little effort to publicize or distribute the work of authors willing to subsidize their own literary careers. Over the years Roussel paid the firm colossal sums of money both to cover printing costs and to place adverts in journals and newspapers. There seems to have been no campaign, however, to bring *La Doublure* to the public's attention. The book sank without trace, and Roussel, as he put it in 'Comment j'ai écrit . . .', 'plummeted to earth from the prodigious heights of glory.'

---

of Madame Roussel's friend Paul Bourget, who was one of Lemerre's best-selling authors. Roussel's decision to remain with the firm for the rest of his life might be seen as evidence of his cult of 'precedents' (R & Co, p. 84), which he felt obliged him for ever after to fulfil commitments or repeat certain actions. Lemerre's exorbitant bills ended up playing a significant part in Roussel's financial ruin, and even decades after his death the firm appears to have been anxious to conceal details of its dealings with him. John Ashbery records visiting their offices in 1959 and asking to consult their Roussel files. He was told that this was impossible without Michel Ney's permission, which he then obtained, but was informed on his return that no documents relating to Roussel survived. Several months later the firm closed down and its archives were, apparently, destroyed (DG, p. 102/AT4, pp. 90–91).

# CHAPTER 3

# Prospecting

The two uncomplimentary reviews of *La Doublure* were not the only critical judgement passed on Roussel's ill-fated literary début. Among those to whom he sent a copy of the book was Marcel Proust, who responded in the following carefully barbed terms:

> Like the Infant-Hero of the Fable, you carry without faltering the weight of a formidable poetic apparatus. You have, which is rare these days, inspiration, and you write, without losing breath, a hundred verses where another writes ten lines.

Roussel evidently missed, or decided to overlook, Proust's deftly weighted ironies, and treated the remark as a handsome tribute to his fecund imagination. Proust's letter has not been recovered, so its full contents are not known, but this extract figures prominently in the compilation of admiring – and not so admiring – citations that Roussel appended, thirty years later, to *L'Étoile au front*.*

---

* The last of these, that appended to *Nouvelles Impressions d'Afrique*, is reprinted at the end of Philippe G. Kerbellec's *Comment Lire Raymond Roussel* (Paris: Jean-Jacques Pauvert, 1988), p. 249. Of course, Proust's *À la Recherche* . . . might itself be characterized as expanding with an analogously extreme fullness. At the time of this letter, however, Proust, although six years Roussel's senior, had only published a miscellaneous collection of stories, *Les Plaisirs et les Jours* (1896), illustrated by Madeleine Lemaire, who seven years later would provide the drawing that ornamented Roussel's 'Le Concert' in *Le Gaulois du Dimanche* (27–28 June, 1903). Madeleine Lemaire had long been a friend of the Roussel family, and had painted a portrait of young Raymond aged about four; fifty years on, for unknown reasons, he decided to use this picture to illustrate the newspaper items with which *Nouvelles Impressions d'Afrique* was advertised. It was perhaps through Madeleine Lemaire that Roussel met Reynaldo Hahn, with whom Proust enjoyed, in Edmund White's words, 'one of the few equal and reciprocated and sustained sexual and romantic relationships of his life' (*Proust*, London: Weidenfeld & Nicolson, 1999, p. 63) and on whom he modelled several characters in *Jean*

The failure of *La Doublure* plunged Roussel into what he describes in 'Comment j'ai écrit...' as 'a dreadful nervous illness'. It did not, however, fundamentally weaken his faith either in the merits of the book or in his ultimate literary destiny.* Roussel was no more able to lay aside his 'formidable poetic apparatus' than the Infant-Hero to evade his mythical fate. While writing *La Doublure* Roussel had felt himself to be 'in a state of unheard-of bliss, one blow of the pickaxe had opened up a whole seam'; the next ten years he mainly devoted to the more agonizing process of 'prospecting' for literary gold, arduously sifting and panning through vast tracts of language in search of 'le gros lot' (the dazzling prize). This development had itself been predicted by *Mon Âme*: Roussel suddenly found himself no longer the triumphant creative genius of the poem's first section, working the endlessly resourceful mine of his inner being, but rather the hapless victim of the second part, condemned to produce language in the remote hope he might eventually rediscover those delirious 'sensations of art' he had enjoyed during the composition of *La Doublure*.

The full extent of Roussel's prospecting has only recently become clear. In 'Comment j'ai écrit...' he merely remarks:

---

*Santeuil*, his unfinished first novel finally published in 1952. In his notebook Leiris records that, according to his mother, Roussel and Hahn's relationship 'gave rise to much gossip' (R&CO, p. 129). Reynaldo Hahn's songs were in the repertoire of those performed by Roussel to his own piano accompaniment, and from 1902 onwards Hahn was a regular attender of Madame Roussel's salon. Roussel sent Hahn copies of a number of his books, inscribed with typically fulsome dedications: 'To the first man who has ever composed immortal masterpieces in adolescence, a friendly memento from a very great admirer, and very feeble interpreter'; 'To the genius, Reynaldo Hahn, the greatest musician alive, his enthusiastic old friend'; 'To Reynaldo Hahn the most miraculous musician of the past, the present and the future, a friendly token of my esteem' (FR, Cat. no.4881, f.36).

* According to Janet, Roussel frequently took comfort in Henri Bergson's discussion of 'spiritual energy': 'One values praise and honours exactly to the extent that one is not sure of having succeeded ... Someone who is sure, absolutely sure, he has created a powerful and lasting work is not interested in eulogies, and feels himself above glory, because he knows he has it, and because the pleasure he experiences is like a divine joy' (CJ, p. 131/AT4, p. 40). On the other hand, Roussel spent enormous amounts of time and money attempting to persuade the Parisian public to accord him the 'eulogies' Bergson's genius feels able to despise.

I started working again, but in a manner more judicious than that which had brought on my breakdown from over-exertion. For several years I engaged in prospecting. None of my works satisfied me, apart from *Chiquenaude*, which I published around 1900.

The discovery of *La Seine*, more *Textes-genèse*, more *Têtes de Carton*, another poem in the manner of *La Vue* based on the picture ornamenting a hatter's business card and, above all, of the huge, sprawling *Les Noces*, has radically expanded our understanding of the aesthetic imperatives that led to Roussel's evolution of the *procédé*. It seems clear that his obsession with double meanings developed out of his gradually increasing awareness that undoubled language – language not fitted with a lining – could never aesthetically satisfy him. These newly found texts conclusively prove that Roussel originated the *procédé* not in order to stimulate his imagination, but as a means of underpinning its proliferative excesses. It allowed him to escape the linguistic nightmare embodied in section II of *Mon Âme*:

> Des vers se forment dans mon âme,
> N'ayant qu'un sens quelconque, feint,
> Mais, quoique je lutte et m'en blâme,
> À les faire je suis constraint.

> (lines 325–8)

Verses form in my soul/ Which have only a commonplace, spurious meaning,/ But, however I struggle and blame myself,/ I am forced to keep making them.

---

Although Roussel suggests in 'Comment j'ai écrit . . .' that he abandoned music altogether when he was seventeen, he in fact remained a student of the Conservatoire until the summer of 1898, when, in the final competition he entered there, he was awarded a *premier accessit* for his performances of Chopin's Premier Scherzo and the finale of Beethoven's Sonata in F. In the autumn he reported to the 72nd infantry regiment at Amiens for his three years of military service. In September 1900 he managed to arrange a transfer to the 1st regiment of Engineers based in Versailles (see Plate 6). It was just after this move that Lemerre issued the short story 'Chiquenaude' as a twenty-four-page booklet. If Roussel had hopes that this slim *plaquette* might prove more attractive to the book-buying public than the weighty *La Doublure*, he was to be again disappointed: thirty-two years later Lemerre was still trying to dispose of unsold stock.

'Chiquenaude' is the first text Roussel published that makes use of the *procédé*. There is no knowing why he preferred it to the other *Textes-genèse* composed at the same time, which only appeared after his death in a section of 'Comment j'ai écrit . . .' punningly entitled *Textes de grande jeunesse ou Textes-genèse*. Perhaps it was because the story shares a number of elements with *La Doublure* and its composition momentarily revived Roussel's ecstatic self-belief: its narrative includes an understudy who performs the role of Méphisto in a pantomime, just as Gaspard did in the final section of *La Doublure*. On the other hand, Roussel sternly declares in 'Comment j'ai écrit . . .' that it is 'pointless to search for any links between the book *La Doublure* and the story "Chiquenaude"; there are none.' Like 'Nanon', 'Une Page de Folk-lore Breton', and the seventeen *Textes-genèse*, 'Chiquenaude' fulfils the requirements of the most elementary form of the *procédé*: in all these stories the opening and concluding words are the same with the exception of a single letter – or, as here, two – but most of the key words are used in a different sense. Chiquenaude (literally, flick of the finger) is the name of a fairy godmother in a pantomime called *Forban talon rouge* (Red-heeled Buccaneer) to which the narrator has contributed a poem to be recited by the character Méphisto. The night he attends the show the actor who normally plays this part has fallen ill, and an understudy deputizes. The story begins:

> Les vers de la doublure dans la pièce du *Forban talon rouge* avaient été composés par moi. (The verses of the understudy in the play *Forban talon rouge* had been composed by me.)

These verses are an exultant chant with which Méphisto taunts each antagonist who dares him to single combat. Méphisto knows he can never lose as long as he is wearing his enchanted red costume, which repels all sword-thrusts. Through prolonged wear the costume has become rather tattered, but Méphisto is able to patch up frayed areas with a supply of this magic red cloth, and so preserve his invulnerability. His success thus depends on preserving his red clothing, and its lining, intact. The situation reverses that of Roussel, who was afflicted after the failure of *La Doublure* by 'a kind of skin disease, which took the form of a rash covering my entire body,' diagnosed by Roussel's mother as measles (*la rougeole*). Like Roussel, Méphisto is laid low by the failure of the very *doublure* that promised him invincible immortality.

In the play of *Forban talon rouge*, Méphisto shares a night of passion with Foire, the girlfriend of Panache, the red-heeled buccaneer of the play's title. While Méphisto and Foire sleep, Chiquenaude, Panache's fairy godmother, sews into the lining of one of the legs of Méphisto's red suit a rotten, worm-eaten piece of flannel. Panache surprises the lovers and challenges Méphisto to a duel. By this time the worms from the inserted flannel have eaten a number of holes in the leg of the magic costume; Panache's poisoned sword passes through one of these into his opponent's thigh, and Méphisto falls instantly dead. The story ends with Chiquenaude gloating over the fatally riddled square of cloth:

> Les vers de la doublure dans la pièce du fort pantalon rouge . . .! (The worms in the lining of the piece of strong red trouser . . .!)

The puns with which 'Chiquenaude' and the other *Textes-genèse* open and close can themselves be seen as *vers* in both senses of the word, verse-worms operating within the understudy's lining. They intimate an alternative logic of connection buried within the materiality of language, yet also eat away at the story they enclose, as if narrative were mere fodder for voracious word-games. Like the carnival in *La Doublure*, the *Textes-genèse* transform all they present into a charade whose solution is like the clicking shut of an empty box. Many of their double entendres derive from some kind of artistic rendering of the events or characters described in the story. A number feature a sketcher whose work needs some slight emendation. In 'La peau de la raie' the narrator is attempting to catch a certain skate that can be seen frolicking in the limpid waters beneath the point from which he's fishing:

La peau de la raie sous la pointe du Rayon-Vert miroitait en plein soleil du mois d'août. (The skin of the skate beneath Rayon-Vert point gleamed beneath the full August sun.)

As he fishes, an acquaintance, Madame Bosse, dashes off a caricature of the narrator. To evoke the name of the point, she uses a green pencil for her sketch. When shown it, the narrator complains that she has made him look too bald; in the picture his thin locks are grotesquely parted to leave visible a large expanse of white skull. He asks her to add some more hair to the drawing. Madame Bosse accordingly sets about making the required adjustments:

– Il faut qu'elle passe tout entière dessous, tout entière, n'est-ce pas?
– Qui, elle? . . . demanda Mme Bosse. Par-dessous quoi? . . . D'une voix impatiente je répondis en frappant le sol du bout de mon pied:
– La peau de la raie sous la pointe du crayon vert.

('It must all pass underneath, mustn't it?'
'What must?' asked Mme Bosse: 'Underneath what?'
In an impatient voice I replied, stamping the ground with my foot:
'The skin of the parting beneath the point of the green pencil.')

Parlour games, practical jokes, carnival costumes and theatrical performances also furnish Roussel with opportunities to turn each text's opening words inside out. In a story such as 'Parmi les Noirs' the materiality and doubleness of language that underlie the *procédé* register on a variety of levels within the narrative itself. Its cryptograms emphasize the physical aspects of words, and their limitless capacity to become estranged and even antithetical: implicit in the white letters on the cushions of the billiard table are the black hordes of the plunderer.

The story is set on a rainy day during a house party in the country. To pass the time, the host, Flambeau, suggests they play a complicated word-game:

A question was to be posed in writing to someone, and this person was then shut in the [billiard] room next door. After ten minutes exactly, the door was opened, and the person had to give their response to the question in the form of a rebus.

Whoever guesses the answer is then in turn set a question to which they have to produce a riddling reply. The first contestant, the painter Débarras, is asked if he prefers water-colours or pastels, and why. His response begins with the musical notation for LA, followed by the letters *coi*, then the musical notation for RÉ, followed by a picture of a lama, a meadow (*pré*), iron bars in a bag (*fer en sac*), the letters OSE SA SA, a very thin (*fine*) S, and a drawing of an old man with SONEC written on his body carrying a heavy burden and – in a cartoon speech-bubble – pleading for help, followed by another LA. These pictures and letters phonetically yield LA – coi – RÉ – lamà – pré – fer en sac – OSE – deux SA – fine S – aide Sonec – LA, which in turn becomes, 'L'aquarelle a ma préférence à cause de sa finesse et de son éclat' ('I prefer water-colours because of their subtlety and vividness').

Clearly Roussel's *procédé* owes much to cryptograms of this sort; both involve breaking down words into their constituent sounds, and this fragmentation then enables double meanings to proliferate at will. The narrator, however, has no talent for drawing, and therefore does not inscribe his puzzle on paper. He is asked what he considers the most moving book published during the year. His answer consists of seemingly meaningless letters chalked on the worn cushions of the billiard table, which happens to be rather the worse for wear. It as at this moment that the story opens:

Les lettres du blanc sur les bandes du vieux billard formaient un incompréhensible assemblage. J'en étais déjà à mon sixième tour et je voyais avec plaisir les mots baroques que j'obtenais avec mon système pourtant si simple.

– Quel charabia! pensais-je. Personne ne trouvera la clé et Balancier lui-même n'y comprendra rien.

(The white letters on the cushions of the old billiard table formed an incomprehensible grouping. I had just completed my sixth revolution, and I was delighted to see what outlandish words my very simple system had produced.

'What gibberish!' I thought to myself. No one would find the key, and even Balancier himself would not be able to understand it.)

By writing each letter in sequence on the four cushions he obtains: LEEBCLASIPA, ETSLSENDEIR, STDAUSDUULD, LRUNRBEVXL (*Les lettres du blanc sur les bandes du vieux pillard*). The narrator's cryptogram is thus itself the opening (bar one letter) and closing words of the story. The novel it alludes to, called *Parmi les Noirs*, was written by Balancier, himself a member of the house party, and it is of course Balancier who solves the narrator's enigma. The story folds into itself at every turn, but also generates its diametrical opposite, the antithetical world of black Africa. Balancier's novel describes the tribulations of a sea captain named Compas (Compass), whose ship founders in a hurricane off the coast of Africa. The crew escape in lifeboats, but Compas refuses to abandon his command:

> He watches his companions rapidly disappear, and soon he has lost all sight of them. A gust of wind breaks his mast, which, in falling, wounds him in the head. He collapses unconscious to the deck. When he comes to, he finds himself surrounded by various black Africans who are dressing his wound. His boat, wrecked on the shore, is no more than a crumbling heap of flotsam. However, certain parts of the cargo are worth salvaging, and another, larger group of blacks are busy carrying away all sorts of items on their backs.

Compas's crisis proves, like Méphisto's, analogous to that suffered by Roussel. Both Roussel and Compas endure 'a terribly violent shock', as he puts it in 'Comment j'ai écrit . . .', and find themselves alone in the inverted realm of fragments prefigured in Section II of *Mon Âme*. Indeed, Compas's life under the irascible chief Tombola (whose name even figures the *grand lot* of Roussel's *gloire*) seems to shadow forth the torments of prospecting that drove him to writhe on the floor in fits of rage. On meeting his ferocious captor, Compas explains that he wishes to be on his way: at this

> Tombola grows angry, and gives orders that Compas be kept under surveillance. And so begins a wandering life full of hardships and dangers. Tombola holds absolute sway over a vast horde of black followers, with whom he pillages all he finds in his path ... Compas witnesses endless new cruelties, yet without ever becoming inured to such sights. As soon as a village is espied, Tombola attacks with his innumerable troops, who soon overwhelm it. There follow hideous scenes of cannibalism. Neither old, young nor adult are spared, and Tombola is the first to feast on their human flesh. The only ones not killed are those who are enlisted as recruits. All possible booty is seized, and, before leaving, the pillagers set fire to the four corners of the unfortunate hamlet.

Just as Méphisto is undone by the worms that gnaw away at his protective lining, so Compas is forced to witness an equivalent disintegration and ingestion. Tombola's enemies are eaten or recruited; either way they are absorbed into the body of his pillaging band. But while Méphisto is destroyed by his *vers*, his worms or verses, Compas survives by writing letters *about les bandes du vieux pillard*, the hordes of the old plunderer, letters later duplicated in white chalk on the cushioned linings (*bandes*) of the billiard table with which the story begins. The *procédé* that enables this doubling of the lining is more, then, than just a parlour game, but linguistically fused with the continued existence of the *blanc*, be he Compas or Roussel.

Compas sends his letters off to his wife by carrier-pigeon. We are not actually told if they arrive or not, but we do know that they manage to cross into the realm of art, for it is these letters which constitute the text of Balancier's novel *Parmi les Noirs*, to which the narrator's riddle in turn alludes. Novel and rebus form neatly poised, mutually dependent polarities worthy of a scale-maker (*balancier*): the black printed letters of the novel made up of letters written about blacks are inverted into the white letters alluding to the letters of a white man printed on white paper; at every stage white and black reflect and oppose each other, for the unassimilable white letters of the protective lining exist only in relation to the letters from Africa describing irrepressible black feats of absorption. It is not only the story's opening and closing words that incarnate its duality: mirrorings and antitheses radiate from its primary puns in all conceivable directions.

In a headnote introducing the *Textes-genèse*, Roussel describes 'Parmi les Noirs' as the 'embryo' of *Impressions d'Afrique*, while in 'Comment j'ai écrit . . .' he explains in detail how the opening scene of his first prose novel developed out of the *billard/pillard* motif. The essay clearly represents 'Parmi les Noirs' as the original source of the *procédé*, and yet it seems not to have satisfied Roussel to the extent that 'Chiquenaude' did, the only work between *La Doublure* (1897) and *La Vue* (1904) which Roussel felt merited publication. It seems unlikely he could have foreseen at the time of composition that the story would turn out to contain 'the entire genesis' of *Impressions d'Afrique*, composed ten years later. The tale does predict, however, the ambivalence Roussel would come to feel about the cryptic procedures underlying his novels and plays. As the narrator contemplates his scrambled letters, he delights in the thought that even Balancier will be utterly confounded by his ingenuity. But while the others puzzle over the seemingly nonsensical chalked letters, the novelist carefully copies them down in his notebook and retires to a corner to decipher them:

> Soon his face brightened and I saw his lips carefully articulate several words.
>
> 'He has the key,' I said to myself, 'it's only a matter of seconds now.'
>
> In fact, at that very moment, Balancier threw me a knowing look and announced out loud that he had found the solution.

Could Roussel have already dreaded such a moment, even before the development of the second phase of the *procédé*, which, unlike the first version deployed in 'Chiquenaude' and 'Parmi les Noirs' and the other *Textes-genèse*, required that its own workings be concealed within the narratives it generated? Perhaps he sensed at the time of composition that the story might become 'the key' to later aesthetic cryptograms which would only protect against the fragmentation and cannibalism they transpose as long as they remained undecoded.

The *Textes-genèse* exploit the haphazard duplicities of language – the fact that the same word can have two unrelated meanings – to fulfil their ingenious patterns of self-enclosure. Yet these puns, which on one level illustrate the arbitrary and unstable nature of words, serve also as a defence against the random or merely sequential. The details of each story are deliberately focused by Roussel's need to find a means of linking, say, 'Le choc des gouttes sur le pépin du citron' (The impact of the [lemon] drops on the pip of the lemon), to 'Le choc des gouttes sur le pépin du mitron' (The fall of the [rain] drops on the umbrella of the baker's assistant). These double meanings literally underwrite the narratives they inspire; each story concludes at the moment it achieves its predestined, near-perfect rhyme.

Some interesting comparisons can be drawn between such methods and the kinds of linguistic and libidinal economies analysed by Roland Barthes in his studies of Sade, Loyola, and Fourrier. The transformations Roussel's *procédé* makes possible are achieved not through a Rimbaldian 'alchemy of the verb' or a Joycean fusion of sounds and meanings, but through elaborate, painstaking processes of combination: Barthes notes of his three authors that they 'deduct, combine, arrange, endlessly produce rules of assemblage; they substitute syntax, *composition*, for creation.' In the *Textes-genèse*, Roussel's foregrounding of the stories' origins in the materiality of language makes clear the extent to which the narratives fulfil an analogous 'materialist rite', to use Barthes's term, a rite that ultimately articulates an order Barthes defines in formalist terms as 'metrical'.

It was almost a decade, however, before Roussel developed from such puns and rhymes an all-encompassing 'metrical order', his *procédé poétique*, and what might be called Roussel's *Textes-avortés* were perhaps almost as important to its evolution as his *Textes-genèse*. The two vast compositions, *La Seine* and *Les Noces*, can be seen as charting a kind of *via negativa* to the promised land of the *procédé*; they embody the terrors and dangers of a language that is undoubled, and thus driven to prolong itself indefinitely. While the *Textes-genèse* circle neatly back to their beginnings, like serpents with their tails (and their tales) in their mouths, *La Seine* and *Les Noces* explore an opposite ideal, that of an art coterminous with existence.

Although neither *La Seine* nor *Les Noces* is dated, both works clearly belong to Roussel's periods of prospecting. It seems likely that *La Seine* was written between the *Textes-genèse* and *La Vue* (1900–03). *Les Noces* is harder to date, but was probably composed either just after the publication of *La Doublure* (1897–1900), or between *La Vue* and *Impressions d'Afrique* (1904–08), when he 'again set about prospecting for several years'. Neither work could be said to bear out Roussel's claim in 'Comment j'ai écrit . . .' that after his crisis he set about working 'in a more judicious manner': these two colossal manuscripts rather prove yet again that Roussel was congenitally incapable of confining his imagination within the parameters of the 'judicious', for both *La Seine* and *Les Noces* proliferate in all directions until all sense of perspective is overwhelmed by the unstoppable flood of new characters, new narratives, new descriptions of anything and everything.

*La Seine* is a verse play that runs to around seven thousand lines. Its opening suggests a wholly standard domestic drama. Geneviève sits sewing at home. The doorbell rings; it is her husband Raoul, who has lost his front-door key. The happy couple briefly review the origins and development of their relationship; like Nanon and Sylvestre, they fell in love at an early age, playing together as brother and sister for days on end. Now they are a delightfully contented married couple with a fine young son, Charlot.

The dutiful Geneviève leaves to visit her mother for the evening, and Raoul immediately confesses in soliloquy that he is leading a 'double life' (line 154):

c'est coupable et je veux
Chaque jour vaincre mon désir; mais ses cheveux,
Ses lèvres, son regard surtout, fixe ou mobile,
Dont elle sait jouer avec un charme habile,
Et ses dents . . . rien qu'en y pensant je deviens fou.

(lines 163–7)

it is wrong of me, and I wish/ Each day I could overcome my desire;
but her hair,/ Her lips, above all her glances, whether fixed or
shifting,/ Which she knows how to vary with artful charm,/ And
her teeth . . . simply thinking about these things makes me frantic.

He resolves to write his mistress a letter ending their affair, at
which moment she arrives in the house: 'Ici! Toi! Ciel! . . .' he
bursts out (line 226):

RAOUL:   Mais comment donc es-tu
         Entrée?
JEANNE:   Avec ta clé; quand tu t'es dévêtu
         Ce matin j'ai fouillé derrière toi tes poches
         Pour l'avoir . . .

(lines 243–6)

R: But how did you/ Get in? J: With your key; when you undressed/
This morning, I searched your pockets behind your back/ To get
it . . .

Raoul's purloined key thus simultaneously initiates the action
of *La Seine* and signals the end of Raoul's double life, just as
Gaspard's difficulties with his sword wreck his career as an
understudy and provide the origin of the events described in *La
Doublure*. Jeanne persuades Raoul to abandon his wife, child
and home, by threatening to return to her former life on the
streets. Yet, in the context of the overall play, Raoul's decision
to leave is significant more in relation to the digressions it
appears to license than to the plot it supposedly sets in motion.
The adulterous couple depart, and through the front door of
the flat, which has been left open, the audience overhears a long,
desultory discussion between a miscellaneous group of young
painters. For the next six thousand lines of the play the melodramatic implications of its opening are wholly suspended. Only

in the short final scene – again as in *La Doublure* – does Roussel return to his primary narrative.

The enormous second act is set in the concert hall of the Moulin Rouge. This act alone features almost four hundred named characters. They mingle casually, exchanging small talk, anecdotes and observations about the music, or the crowd, or the dancers, or anything that catches their attention. Roussel interleaves these languorous colloquies so that the reader – for *La Seine* has yet to be performed – is forced to switch attention back and forth among the various, ever-shifting clusters of characters. The method looks forward to the choric dispersal of narrative deployed in his first prose drama, *L'Étoile au front*, where the characters share out stories almost as if playing a game of Chinese whispers, and also to the multiple levels of perspective Roussel achieved through his use of brackets and footnotes in *Nouvelles Impressions d'Afrique*. He seems untroubled by the meandering banality of most of the conversations and interchanges. Jeanne, for instance, provides a running commentary on the progress of her game of patience.

JEANNE:   C'est ce maudit valet
          De cœur qui gêne tout; ce petit gringalet,
          Où pourrait-on le mettre?

(lines 1199–201)

It's this accursed jack/ Of hearts who is holding everything up; this little whipper-snapper,/ Where can he be put?

Ce sept de cœur aurait bien dû venir plus tôt,
Franchement; je pouvais dégarnir jusqu'en haut,
Tandis que maintenant je ne sais où le mettre . . .

   (lines 1239–41)

This seven of hearts ought to have come much earlier,/ To tell the truth; I would have been able to get rid of it above,/ Whereas now I don't know where to put it . . .

Le huit aussi marche . . . c'est un progrès
Très grand . . .

(lines 1255–6)

The eight also fits . . . this is progress/ Of a serious kind . . .

                        C'est la dame
De trèfle qui nous manque à présent; en l'ayant,
Regarde, tout ce qu'on ferait, c'est effrayant!
(*Tirant une carte*)
Ce n'est pas celle-là? Non . . .

                                 (lines 1374–7)

It's the queen/ Of clubs I'm missing at present; if I had her,/ Look, there's so much I could do, it's dreadful! (Drawing a card)/ This is not her? No . . .

                       Abondance
De trèfle: nous allons sûr la rater, je crois;
Et toi?
RAOUL:
           C'est bien possible à cause de ces rois
Qui sont très encombrants, voilà ce qui nous gêne
Surtout, pour le moment.

                                 (lines 1434–8)

A plethora/ Of clubs; we're sure to fail, I think;/ And you? R: It's very possible because of these kings/ Who are a real nuisance, they're the ones holding us up/ Mainly, at the moment . . .

These remarks – and many more of a similar kind – are spread over some twenty pages, and interspersed amid equally drab stretches of mundane chit-chat. Yet one also becomes paradoxically aware that the play's ability to capture the random flow of society *causerie* derives from its strict use of alexandrines. The regular rhymes seem to allow Roussel to neutralize all other expectations; as in *La Doublure*, it is only the artifice of verse that makes possible the purely prosaic.

Analogously, the play's abrogation of its own narrative impetus makes it wholly hospitable to the stories the characters relate to each other. Throughout Acts II and III (set in the Bois de Boulogne), which together occupy six thousand of its seven thousand lines, and during which nothing happens in relation to its central plot, the play becomes the medium through which successive narratives are unfolded, rather as in *La Vue* the tiny picture set into the lens of a pen-holder becomes the medium through which Roussel creates his diverse and energetic portrait of a seaside town. In both *La Seine* and *La Vue*, stasis and narrative seem mutually dependent upon each other; it is only because the action is frozen that the inner descriptions and stories are released, and it is these digressions that, like Scheherazade's tales of the Arabian nights, block, or at least delay and delay, the progress of the main plot that frames them. Indeed, as for Scheherazade, or Compas in 'Parmi les Noirs,' who is cushioned from his pillaging captors by his literally wandering missives, or the narrator, who hopes to be saved by his letter-dispersing code, these digressions come to seem a form of self-preservation. In Act IV of *La Seine*, Raoul, by now abandoned by Jeanne, finds himself alone, as Gaspard did, with the elements:

> RAOUL: J'ai l'air autour de moi, partout . . . je sens le sol
> Ferme lorsque je marche . . .
>
>> En bas la Seine passe . . .
>
>> (*Il lève la tête.*)
>
> Le ciel! . . . Je vois le ciel . . . les étoiles . . . l'espace . . .
>> (*Il regarde autour de lui.*)
>
> Personne? Non.
>
>> C'est l'heure . . .
>
>>> Il faut . . . je veux . . . je veux
>
>> (*Il enjambe le parapet.*)
>
> Adieu, Jeanne . . . ma Jeanne aimée . . .
>> (*Il porte la boucle à ses lèvres.*)
>
>> Oh, ses cheveux! . . .
>
>> (*Il se précipite.*)

(lines 6927–31)

I have the air around me, everywhere . . . I feel the earth/ Solid beneath my feet . . . Below the Seine passes. (*He lifts his head.*)/ The sky! . . . I see the sky . . . the stars . . . space . . . *(He looks about him)*/ No one? No. It's time . . . I must . . . I wish . . . I wish . . . (*He climbs on to the parapet.*)/ Farewell, Jeanne . . . my beloved Jeanne . . . (*He brings the lock of hair to his lips.*) Oh, her hair . . . (*He hurls himself over.*)

He will thus become part of the flow of nature rather than the pageant of narrative, a victim of physical rather than linguistic disintegration. And Roussel's final stage direction pointedly illustrates the indifference of both to the anguished lover's fate:

> A silence. Soon someone whistling a popular song can be heard in the distance. A boy appears, crosses the bridge, and exits, all the time whistling. The whistling slowly fades. The curtain falls.

Raoul's demise might be considered the result of Roussel's failure to fuse the material and the representative levels of language. While the *procédé*, even in its elementary form in the *Textes-genèse*, generates episodes that are inherently doubled or lined, the inset stories of *La Seine* are in direct opposition to the progress of the story's primary narrative. There is no mediation between them of the sort effected by the puns that open and close each *Texte-genèse*. The play's antitheses can never meet, can only be juxtaposed; the absolute nature of this opposition is clearest in the final act, where Roussel intercuts Raoul's tortured soliloquies with the casual chatter of numerous passers-by. The need for some means of forcing polarities to interpenetrate also underlies the intriguing story of the ship's boy wrecked, like Compas and the Incomparables, on the coast of equatorial Africa. The episode is told by a character called Daman,* and is further recessed by being a description of a series of engravings. This time it is not a hurricane but pirates who precipitate the disaster:

> Le bateau s'enfonçait tout de suite et coulait,
> En ne laissant qu'un grand bouillonnement de mousse;
> Sauvé tranquillement sur une épave, un mousse
> Abordait dans un lieu désert, nu comme un ver,
> S'étant dévêtu pour nager.

(lines 4324–8)

---

* Odd names crop up in all Roussel's texts, and we know he had extreme difficulty in arriving at each final choice. Leiris records that he sometimes asked Eugène Vallée, the overseer at the Lemerre printing house, to fill in the blanks or initials he had left in the manuscript, but then invariably replaced Vallée's suggestions with other names (R & CO, p. 206). *La Seine* contains an especially eccentric range: Ernest Arson, Buss, Bopp, Burc, Bals, Roolf, Pauline Bux, Orry, Raga, Saerck, Èche, Renée Wunster, Lay … The manuscripts offer no indication as to how he arrived at these names.

The boat foundered and sank at once/ Leaving only a churning whirlpool of foam;/ Calmly saved on a bit of wreckage, a cabin boy/ Landed on a deserted shore, naked as a worm,/ Having stripped off to swim.

The perfect rhyme of *mousse/mousse* gestures towards the patterned realm of the *procédé*: the white cabin boy escapes from the white froth of the shipwreck and is washed up on the shores of black Africa. He climbs a hill and witnesses the local inhabitants feasting 'sur un homme blanc, barbu' (on a bearded white man) (line 4340). Fortunately, he has a can of boot-polish that has been driven ashore with the wreckage, and he immediately sets about blacking his body. When only half-way through this operation he is surprised by members of the cannibal tribe, but instead of capturing and devouring him, they fall to their knees in wonder, and treat him like a god:

> l'étrangeté
> De ce jouvenceau noir et blanc plongeait la race
> Dans un étonnement sans borne . . .

(lines 4380–82)

the strangeness/ Of this black and white youth plunged the tribe/ Into limitless astonishment . . .

At a banquet to celebrate his sudden elevation, the half-white, half-black cabin boy turned chieftain happily feasts on the flesh of young members of the tribe who had themselves hoped to eat him, and revels in his 'superbe destin' (line 4388). It would only be by discovering some means of unifying such divisions within language itself – i.e. the *procédé* – that Roussel would see a way to fulfilling his own equally 'magnificent destiny'.

Yet Roussel's openness in *La Seine* to drift and contingency does exert a peculiar kind of fascination. Towards the end of Act II a character called Clotilde Park explains to an acquaintance, Nicourt, how she enjoys watching the play of dust motes in sunlight, in terms that clearly reflect Roussel's experience of *la gloire*:

> j'ai bien médité
> En regardant ce long endroit plein de lumière
> Remuante. . . . Je suis du reste coutumière

De ses réflexions profondes et sans fin;
Je resterais ainsi sans éprouver la faim,
La soif ni la fatigue un temps inconcevable.
Chaque grain de poussière était vite introuvable
Sitôt qu'il dépassait la ligne où le rayon
Finissait, pour entrer dans l'ombre.

(lines 5256–64)

I have thought deeply/ While watching this long space full of light/ Seething with activity ... I am, besides, in the habit/ Of engaging in deep, endless meditations;/ I would remain thus, without feeling hungry,/ Thirsty or tired for inconceivable amounts of time./ Each grain of dust quickly became untraceable/ As soon as it passed beyond the line where the beam of light/ Finished, and entered into the shadow.

The multitudinous characters in *La Seine* are presented with just this suspense and detachment: they float in and out of focus, beyond the reach of all perspective and barely distinguishable from each other. Clotilde is particularly entranced by a certain 'très mince' (very slender) (line 5280) mote whose motions seem to her 'rempli de majesté' (full of majesty) (line 5288); after all manner of agile and dignified manoeuvres within a shaft of light he finally retires:

puis il est entré dans la nuit noire,
Dans l'oubli, comme pour renoncer à la gloire
De briller.

(lines 5297–9)

then he entered into black night,/ Into oblivion, as if to renounce the glory/ Of shining.

Roussel was in fact loath to allow his leading dust mote, Raoul, to enter the darkness for ever. A couple of short fragments entitled *La Tonsure* suggest he had plans to expand the play yet further. In the first of these Raoul reappears as L'Abbé Mathieu; instead of drowning himself he has joined a monastery, where he is discovered by a repentant Jeanne who begs his return. In the second fragment he has taken the further precaution of joining a Trappist monastery, but is still tormented by the image of his lost love:

Trappiste!

Je suis trappiste, seul et sans parler jamais
A personne!
Ô ma Jeanne, ô Dieu que je t'aimais.

(lines 59–61)

Trappist!/ I am a trappist, alone and unable ever to speak/ To
anyone!// O my Jeanne, o God, how I loved you.

By the end of this monologue he has lost his wits altogether:
he oscillates between charged erotic memories and nightmarish
visions of Jeanne deformed and limping; her body is all clammy,
her forehead carbuncled and grossly swollen; her right arm
lengthens and starts twirling crazily. The fragment concludes on
a note of hysterical revulsion and self-division: as he feverishly
attempts to embrace an imaginary Jeanne, Raoul finds himself
instead recoiling in disgust from the touch of her skin.

———

Roussel was the most secretive and secret-loving of men, particularly in all matters regarding his own sexuality.* One of the
main themes of his discussions with Janet seems to have been
the erosion of double standards in public life:

He is made indignant by the exhibition of naked women
which is in vogue in some theatres; he cannot think without
sadness of the young women of good families who assist in
the care of the wounded in ambulances, who paint in
studios and are therefore exposed to the sight of human
nakedness. 'How can anyone allow young girls to look at
half-naked athletes? All swimming competitions ought to be
banned, we ought to curb the licentiousness of certain
posters, and make severe laws against nudity.' It might be
thought such ideas were those of a scrupulous moralist:
not at all. Martial does not suffer himself from any sexual
scruples, nor is he bothered by the thought of the loose living

* For further discussion of homosexuality in the context of the period, see Eve
Kosofsky Sedgwick's *Epistemology of the Closet* (London: Penguin, 1994,
first published 1990), in particular Chapter 5, 'Proust and the Spectacle of the
Closet', pp. 213–51.

of others; when he protests against public nudity, he is not at all worried that these shows might corrupt society: 'That those who engage in their forbidden acts in private rooms know all the while that they are forbidden, that they might be punished, or at least condemned by respectable members of society – that is perfect. But that anyone can see naked flesh, that anyone can get sexual thrills simply by watching a public spectacle, without threat of punishment, with the consent of their parents and while claiming all the while to be chaste – that is unacceptable. Everything that has to do with love ought to remain rare, forbidden, inaccessible: for a young girl to see a naked man ought to be a stroke of extraordinary good fortune, not something that happens every day in a hospital or painter's studio. If women's breasts are openly on display in public, there is no thrill in catching a sudden glimpse of them. We mustn't strip away the charm of the taboo, or lose the cult of the secret garden. That would be to devalue sex altogether, to botch the whole business.'*

Indeed, his obsession with concealing the delights of the forbidden fruit appears to have extended even to his relationship with his psychoanalyst; at no point does Janet suggest that he was aware of Roussel's homosexuality, and therefore not himself tempted by 'women's breasts'.

What information we have about Roussel's predilections comes mainly from Charlotte Dufrène, his *maîtresse de convenance*. Dufrène was introduced to Roussel by his brother-in-law, Charles Ney, Germaine's second husband, in 1910, although the relationship was probably organized principally by Madame Roussel. As his paid companion she was obliged to accompany him to the theatre, the opera and sometimes on his travels, for which she received a monthly salary and a flat in the eighth

---

* This might be seen as connecting him with the Sadian libertine: 'In their pleasures,' as Barthes notes, 'all libertines have an overwhelming urge to hide the Female's sexual organs scrupulously' (SFL, p. 123). One thinks also of the relationship between forbidden sexual encounters and punning in Wilde; from this perspective the *procédé* becomes a linguistic form of Bunburying.

*arrondissement*, close to the Roussel residence on rue de Chaillot. Despite the mercantile nature of their arrangement and the lack of physical intimacy, she was probably closer to Roussel – though that may not be saying a great deal – during the latter half of his life than any of his friends or family. His final book, *Comment j'ai écrit certains de mes livres*, is dedicated 'A mon amie Charlotte Dufrène.'*

In the course of her interview with Michel Leiris, Dufrène revealed that Roussel was principally interested in 'les cottes bleues et les uniformes de marin à pompon rouge' – that is, blue-collar workers and sailors. She also recalled hearing of an incident involving a stable boy that caused 'a scandal that had to be hushed up'. The stable boy was probably Louis Blanc, who in 1903 was sentenced to five years in prison for extortion. Roussel testified that he had handed over 90,000 francs, only to receive a request for a further 100,000 francs. Dufrène intimated to Leiris that Roussel was a frequent target for blackmailers, and even that many of his trips abroad were motivated by the need to escape their demands. It is possible that his spells in the army were the result of similar difficulties. Dufrène also expressed her conviction that Roussel had never slept with a woman; one evening he pointed out a decayed street scavenger, and declared he'd prefer such a life to having to marry even the richest and most beautiful of the opposite sex.

———

* Charlotte Dufrène was born Charlotte Fredez in Paris in 1880, to strict Catholic parents, and attended a religious boarding-school. Before (and perhaps for a while after) meeting Roussel she was the mistress of the Count de Vallon. She was not, she told Leiris, Roussel's first female companion: when he was around twenty his mother provided him with a mistress, but she soon broke off the relationship, complaining she could no longer bear to listen to her supposed lover's recitation of interminably long poems, and demanding compensation of 100,000 francs from Madame Roussel (R & CO, p. 81). Dufrène frankly admitted to Leiris in 1964 that she had never had any interest in Roussel's writings, and was amazed when he told her a magazine (*Bizarre*) had recently devoted a special issue to him. She related also how his sartorial fastidiousness extended to her as well: she was only to wear the white gloves in which he liked to see her once, and when she had donned a new costume for an outing together, he would squeeze himself into a corner of the car 'as if afraid he might touch her and ruin the outfit, at which he would gaze in admiration' (R & CO, p. 313).

Blackmail lies at the heart of the extremely violent play that Claude and Luce attend in the third section of Roussel's unfinished *Les Noces*. This vast opus exists in various stages of composition and revision, from sketchy worksheets to clean fair copies. Hundreds of pages of its final section, 'À l'Ambigu', are only roughly drafted: many consist of a few scattered words per line, and some of not much more than rhyme words listed down the right-hand side of the page. The whole cycle consists of some 2,900 pages of manuscript material, now published in two fat volumes, V and VI, of the complete edition.

Its main plot is not, however, particularly complex. Claude works in a bookshop and Luce as a seamstress. One Easter Monday they take a trip on a pleasure boat to the Bois de Vincennes. Parts I ('En bateau-mouche') and II ('Au bois de Vincennes') both consist of crazily minute descriptions of every aspect of this outing. Roussel devotes pages and pages, for example, to charting the progress of a series of soap-bubbles blown by a young boy on the terrace of a café where the couple stop for a drink. Like the dust motes whose evolutions so fascinate Clotilde Park in *La Seine*, the bubbles' distorted, ever-changing reflections suggest the impossibly inclusive nature of the aesthetic ideals motivating Roussel during his periods of prospecting. He painstakingly charts the minute differences that the size and form of each bubble have upon the objects mirrored in its fragile, transparent membrane. Furthermore, because each bubble is in motion, the images perpetually alter according to the strength and direction of the air currents sustaining them; thus people and objects shrink and grow, appear and disappear as the breeze determines. The movement of the bubbles

> provoque tantôt le rapetissement
> Des objets, tantôt leur croissance calme et prompte
> Selon la volunté du caprice qui dompte
> La bulle en la faisant remuer: et selon
> Le sens qu'il donne.

(lines 5188–92)

causes sometimes the shrinking/ Of the objects reflected, sometimes their calm, prompt expansion/ According to the impulse of the

capricious breeze which controls/ Each bubble's movement, and
according/ To the direction it takes.

A bubble floats past a bit of melon rind on a plate, which is
immediately reflected on its watery surface. A curious dog then
pokes his nose towards the melon, looking for scraps:

> Dans la bulle, son corps se courbe, son poil ras
> Est brillant et soyeux; presque aussitôt un bras
> S'avance, dont la main prend le chien sous le ventre . . .

> (lines 5207–9)

In the bubble, his body appears bent, his smooth fur/ Is shining
and silky; almost immediately an arm/ Advances, and a hand takes
hold of the dog under the stomach . . .

As in *La Seine*, this kind of obsession with circumstantial detail
continually overwhelms the story line's all but arrested progress.
Part II breaks off late at night in the wood, with Luce seemingly
on the point of succumbing to Claude. Roussel describes their
kissing as neutrally and precisely as he had the foreplay of
Gaspard and Roberte in *La Doublure*. And a fragment ('Sur le
quai . . .') appended to this section presents a different evening
that ends in a similar manner, though rather more explicitly: in
this episode they return to Luce's lodgings; Claude locks the
door, and asks

>           'Tu vas me craindre
> Encore?' Elle dit: 'Non, je t'aime.' D'un baiser
> Au front, près des cheveux il cherche à l'apaiser
> Mais elle, quelque temps, résiste tout émue
> Regardant fixement la flamme qui remue . . .

> (lines 370–74)

'Will you be afraid of me/ For ever?' She says: 'No, I love you.'
With a kiss/ On the forehead, near her hair, he tries to soothe her,/
But she, for some time, resists, overcome by emotion,/ Staring
fixedly at the trembling flame . . .

A rough outline, headed *Les Noces* – the only indication of the
poem's working title – suggests Roussel intended the cycle to
end, like *La Seine* and *La Doublure*, tragically: Claude has left
to become a soldier in Africa; Luce is pregnant, dismissed from

her employment, homeless, and preparing to sleep *à la belle étoile*. Another draft of the ending is appended to the outline of the second half of the play presented in 'À l'Ambigu': here the destitute and visibly pregnant Luce is about to confront Claude – who has abandoned her for a new lover (denoted simply by the letter Y) – in one of the café-concert halls of the Moulin Rouge.

The Théâtre de l'Ambigu was one of Paris's most popular venues at the turn of the nineteenth and twentieth centuries. It specialized in melodramas. In the third section of *Les Noces* Roussel sets about describing the performance – attended by Claude and Luce – of a particularly gruesome and convoluted piece that involves blackmail, kidnap, murders, a vast array of unsavoury low-lifers and a detective – one Bridier – who, though a master of disguise, takes an inordinate time amassing evidence before closing in on the play's chief criminal (Frisette). Acts I, II and the beginning of Act III have been fair-copied, and there even exists a revised, expanded version of Act I. A further five thousand lines describing the action of the rest of Act III and Act IV have been roughly drafted: the events of the rest of the play (Acts V and VI) can only be gleaned from an extensive prose synopsis of its complicated dénouement.

Roussel adored the popular theatre, and often attended the same boulevard shows dozens of times in succession. He was, according to Michel Leiris, especially fond of melodramas such as *La Bouquetière des Innocents*, which he saw between ten and fifteen times, and *La Tour de Nesle*. It seems likely it was the combination of violence and artifice that most enchanted him. As the play performed in 'À l'Ambigu' heads towards a gory murder, Luce confides to Claude:

> Nous allons, j'espère, avoir un crime
> Terrifiant pour la vue et tout à fait beau,
> Avec l'arme semblant pénétrer dans la peau,
> Et l'assassin montrant au public sa main sale
> De sang.

(lines 2663–7)

We are going to have, I hope, a crime/ That is terrifying to watch, and altogether awful,/ With the weapon seeming to penetrate the

skin,/ And the assassin showing to the audience his hand stained/
With blood.

In his descriptions of stage action Roussel consistently refers to
the theatrical contrivances deployed in each scene to produce a
semblance of reality. Cadouru assassinates poor Simone in style:

> il la crible
> De grands coups de couteau dans la poitrine . . . Alors
> Le silence se fait, dedans comme dehors;
> Sur le long peignoir blanc, un sang factice coule;
> Simone fait des pas inconséquents, puis roule
> Sur le tapis et reste en place sur le dos,
> Comme morte . . .

(lines 2823–9)

he riddles her/ With fierce knife thrusts in the chest . . . Then/ Silence
falls, inside and outside;/ All down her white dressing-gown,
artificial blood flows;/ Simone makes a few tottering steps, then
rolls/ On the carpet and remains on her back/ As if dead . . .

And Claude, for one, is impressed by the verisimilitude of the
actor's performance:

> C'est un homme adroit, il vous supprime
> Lestement; on croirait qu'il a vraiment blessé
> Simone

(lines 2963–5)

He's a dexterous fellow, and kills/ Very nimbly; it's easy to believe
he really hurt/ Simone

he notes approvingly to Luce.

Thus, by presenting in a poem a theatrical performance,
Roussel found yet another means of delineating the gap between
representation and reality that so obsessed him in *La Doublure*.
But whereas the floats and masqueraders succeed each other
with no particular narrative logic – and the same could be said
of the conversations and anecdotes that make up most of *La
Seine*, and indeed of the scenes described in *La Vue* – in 'À
l'Ambigu' Roussel begins to explore ways of layering the different strands of his material: reading the poem involves keeping
an increasingly demanding number of different plots in the mind,

and in this it looks forward to Roussel's use of what Leiris called 'multiples tiroirs' (multiple drawers/episodes), the principal structuring technique of *Impressions d'Afrique*, and in a still more sophisticated form, of *Nouvelles Impressions d'Afrique*.

'À l'Ambigu' also makes clear Roussel's complete lack of interest in moral issues, inner motivations and character development. 'He hated', recalls Leiris, 'psychological plays, the drama of "ideas".' The complexities of the plot absorb all his attention. The characters perform the most nefarious deeds without scruples or remorse. In Act IV the illicit lovers l'Enfant de Chœur and Françoise finally succeed in murdering l'Enfant de Chœur's official partner, Isabelle, who has made her will in his favour. As in Zola's *Thérèse Raquin*, they stage the killing as a boating accident, but whereas Laurent is forever haunted by the ghost of Camille, l'Enfant de Chœur merely observes, 'Nous avons bien fait/ de la tuer, c'etait une vilaine femme' (We did well/ to kill her, she was a nasty woman) (lines 8642–3), and sets about spending his prospective inheritance with gay abandon. The only witness of their crime, the ugly, evil Frisette, is – rather implausibly – madly in love with Françoise, and he uses this knowledge to blackmail her into sleeping with him. Frisette is the play's arch-criminal, and the only one eventually – or almost – brought to justice: he is tried and condemned to death for various crimes, but escapes from prison and appears, brandishing a revolver, in the cabaret where Françoise – who has recently taken up singing – is about to make her debut. When Bridier and the police arrive on his tail, he shoots himself. Françoise and l'Enfant de Chœur's crime goes unpunished.

These later developments are outlined in the prose synopsis, and would have added at least another six or seven thousand lines to the 8,760 either completed or drafted. Yet this synopsis suggests Roussel planned for *Les Noces* two further sections still: a scene between Claude and Luce in the wood (either a return to the Bois de Vincennes or perhaps an outing to the Bois de Boulogne) in which they make 'nouveaux serments' – that is, yet more avowals to each other – and discuss the drowning of Isabelle by Françoise and L'Enfant de Chœur; and the final scene at the Moulin Rouge in which Luce was to confront Claude and his new lover.

Like *La Seine*, *Les Noces* illustrates Roussel's compulsion during his period of prospecting to reflect the immeasurable diversity of existence by producing a seemingly endless flow of alexandrines. The sheer scale of what I have called Roussel's *Textes-avortés* brings to mind Barthes's discussion of Ignatius Loyola's language in the *Exercises*, 'subdividing, bifurcating and trifurcating, combining every strictly semantic operation designed to combat relentlessly the vague and the empty.' The metronomic tick of Roussel's alexandrines function analogously, formally underwriting his remorseless enumeration of minutiae. Yet clearly at some point during the composition of *Les Noces* he realized that a language committed to depthless proliferation could never achieve the sensations of art he was seeking. *Les Noces* and *La Seine* both seem attempts to use rhyme like some relentless amoeba, ever expanding through continuous self-division, in the hope of creating a literary language both unlimited and unstoppable. Evidently it was the failure of these two *inédits*, as much as the success of the *Textes-genèse*, that made possible the evolution of the *procédé*; and as we shall see in the next chapter, Claude of *Les Noces* proved in the end as significant a catalyst of *Impressions d'Afrique* as the *billard/pillard* rhyme of 'Parmi les Noirs'.

━━━━━━

Various symmetries emerge from any consideration of the works that Roussel ultimately decided were worthy of publication. His prose texts and his books of poems can both be seen to form triptychs: under the aegis of the *procédé* we have the *Textes-genèse*, which lead to the novels, which lead to the plays. His poems form an equivalent trinity: *La Doublure*, *La Vue* and *Nouvelles Impressions d'Afrique*. These works, as Roussel firmly insists in 'Comment j'ai écrit . . .', 'make no use whatsoever of the *procédé*.'

*La Vue*, the middle panel of Roussel's poetic triptych, itself consists of three long poems: 'La Vue', 'Le Concert' and 'La Source.' The first two were published in the *Gaulois du Dimanche* on the 18–19 April and 27–8 June 1903 respectively. 'La Source', the last of the three to be written, appeared only in the volume issued by Lemerre the following year. Roussel must have hoped that publication in a popular newspaper would help relaunch his literary career, and he notes in 'Comment j'ai écrit . . .' that when the title poem appeared in *Le Gaulois* it 'was noticed by certain scholars'. Sales, however, were slow even by Roussel's standards: the modest print run of 550 copies was not exhausted until 1953, almost fifty years after publication and twenty years after Roussel's own death.

The three poems collected in the book are all based on the same premise: in each Roussel describes in fanatical, indeed impossible, detail a miniature representation. The two thousand lines of 'La Vue' are devoted to a minute photograph of a beach scene set into the lens of a souvenir pen-holder:

> Quelquefois un reflet momentané s'allume
> Dans la vue enchâssée au fond du porte-plume
> Contre lequel mon œil bien ouvert est collé
> À très peu de distance, à peine reculé;

> (lines 1–4)

Sometimes a momentary gleam suddenly shines/ Into the view set into the bottom of a penholder/ Against which my wide-open eye is glued/ Very close, almost touching it.

The penholder* itself is white, but streaked with stains of red ink that resemble blood. Despite the tininess of the photo, 'tout enfle' (all swells) (line 13) when the curious eye peers into it. In 'Le Concert' Roussel examines equally meticulously the sketch of a hotel adorning the heading of a letter written on the hotel's stationery, while in 'La Source' he presents the spa pictured on the label of a bottle of mineral water. Whereas the images

---

* In his autobiographical story 'First Love', collected in *Nabokov's Dozen* (1958) and in *The Stories of Vladimir Nabokov* (London: Weidenfeld & Nicolson, 1996), Nabokov records visiting Biarritz in 1909, where he too purchased a penholder: 'Among the trivial souvenirs acquired at Biarritz before leaving, my favorite was not the small bull of black stone and not the sonorous sea-shell but something which now seems almost symbolic – a meerschaum penholder with a tiny peephole of crystal in its ornamental part. One held it quite close to one's eye, screwing up the other, and when one had got rid of the shimmer of one's own lashes, a miraculous photographic view of the bay and of the line of cliffs ending in a lighthouse could be seen inside' (*The Stories of Vladimir Nabokov*, p. 610).

reflected in the floating soap-bubbles of *Les Noces* are in a state of perpetual flux, either expanding or diminishing, and the life they distortingly mirror is itself in motion and continuing around them, the three scenes depicted in 'La Vue', 'Le Concert' and 'La Source' are eerily frozen, beyond the reach of time and change. One of the first characters we meet on the beach is a child who has just hurled a stick for his dog – a recently barbered poodle – to chase. Towards its conclusion, the poem circles back to the same spot of beach, where the boy is still in the act of throwing the bit of driftwood and his eager dog still on the point of setting off in pursuit.

The immobility of these scenes contrasts with the poet's own vulnerability to the attritions of loss. Like the *Textes-genèse*, the poems return to their origins. By poring over the tiny photograph the poet is able to screen out his immediate circumstances:

> Mon œil gauche fermé complètement m'empêche
> De me préoccuper ailleurs, d'être distrait
> Par un autre spectacle ou par un autre attrait
> Survenant au dehors et vus par la fenêtre
> Entr'ouverte devant moi.

(lines 18–22)

My left eye is firmly closed, and this prevents me/ From giving my attention to anything else, from being distracted/ By another spectacle or by another attraction/ Happening outside, which I might see through the window/ Half-open before me.

The crazily precise observations prolong and complicate themselves in defiance of both the present and the strictures of common sense. Roussel describes not only the promenaders on the beach, but a yacht and various small craft in the offing. We learn of a fisherman who is becalmed out at sea that his jacket is tight under the arms and worn at the cuffs, that his beard is rather untidy and that his left eyebrow is slightly shaggier than his right. The captain of a boat that is further out, and partially obscured by the smoke of the yacht's engine, sports a brown goatee in which one can just make out a few grey hairs. On shore, a boy paddling in the waves carries a bucket with a picture on it of a happy, strong-limbed farmer sowing seeds in a field, and in the distance a church steeple and a number of low roofs. Up on the headland, an old horse-drawn landau contains a slightly rheumatic dowager, a bony prude wearing pince-nez spectacles, and a fat man in brand-new clothes carrying a cane whose ivory pommel has been fashioned to represent the head of a laughing Chinaman. No detail seems too trivial for Roussel's 'curious eye', and these poems give the impression they might continue indefinitely, entranced by their own powers of perception. In 'La Vue' it is eventually the weather that forces the poet to confront the powerful grief against which the patient business of registering the minutiae of the scene has defended him: the sky suddenly clouds over, and both inner and outer worlds are shrouded in darkness.

> En ce moment l'éclat
> Décroît au fond du verre et tout devient plus sombre;
> Sur la plage s'étend, partout égale, une ombre;
> Mon bras levé retombe, entraînant avec lui
> La porte-plume et son paysage enfoui
> Dans l'extrémité blanche aux taches d'encre rouge;
> Dans le ciel un amas de grosses vapeurs bouge...

(lines 2040–46)

At this moment the brightness/ Fades at the bottom of the glass and all becomes dark;/ Across the beach extends, evenly throughout, a shadow;/ My lifted arm falls, dragging with it/ The pen-holder and its landscape hidden/ In the white tip stained with red ink;/ In the sky a mass of heavy vapours stirs...

Only as the scene disappears does Roussel reveal its personal significance for him:

> car c'est l'exhalaison
> Des sentiments vécus de toute une saison
> Qui pour moi sort avec puissance de la vue,
> Grâce à l'intensité subitement accrue
> Du souvenir vivace et latent d'un été
> Déjà mort, déjà loin de moi, vite emporté.

(lines 2051–6)

For it is the distillation/ Of feelings experienced throughout a season/ Which emerges for me with such power from the view,/

Owing to the intensity suddenly acquired/ By the memory, undying and latent, of a summer/ Already dead, already far from me, carried quickly away.

The opening and close of 'Le Concert' position the poem as a similarly doomed search for lost time. As midnight strikes, the poet contemplates various packets of correspondence; he holds in his hand a letter especially dear to him, whose contents he knows by heart:

> Oubliant le moment présent, je me retrempe
> Dans les vieux souvenirs d'heureux jours disparus.
>
> (lines 2–3)

Forgetting the present time, I again steep myself/ In old memories of vanished, happy days.

The letterhead of the cherished missive that occupies the poem's one thousand lines offers only a temporary, if prolix, prelude to his confrontation with the absent beloved's words. After comprehensively speculating on the manners, clothes and characters of the arriving guests, of the hotel staff, of groups of residents relaxing on their balconies, of various passers-by, of three children playing at marbles and of a dreamy canoeist paddling on a distant lake, and then launching into a full and lively description of an orchestra performing on the bandstand of a nearby park, the poet finally turns to the letter itself:

> Puis, tout bas, je relis pour la centième fois,
> Essayant d'évoquer, à chaque mot, la voix.
>
> (lines 1067–8)

Then, in a low whisper, I begin rereading for the hundredth time,/ Trying to evoke, with each word, the lost voice.

In 'La Source,' which is set in a restaurant, a waiter suddenly whisks away the bottle of mineral water on whose illustrated label Roussel seems to have found enough material for any number of pictures by Frith or Renoir, plunging him back into the difficult, solitary present; the poet is constrained to acknowledge the presence of his fellow-diners, with whom the poem began:

L'américain, vautré plus que jamais, allume
Un cigare; le couple émoustillé, là-bas,
Chuchote toujours des choses qu'on n'entend pas.

(lines 1010–13)

> The American, who is sprawling more than ever, lights/ A cigar;
> the excited couple, beyond,/ Still whisper things which can't be
> heard.

By framing the poems in this way, Roussel establishes a wholly
antithetical relationship between the real time of the poet supposedly studying the minute reproductions and the timelessness
of the Belle Époque scenes he contemplates. The device doubles
the poems, rather as the puns of the *Textes-genèse* double the
narratives that bridge their different meanings: both the puns of
the stories and the mechanically generated images of the poems
function as a kind of arbitrary but all-transforming eye of the
needle through which Roussel's writing must pass if it is to
attain reality's polar opposite, the looking-glass heaven of art.
The poems transpose the verbal sleights of hand that eventually
developed into the *procédé* to the dimension of the visual. In
'Comment j'ai écrit . . . ' Roussel revealed that his linguistic
prospecting often 'tortured' him to the point of self-violence and
despair; the 'blood-like stains' of red ink that disfigure the white
pen-holder suggest that the search for a means of releasing the
'curious eye' was equally tormented.

Roussel does not specify the name or location of the beach
depicted in 'La Vue', but there seems no doubt the poem is
based on recollections of the Roussel family's annual holidays
in Biarritz. Madame Roussel was so fond of this extremely
fashionable resort that in 1907 she purchased a large plot of
land on the seafront and had an architect design a vast five-
storey villa that still stands today. In the event, this palatial
residence, which included among its lavish appointments mini-
baths for Madame Roussel's collection of chihuahuas, was
finished only shortly before her death there in 1911.*

Roussel's personal affiliation with the scene, though suddenly
avowed in the poem's final lines, could not be said to inflect his

---

* For further details of Villa Begoña, as it is now called, see FC, pp. 139–42.

presentation of its topography or characters; the poem proceeds with an even-handed, impersonal rigour, scrupulously itemizing distances, clothing, gestures, natural and human features, expressions, accoutrements. The variety, distinctiveness and energy of the various individuals and groups is effectively countered by the poem's silence and stillness; its expressive power seems both dependent upon and determined by a fundamental and chilling constraint. These contradictions surface most forcefully in Roussel's description of a family in full mourning. The protective mother presses her cosseted youngest child against her skirts, fearful of letting him out of her sight:

>           elle baisse
> Les yeux vers lui qui, sans résistance, se laisse
> Choyer et dorloter longtemps; il est enclin
> Aux caresses, grâce à son naturel câlin;
> C'est l'enfant débordant de douce insouciance,
> À qui jamais la rude et dure surveillance
> N'a pesé, qui se sait idolâtré, gâté,
> Pour les dons qu'il possède et pour cette beauté
> Dont s'exhale, sitôt qu'il paraît, le grand charme;
> Personne au monde ne fait pour lui le gendarme,
> Dans l'ensorcellement sûr de son regard noir;
> A l'avance il sait bien que pourvu qu'il se montre
> N'importe où, même aux gens inconnus qu'il rencontre,
> Il sera le héros d'un moment, séduira,
> Et que, s'il y met du sien, on lui sourira;
> Tout lui paraît doré dans le monde . . .

>             (lines 1565–81)

She lowers/ Her eyes towards him, who, unresisting, allows himself/ To be petted and fondled for a long time; he is much/ Doted on, being naturally winning;/ He is a child overflowing with carefree sweetness,/ On whom rude and heavy supervision/ Has never weighed, who knows himself idolized, spoiled,/ Because of the gifts he possesses, and because of this beauty/ From which emanates, as soon as he appears, such great charm;/ No one in the world polices his movements,/ He is confident in his marvellous power,/ In the sure enchantment of his dark gaze,/ In advance he knows that whenever he shows himself,/ No matter where, even to strangers he is meeting for the first time,/ He will be the hero of the moment,

will seduce everyone,/ And that, as long as he plays his part,
people will smile at him;/ All the world seems gilded to him . . .

Clearly this pampered young prodigy's sense of election can be
related to the omnipotence Roussel felt under the influence of
*la gloire* soon after his father's death. On a more general level,
the bereaved young boy's fearless conviction of his Midas-like
ability to experience the world 'tout . . . doré,' to bewitch all he
meets with his 'regard noir', make him appear like an emblem
for the poetic processes at work in all three poems collected in
*La Vue*: the panoptic, entranced and entrancing gaze of the poet
dominates and immobilizes whatever it describes. In these poems
poetry and death strike a curious pact: the buried memories and
losses they refuse to disclose may be broached, Roussel implies,
only at the cost of life itself – 'un été/ Déjà mort, déjà loin de
moi, vite emporté'.

# CHAPTER 4

# Impressions of Africa

Raymond Roussel first visited Africa in 1906, when he was twenty-nine. Most of his travelling up to this point had been as a companion to his mother on her fashionable peregrinations from Monte Carlo to Biarritz to Carlsbad to Cannes. Roussel's two-month excursion to Italy and Egypt was probably the longest period they had yet spent apart from each other. Roussel did not, however, set off alone: he was accompanied by Doctor Mattin, who just over four years later also travelled with Raymond and Madame Roussel on their final voyage together to India and Ceylon. Given the extreme anxiety they shared about all health matters, it seems likely that Doctor Mattin undertook these journeys at least partly in a professional capacity.*

Roussel and Mattin arrived in Alexandria from Naples on 16 November, and on the 22nd embarked on a boat trip up the Nile as far as the first cataract, just beyond Aswan, which they reached on 8 December; the journey back downstream took only a week, and they spent a further week in Cairo before beginning the return journey to Europe on 21 December. Over two decades later in 'Comment j'ai écrit . . .' Roussel was to pride himself on his refusal to derive anything from his travels for his books, but at this stage of his prospecting he seems to have believed it might prove worthwhile to record his tourist's impressions of Egypt. At any rate, he decided to keep a journal of the trip, and this was preserved among his private papers and manuscripts.

Roussel's daily entries in this journal reveal virtually nothing of his affective responses to the country; instead, they consist

---

* Leiris records in his *Cahier Roussel* that, after the death of Roussel's older brother from tuberculosis, Madame Roussel insisted that her surviving son should undergo a medical examination *every day* (R & Co, p. 80).

more or less entirely of dispassionate observations and itineraries. This is how he relates their excursion to the Valley of the Kings on 2 December:

> Crossed the Nile by boat – Hired donkeys – Went to see the Valley of the Kings – Cold lunch – sun – heat.

In Cairo he attended a performance of *Aïda* in a noisome theatre, and noted tartly, 'the performers did not know their parts'. He also records visiting the spot on the Nile where Moses was supposed to have been discovered among the bulrushes, a tourist location also pointed out to Raoul and Jeanne in the draft of an unfinished poem that begins 'Sur le Nil . . .'

Raoul and Jeanne, Claude and Luce, Gaspard and Roberte: the young couples who feature in Roussel's long early verse works are more or less interchangeable. In a longer fragment (over 800 lines) called 'À Belleville' Claude is paired not with Luce, but Jeanne. This Claude starts the poem as one of a three-man criminal gang; they plan to rob a rich, miserly old woman who lives in a cottage near Versailles. While his two fellow-crooks enter the premises, Claude keeps watch outside. The burglary goes horribly wrong: they are surprised by the woman, who lets out a terrible cry that wakens the neighbourhood before they manage to murder her. The three escape into the woods empty-handed, but Claude later shops his companions to the police for immunity and a reward. He bets this money on the gaming tables of Monte Carlo, and finds 'la chance le favorise/ sans cesse il gagne' (luck favours him/ he keeps winning and winning) (lines 177–8). He embarks on a successful courtship of a young florist (Jeanne) and, needless to say, they pretty soon find themselves in Nice at carnival time, where Roussel forgets his hero is called Claude and starts calling him Raoul instead.

'Sur le Nil' traces a similar trajectory. Raoul, like Claude, acquires a fortune by gambling in the casino at Monte Carlo. His winnings enable him and his girlfriend Jeanne to embark for Alexandria – on a boat called *Le Lutin* (elf or goblin) that anticipates the *Sylphide* (sprite) of early drafts of *Impressions d'Afrique*. Like Roussel and Mattin, Raoul and Jeanne set off on a journey up the Nile, but they seem on the point of broaching a world significantly different from both the drily observed scenes of Roussel's journal and the scrupulously denoted inversions of carnival that fill *La Doublure*, 'À Belleville', 'À Paris', 'L'Inconsolable', *Têtes de Carton du Carnaval de Nice* and various other carnival fragments. 'On se sent vivre,' declares Raoul*,

dans ce climat on est ivre

de clarté

Quand on est loin de tout dans ces pays de rêve

c'est une          trêve

dont il faut profiter de son mieux

En se livrant à l'aise au seul régal des yeux

á pareille distance

de               l'existence

Doit être envisagée     en tout comme un roman

(lines 78–87)

in this climate . . . one is drunk/ . . . on light/ When one is far from everything in these countries of dream/ . . . it is . . . a respite/ . . . from which it is important to profit as much as one can/ Surrendering to ease, to the simple feasting of one's eyes/ . . . at such a distance/ from . . . existence/ Must be seen . . . in every way like a novel

In his essay 'Énigmes et transparence', Alain Robbe-Grillet relates the pure 'depthlessness' of Roussel's fiction to its mysterious lack of chiaroscuro: Roussel's stories, Robbe-Grillet suggests, 'leave neither shadow nor reflection behind them.' Cocteau similarly argues that Roussel's style leaves 'no intriguing shadow' but creates a kind of pure 'illumination'. Revelling in the Egyptian sunlight, Claude appears on the very verge of discovering the 'pays de rêve' of Roussel's fiction, the shadowless realm in which every aspect of existence is transfigured into narrative, 'tout comme un roman'. And the unremarkable inlet on the Nile where Moses was reported to have been found looks forward to the innumerable unlikely items and places in

---

*Despite their incomplete state, most of Roussel's fragments can be followed relatively easily. I have attempted roughly to reproduce the layout of Roussel's original manuscript. In the translation ellipses indicate a blank space in the French.

Roussel's novels and plays that acquire legendary status when their history is explained:

<pre>
                              et l'endroit prend soudain
        – malgré l'impression        et morte
     qui se dégage de            – une sorte
        de prestige            à leurs yeux
       tout à coup plus rêveurs plus curieux
     quand le guide leur dit: 'c'est la place précise
        où dit-on            Moïse
              fut sauvé des eaux
              dans sa corbeille de roseaux
</pre>

(lines 104–12)

and the place suddenly acquires/ – despite its appearance ... and dead/ ... which emanates from ... – a sort/ ... of prestige ... to their eyes/ ... suddenly more dreamy, more curious/ ... when the guide says to them: 'This is the exact spot/ where, people say ... Moses/ ... was rescued from the waters/ ... in his basket of rushes.

Raoul (who at one point is called Claude in this draft) is impressed by the legendary glory that now irradiates the inlet, but Jeanne is sceptical: 'on ne peut être sûr,' she observes, at which point the fragment breaks off.

Nearly all the heroes of Roussel's early poems enact roughly the same narrative. Gaspard in *La Doublure*, Raoul in *La Seine*, the Claude/Raoul of 'À Belleville' and the Raoul/Claude of 'Sur le Nil' each undergo a crisis that propels them into a world in which the earlier laws of their existence are suspended. Gaspard's public failure to resheathe his sword, Raoul's defection from his wife and child, Claude/Raoul's betrayal of his comrades, Raoul/Claude's amazing luck at the casino, can all be considered in relation to the grand crisis of Roussel's life that led him to believe he had won the most dazzling prize of all, but then plunged him from the heights of bliss to the depths of despair. The Gaspard of *La Doublure* and the Raoul of *La Seine* both end up paying heavily for their derelictions, themselves abandoned by the lovers who encouraged them to forsake their normal lives; in their final scenes they bitterly rue the lost happiness they shared as part of a couple, adrift in the holiday realm of carnival or the café-concert hall of the Moulin Rouge, or for

Claude and Luce in 'À l'Ambigu,' the extravagant excitements of melodrama. Yet within these endlessly expansive spaces the gender differences between the two lovers all but evaporate. Eventually, but only to bring these colossal texts to conclusion, Roussel had to reinvoke the polarities of male and female so the relationships could be broken up.

But why, he seems to have wondered towards the end of his period of prospecting, should they be broken up? Immanent in Roussel's experience of *la gloire* was a unified radiance capable of 'illuminating the entire universe', a 'moral sunlight' equivalent to the 'clarté' that exhilarates Raoul in 'Sur le Nil', or the golden sun that is the emblem of the Incomparables. Godlike, he contained within himself the competing energies of an 'unheard-of bliss,' a bliss embodied in the early poems in the relationship between the couples. But just as the *procédé* involved revealing two meanings in one word, so to reach the 'pays de rêves' it was equally important to be both genders simultaneously.

It is clear from Roussel's manuscripts that transvestitism was as vital a condition for entering the narrative paradise 'en tout comme un roman' (in every way like a novel) as an awareness of the multiple possible meanings of words or sounds. It is Claude, the one male character whom Roussel planned to make the leaver rather than the left, who initiates this process of cross-dressing. In a fragment of some forty lines ('À l'Eldorado') Claude is pictured in his dressing-room preparing to go on stage at the Eldorado theatre in Nice. A number of the rhymes and details recall Gaspard in his dressing-room in Part I of *La Doublure*, only while Gaspard is removing his make-up having dismally failed to impersonate a young man capable of returning his weapon smoothly to its scabbard, Claude is in the act of adorning himself as a young woman; and whereas Gaspard broods morosely on the catcalls still ringing in his ears, Claude is the 'héros de toutes les causeries' (the hero of everyone's chatter). Roussel presents him in the act of completing his toilette:

> son accoutrement
> qui le transforme     élégamment

```
                         en femme
    ses yeux             flamme
           sont          doux
     sous sa perruque      d'un blond roux
     et montrent        une nuance verte
             sa robe bleue est ouverte
       une traîne      dont      la longeur
                    ; à la rigueur
  a face de  19 ans          encore imberbe
       profil fin          superbe
             peut donner l'illusion
                    l'indécision
       sur               sexe
       le      doute  rende plus complexe
   quand sa voix      timbre   charmant
                    de diamant
   résonne

                              personne
     ne résiste           dès lors
       au doute crée par ses dehors
```

(lines 27–48)

his dress/ which transforms him . . . elegantly/ . . . into a woman/
his eyes . . . flame/ . . . are . . . soft/ . . . under his wig . . . of a
reddish blond/ . . . and show . . . a hint of green/ . . . his blue dress
is open/ . . . a train . . . whose . . . length/ . . . ; at a pinch/ his face
of . . . 19 years . . . still beardless/ . . . fine profile . . . magnificent/
. . . could give the illusion/ . . . the uncertainty/ . . . about . . . the
sex/ . . . the . . . doubt . . . becomes more complex . . . / when his
voice . . . the tone . . . charming/ . . . of diamond/ . . . resonates/ . . .
nobody/ . . . can resist . . . after that/ . . . in relation to the doubt
created by his outside

But to arrive at the Eldorado of his fiction, Roussel had to
perform another reversal: instead of writing novels in verse, he
had to start writing poetry in prose. The Claude Givaudan of
this fragment reappears as Claude Givandou in one of the earliest drafts of an episode relating to *Impressions d'Afrique*, and
he in turn becomes Carmichaël,

  a young man of twenty from Marseilles, already famous for

his remarkable head-voice, which gave the perfect illusion of a woman's pitch. For two years now, Carmichaël had enjoyed enormous success on the stages of café-concert halls throughout France, dressed as a woman and singing, each in its requisite tessitura and with immeasurable suppleness and virtuosity, all the most testing passages in the soprano repertoire.

Indeed, Claude's androgyny is eventually replicated in the heart of Roussel's Africa: the supreme regent, Talou, is so impressed by Carmichaël's head-voice that he insists on being taught to sing in the same style. At the gala, dressed, like Claude in 'À l'Eldorado', in a blue dress with a plunging neckline and sporting a wig of magificently waved golden hair, Talou performs Daricelli's *Aubade* – 'a piece demanding the most perilous feats of vocalization' – in a pure, shrilling falsetto.

———

'In the end,' Cocteau observed in *Opium*, '*Impressions d'Afrique* leaves an impression of Africa.' Robert de Montesquiou, on the other hand, complained of the misleading nature of Roussel's title, and wished he had chosen 'an ornamental crest as original as the many bizarre coiffures' featured in the book itself. Roussel certainly – and no doubt very deliberately – never visited equatorial Africa, where his first prose novel is nominally set, though he boasts in 'Comment j'ai écrit . . .' of having travelled not only in Egypt but throughout north Africa. In the tradition of the pure dandy, like Huysman's Des Esseintes or Villiers de l'Isle-Adam's Axel, Roussel's writings are predicated on a fundamental antithesis between imagination and reality, yet we have already seen how Moses' landing spot featured in 'Sur le Nil,' and one entry in particular from his Egyptian journal seems relevant to the genesis of *Impressions d'Afrique*: 'this morning a blind mimic produced a series of animal cries – imitated a steamboat etc'. Imitation, like transvestitism, is a crucial means of entry to Roussel's looking-glass world. It was his achievements as an imitator that he dwelt on in the penultimate paragraph of 'Comment j'ai écrit . . .' when seeking some kind of compensation for the disappointments of his literary career: 'But there,

at least, my success was enormous and complete.' Michel Leiris
learned from Charlotte Dufrène that Roussel

worked for seven years on each of his imitations, preparing
them when he was alone, repeating phrases aloud to catch
the exact intonation and copying gestures, and would end
up achieving an absolute resemblance. I have it from her,
though I never saw it myself, that he could imitate my father
with haunting accuracy.

Imitation figures in various ways in many of the set pieces staged
at the gala. Young Bob Boucharessas (*bouche à ressasse*: mouth
to repeat) is by no means the only entertainer who relies, paradoxically, on imitation to become incomparable. His renditions
of an accelerating train, the cries of domestic animals, the
grating of a saw on stone, afford a 'complete illusion of reality'.
The creation of an 'illusion of reality' by unlikely means or in
some unusual medium constitutes time and again the secret
purpose and justification of the act performed. The clown
Whirligig hurls playing cards at a black cloth coated with a
sticky paste; the cards all land face out, and eventually the
patterns formed by the alignment of the cards and the colours
of the suits reveal an ecclesiastic on the threshold of his house.
Whirligig also fashions a Gothic cloister out of heaps of copper
coins and a wall nine feet long from dominoes, their black and
white faces skilfully alternated to create the appearance of a
procession of clerics: 'A fraternity of Reverends leaving the
tower of an old cloister to visit the parish priest in his rectory,'
is his 'explanation of his three masterpieces'.

On a less figurative level, the circus horse Romulus is able to
repeat, like a parrot, any word or sentence he hears, and even
recite proverbs, fragments of fables, oaths and commonplaces,
though without understanding them. Louise Montalescot's
complex painting machine manages to imitate nature itself: set
up in front of the Gardens of the Béhuliphruen it produces a
canvas which 'seen as a whole, created an impression of singularly intense brilliance while remaining rigorously true to the
original, as each person was able to ascertain by a quick glance
at the actual gardens.' And it is Carmichaël's failure to reproduce
accurately the new strophes of the *Jéroukka*, the epic composed

by Talou celebrating his own exploits, which threatens the novel's happy ending.

Carmichaël and Talou are figured by Roussel as complimentary antitheses in relation to both imitation and cross-dressing. Talou, in his efforts to master Carmichaël's head-voice, 'endeavours to copy slavishly the examples' of falsetto singing set by his teacher, but his real progress begins when he also dons Carmichaël's female costume. Henceforth Talou always studies in the blue gown, and, with Carmichaël 'prompting bar by bar' during the performance, Talou eventually 'acquits himself honourably of his self-imposed task'. Carmichaël, on the other hand, must sing 'The Battle of the Tez' (the new canto of the *Jéroukka* composed by Talou to commemorate his recent victory over Yaour) in male dress – though in his female voice – and half-way through he falters, 'betrayed by his memory, which denied him a word in the series of unintelligible syllables he had conscientiously learned by heart.' As punishment he is sentenced to three hours' detention. Only when he has performed it once again faultlessly are he and the other hostages – whose ransoms have just arrived – allowed to return to France.

Africa and France are represented by Roussel as partners in a similar kind of dialectical relationship: as necessary opposites, their languages can be transliterated and reproduced by the other perfectly, but neither Talou nor Carmichaël understand what they are singing, and in this sense they remain as separate as the double meanings of the *procédé*. Roussel's Africa, needless to say, bears no resemblance to any historical Africa, though Roussel, particularly in the early drafts, makes use of the colonial stereotypes current in adventure fiction, exotic stage-plays and travel narratives of the time.*

These drafts reveal, however, the extent to which the evolution of the novel in fact involved dispensing with the crude caricatures of popular culture generated by the scramble for Africa, and gradually infusing blacks and whites alike with the self-sustaining buoyancy – the *esprit Rousselien* – that characterizes his fiction. In 'Comment j'ai écrit . . .' he presents the evolution

---

* For an illuminating discussion of Roussel's relation to turn-of-the-century French representations of Africa, see Annie Le Brun, VM, pp. 204–12.

of *Impressions d'Afrique* as a mere question of developing further the puns thrown up by 'Parmi les Noirs':

> As regards the genesis of *Impressions d'Afrique*, it can thus be seen to derive from bringing together the words *billard* and *pillard*. The 'pillard' is Talou; the 'bandes' are his warlike hordes; the 'blanc' is Carmichaël (the word *lettres* was not kept).
>
> Then, as a way of expanding this method, I sought new words relating to *billard*, but always with the aim of making use of a meaning other than that which initially presented itself, and each time this provided me with a further creation.
>
> Thus *queue de billard* [billiard cue] supplied me with Talou's gown with its train [another meaning of *queue*] ... I looked for a word to add to the word *bandes* and thought of old strips of cloth in which someone has made darns (*reprises*). And the word *reprises* in its musical sense furnished me with the *Jéroukka*, that epic sung by Talou's *bandes* (warlike hordes) whose music consisted of the continual *reprises* [repetitions] of a short motif.
>
> Searching for a word to go with *blanc* I thought of the glue (*colle*) which sticks the paper to the base of the cube of chalk. And the word *colle*, taken in the sense (which it has in school slang) of detention, gave me the three hours' detention imposed on the *blanc* (Carmichaël) by Talou.

While there is no reason to disbelieve Roussel's statement in the following paragraph that 'this preliminary work was itself difficult and took up a great deal of time', the various drafts of *Impressions d'Afrique* testify to a very different kind of compositional toil: Roussel's fanatically worked manuscripts tell us nothing about the word games underpinning the novel, but demonstrate his utter determination to recast and revise and excise and expand in pursuit of the 'sensations of art', 'the complete illusion of reality', his novel was to afford. 'I bleed over every phrase,' he told Janet, and certainly the inching progress of *Impressions d'Afrique* towards its final form suggests an almost Flaubertian obsession with the *mot juste*, a dedication both unsparing and resolute to the vocation of writing.

Talou VII was originally called Bangoja, and differed little from his prototype, Tombola, in 'Parmi les Noirs'. Bangoja is described as 'a sort of African Nero who combined personal vanity with the pride of omnipotence'. Just as Roussel in his glory compared himself with Napoleon, so this warlord is a poet who insists that any who fall into his hands must be able to recite sections of his ongoing epic poem, the *Bangojade*; whereas Tombola absorbed his captives by devouring them, Bangoja inflicts on all in his power an opposite plight – they have to absorb him by learning his poetry, or suffer some terrible retribution. A number of incidents make Bangoja seem a stereotypical savage chieftain. For instance, when one of the European artistes appears riding a bicycle and brandishing a racket in each hand, with which he bats four shuttlecocks in the air, Bangoja interrupts and attempts the feat himself, only to fall sprawling in the dirt.

Early drafts present Talou's efforts to imitate Claude/Carmichaël's head-voice as similarly ill-fated: their daily lessons prove exasperating to the young Marseillaise, 'who could obtain nothing worthwhile from his royal pupil,' and his public rendition of the song is an excruciating disaster. And whereas in the final version the rituals of Talou's coronation are performed with an impressively solemn dignity, the manuscripts include a couple of accidents that reduce the ceremony to slapstick: one of the Europeans (Ba . . . ) concocts a papal bull sanctioning the right of the African emperor to the lands he has just annexed, but he misspells the regent's name and is roundly berated by the incensed chieftain. The two eldest Boucharessas brothers, Tommy and Hector, whose act consists of juggling rubber balls between each other with drums, momentarily lose control: one of Hector's returns flies over Tommy's head and shatters the Holy Ampulla, a cruet containing olive oil with which Talou has just majestically anointed himself. And proceedings are further disrupted by the ageing historian Tinglet (the original of Juillard), who gets drunk on a bottle of champagne and starts trying to grope the Emperor's wives as they wait to perform their spectacular belch-dance, the Luenn'chétuz.

Roussel's painstaking reworkings of his material reveal a general overall trend: not only does he gradually eliminate vaudevillian mishaps and crude stereotypes, but he makes almost everyone a success. In the final version, only the overweight Latvian ballerina, Olga Tcherwonenkoff, really fails in the course of the gala, and even she offers glimpses of her former talent:

> Under the stiff folds of her tulle skirt, her monstrous legs, moulded in close-fitting pink tights, performed their skilful manoeuvres with sufficient agility and a remnant of their former grace that was rather surprising.
>
> Suddenly, crossing the stage with tiny steps, each foot balanced on the point of the big toe, Olga fell heavily and cried out in anguish.
>
> Doctor Leflaive left our group and rushed on stage, where he was able to diagnose the lamentable state of the invalid, who had been immobilized by *un coup de fouet*, or sudden spasm of pain.

Leaving aside the momentary lapse of memory suffered by Carmichaël, Olga's is the only performance that comes to grief. In the drafts, on the other hand, not all the characters are extraordinarily gifted nonpareils, and several fail miserably. Le Vicomte de Bianchon, for instance, who is cut wholly from the finished novel, is 'an incorrigible gambler; having spent all his wealth on baccarat and at the horse races, he had pooled his last few thousand-franc bills and set off for America, where he hoped to recover his fortune.' Bianchon cannot, however, resist speculating the remnants of his inheritance at the mini-Bourse, despite his ineptitude in composing the alexandrines in which all transactions must be delivered: he bawls 'orders continually, without bothering at all about his prosody, which left much to be desired, and he, on his own, bought and sold more shares than all the other speculators put together.' Just before the gala begins he stakes everything on the ichthyologist Broussier (Martignon in the final version) but the Grand Cordon goes instead to Roger Danglès, the original of Marius Boucharessas: 'this blow completed the ruin of the well-born, miserable man, and carried off the remaining fragments of his fortune. Unwilling to receive our condolences, he went off on his own, completely crestfallen, and in solitude gave himself over to his bitter thoughts.'

Tinglet endures a similar series of humiliations. Having spent his entire life in the vain pursuit of academic distinctions, he seizes the opportunity of the gala to present an interminable lecture on a variety of literary and historical topics (Racine, General Charrette, the Îles de la Sonde); each of these subjects is greeted by an enraged audience with ever more vociferous hoots and a volley of stones. Eventually he beats a retreat to the Royal Lodge where he indignantly complains of his ill-treatment to the Emperor's daughter (called Sanga in the drafts). By the final version, however, the hapless Tinglet has metamorphosed into the remarkable Juillard, a brilliant speaker whose lucid and witty account of the history of the Electors of Brandenburg holds his listeners spellbound.

The manuscripts of *Impressions d'Afrique* allow us to follow the means by which Roussel literally converted failure into success. The distance between Tinglet and Juillard can be seen as equivalent to that between the Gaspard of *La Doublure* and the Claude of 'À l'Eldorado'. Roussel may only have felt 'la gloire' in its full power when composing his novel in verse about the double failures of an understudy, but the discovery of what in 'Comment j'ai écrit . . .' he calls 'ma voie' (my way) entailed the opposite: the description, in a prose lined by the poetic doublings of the *procédé*, of unique and magnificent triumphs.*

* In his discussion of 'Homonymy' in 'Sade II', Barthes offers an interesting analogue to the pleasures Roussel derived from his discovery of the *procédé*: 'In Sadian *art de vivre*, it is not so much a question of multiplying pleasures, of making them revolve, creating out of them a dizzying carousel (this rapid succession will terminate the Party), as of superposing them (this simultaneity would define what we might call sybaritism) . . . "And do you not see that what you are daring to do simultaneously bears the imprint of two or three crimes . . .?" "Well, really, madame, precisely what you have just told me is going to make me come even more pleasurably." This superior pleasure, completely formal, since it is in sum only a mathematical notion, is a language pleasure: that of unfolding a criminal act into different nouns: "I am thus simultaneously committing incest, adultery, sodomy"; it is homonymy that is voluptuous' (SFL, pp. 157–8). The *procédé* makes possible a similar kind of 'superposing', both at the material level of language and in the 'multiple drawers' of the episodes to which it gives rise. However, while Sade achieves an intensification of pleasure by announcing the different crimes implicit in

The first of twenty instalments of *Impressions d'Afrique* appeared in *Le Gaulois du Dimanche* over the weekend 10–11 July 1909, under the picture of a ship foundering in high seas. Clearly Roussel – or his mother – had come to some arrangement with the editor Arthur Meyer, as was no doubt the case with the other works Roussel had published in Meyer's papers. Nevertheless, he was obliged for reasons of space to omit several sections, and the last quarter of the novel was printed in a special 'supplement' on 20–21 November. Roussel observes in 'Comment j'ai écrit . . .' that his novel's initial appearance in *Le Gaulois* 'passed completely unnoticed' and Meyer's desperate resort to a bumper supplement suggests that the four-month serialization had not held the readers' attention.

The novel was issued by Lemerre the following year – although bearing 2 October 1909 as its *date d'achevé d'imprimer* – as always at Roussel's own expense. The pun lurking in the book's title was alluded to by Roussel himself two decades later in the 'sequel', *Nouvelles Impressions d'Afrique*: in the long list of examples of people musing about things, Roussel includes a young author wondering 'Jusqu'à quand ses écrits paraîtront à ses frais' (for how long his writings will appear at his own expense). Roussel's impressions of Africa are also *impressions à fric* [a slang term for money], copies of a book the author has himself paid handsomely to have printed.*

The few who bought the first edition, which, as Roussel lamented in 'Comment j'ai écrit . . .', took twenty-two years to sell out, would have found a small green insert pasted to the top of page 1 of the novel:

## WARNING

Readers not initiated into the art of Raymond Roussel are

---

the one act, Roussel could only savour his homonyms in secret, or by privately anticipating their posthumous disclosure.

* The cost for 1,100 copies was 2,409 francs (FR, cat. no. 4511, f. 5r). Roussel spent a further 6,689.50 francs having the book advertised in newspapers (ibid., f. 7r). This publicity had little impact: he received a letter from Lemerre dated 13 May 1911, informing him that only187 copies had been sold (ibid., f. 9r).

advised to read this book from page 212 to page 455, and then from page 1 to page 211.

This warning harks back to his instruction to readers of *La Doublure* to begin on the first page and finish on the last, and suggests again the relentlessly binary nature of Roussel's figurations. The doubles and failures of his novel in alexandrines must be read as a linear unity; *Impressions d'Afrique*, on the other hand, written in the *procédé*-inspired rhymes of prose, falls into two interchangeable halves, a duality that balances the examples of singularity and success that it relates.

Most of the drafts suggest Roussel originally intended to begin with the shipwreck, and thus, in a sense, it was his own initiation 'into the art of Raymond Roussel' that allowed him to divide the novel that itself derived from the *procédé*'s divisions of language. Its complementary halves also reflect the polarities and conjunctions between black and white, male and female, imitation and uniqueness that structure the novel as a whole; and, as in 'Parmi les Noirs', the catalyst of this initiation is disaster, the shipwreck that strikes the *Lyncée* in mid-Atlantic, in the middle of the eighth night of the ship's passage to Buenos Aires:

> The screw and the steering were broken by the violence of the waves, and after two days of wild drifting the *Lyncée*, propelled like so much dead wreckage, ran aground on the coast of Africa.
>
> No one was missing when the roll was called, but with the ship itself stove in and even its lifeboats out of commission, all hope of returning to sea had to be abandoned.

By withholding details of the originating calamity until Chapter 10 – after all the performances but Carmichaël's second attempt at the *Jéroukka* have been described but not explained – Roussel displaces his own means of entering the novel to its centre, so it becomes a hinge, like the *à* of the *procédé*, between the two halves of the book, between description and explanation. In *La Doublure* and *La Seine* it is the catastrophe which initiates the action – or rather the suspension of all action – that follows, but in *Impressions d'Afrique* the shipwreck serves rather to introduce the process of providing the material presented in the first nine chapters with its expository lining. In this again we see Roussel transforming – at least for those initiated – disaster into success.

The novel opens over three weeks after the shipwreck, towards four o'clock on 25 June. Talou (although we do not learn this until Chapter XVIII) has recently reunited the kingdom founded by his ancestor Souann.* In this overarching narrative of division and restoration Roussel again enacts his obsession with doubles, transvestitism and imitation. Talou VII and his enemy Yaour IX are both descendants of Souann, who on seizing power over the empire of Ponukélé many generations ago had determined to create a dynasty. However, soon after his accession, two ravishing fifteen-year-old Spanish girls, identical twins, find themselves shipwrecked and washed up on the coast near Éjur, the capital of Ponukélé. Souann marries both on the same day, and what's more, the two sisters both give birth at the very same moment nine months later to two sons, Talou and Yaour. The sisters are themselves so alike that Souann cannot be sure which one he slept with first, so, instructed by the Great Spirit, he has two seeds planted simultaneously, one of a palm tree for Talou and one of a rubber tree for Yaour. The stem of the palm tree shows first, and Talou is proclaimed Souann's successor, but when, some years later – after the Spanish twins have died from fever – Souann manages to annex the land adjoining Ponukélé, called Drelchkaff, he cedes this to the unlucky Yaour. On Souann's death, needless to say, Talou asserts his rights to the newly conquered territory of Drelchkaff, and Yaour to Ponukélé, and a long-lasting feud between the two royal houses commences.

Talou VII's victory over Yaour IX enables him to unite the divided kingdom, and, characteristically, he achieves it while dressed (as indeed is his opponent) in women's clothes. On hearing of Talou's transvestite rehearsals of Carmichaël's head-

---

* Here again, but wholly coincidentally, Roussel and Proust meet . . . *Du côté de chez Swann* was published three years later, in 1913, also at the author's own expense.

voice, Yaour professes a burning desire to witness this singular performance. Talou agrees, but learns from Yaour's ambassador Gaïz-dûh that his distant relative secretly plans to use the occasion to infiltrate Éjur and destroy the Ponukéléan army. Yaour arrives with his retinue and is greeted by Talou attired in Carmichaël's blue *robe de chanteuse*, which Yaour admires so effusively that Talou instructs the artistes to provide his rival with a costume similar to his own. This turns out to be one worn by the tragedienne Adinolfa for the character of Marguerite in Goethe's *Faust*. Yaour has just donned the pink woollen gown, the alms purse and the wig of flaxen plaits when a distant commotion indicates that his ambushing troops have themselves been ambushed, and the Battle of the Tez (the name of the river that flows between the two kingdoms) has been joined. Yaour flees, pursued by Talou, and the two regents duel in their exotic drag until Yaour succumbs to a spear thrust, and Talou is able to proclaim himself King of Drelchkaff, since Yaour has died childless. It is with the ceremony commemorating his coronation that *Impressions d'Afrique* begins.

This recombining of the separated halves of Souann's dominions can be seen as mimetic of the compositional processes that generate the narrative:

> 1 *Revers* (lapel) *à marguerite* (daisy, as worn in the buttonhole of a jacket lapel); 2 *revers* (setback, such as a military defeat) *à Marguerite* (woman's name); hence the battle of the Tez lost by Yaour dressed as Faust's Marguerite.

The *procédé* opens a fissure in language which the resulting story must then bridge: every episode is a mini Battle of the Tez, an attempt to heal the division caused by Souann's double lineages:

> 1 *Maison* (house) *à espagnolettes* (window fasteners); 2 *maison* (royal dynasty) *à espagnolettes* (little Spanish girls); hence the two young Spanish twins from whom Talou and Yaour are descended.

By opening with a series of rituals celebrating the achievement of this reunification, Roussel effectively declares again the extent to which his own glory was 'a fact, an established fact, a sensation'; it required no external validation, for it existed on its own terms, beyond all narratives of success or failure. Analogously, there can be no doubt as to the perfect resolution of the puzzles posed by Roussel in the first half of the book, and explicated in the second. As Cocteau pointed out, Roussel's 'surprises' 'rest on a feeling of security.' The only source of narrative tension is the outcome of Carmichaël's second rendition of Talou's verses in praise of his transvestite triumph over Yaour.

It is the unnamed narrator who offers to help Carmichaël memorize the rebarbative verses:

> Fetching from the deserted stage-wings Juillard's chair, I came and sat down under the branches of the sycamore, and offered to help Carmichaël in his task. He instantly held out to me a large, loose sheet of paper on which the barbaric pronunciation of the Ponukéléan text had been meticulously transcribed in French characters. Spurred on by fear of a second failure, he began carefully to recite his strange lesson, humming the tune beneath his breath, while I followed each line syllable by syllable, ready to call attention to the least error, or to prompt with any fragment he might forget.
>
> The crowd, on leaving the place des Trophées, had slowly dispersed throughout Éjur, and, distracted hardly at all by my purely mechanical task, I could not help thinking, in the great silence of the morning, of the many adventures which had filled my life over the last three months.

Again the symmetries and correspondences are striking. The interaction between the two white men might be seen as a recasting of that between the narrator and Balancier in 'Parmi les Noirs': in the story Balancier unscrambled the chalked letters referring to his own book about a white man sending missives to his wife about a black plunderer, whereas in the novel the narrator aids Carmichaël to reproduce – but not decode – the black letters written by the black plunderer about his destruction – while dressed as a white woman – of his similarly costumed black double. The two white men also parallel and invert the unfortunate Spanish twins, who each argued for the primogeniture of their own sons; the partnership of the narrator and Carmichaël intimates the annulment of this division, for together they manage to reproduce the song of Souann's descendant, Talou, that celebrates the healing of that breach. Such mirrorings again mime the workings of the *procédé*, which figures each word as having two sides whose relationship may be conjugated in terms of any number of dualities: conscious/unconscious, black/white, female/male, surface/lining, original/imitation or double. Roussel points out in 'Comment j'ai écrit . . .' that he deliberately chose to derive from each word in his pairings 'a meaning other than the primary meaning'. Nevertheless, the suppressed original meanings linger behind the endless bifurcations of the *procédé*; the peculiar, uncanny dimension of Roussel's fiction that results from this displacement has been best described by John Ashbery in his second article on Roussel. Considering the notorious 'rails en mou de veau' (rails made of calves' lights), he observes:

> Disregarding for the moment the meaning of the French words and the pseudo-rational reason for their being there, we can recognize in them a svelte, secret resonance that implies hidden chambers and secret meanings. The phrase is like a Chinese box that one turns over and over, certain that there is a concealed spring somewhere, that in a moment the lid will fly open, revealing possibly nothing more than its own emptiness, but proving that reality is only a false bottom.

In early drafts of the novel the narrator takes a much more active role in affairs: for instance, it is he, rather than Juillard, who awards the Grand Cordon to the act that draws the most applause from the native audience. His effacement from the text has a similar effect to the sublimation of the primary meaning of the word combinations chosen as sources for the various episodes: for the process of turning language inside out inevitably involves a dissolution and diffusion of subjectivity also. The narrator thus becomes the shadowy negative of the author.

Whereas Roussel prided himself on his masterly impressions of the famous, the narrator takes no part in the gala of the Incomparables and indeed doesn't even buy or sell shares at the mini-Bourse in halting alexandrines – of which Roussel himself had composed some 50,000 by this stage in his career. And while Roussel, as the manuscripts for the novel so clearly illustrate, found himself obsessively driven to explore endless uncharted regions of language in pursuit of his aesthetic ideal, the narrator is a casual traveller whose only motivation is curiosity about the geographical world:

> intending to undertake a long voyage through the curious regions of South America, I had embarked at Marseilles on the *Lyncée*, a large and speedy vessel bound for Buenos Aires.

In adult life Roussel seems to have been immune to all emotional entanglements and intimacies; 'more than anyone,' Leiris remarked in an essay written shortly after Roussel's death, 'he must have felt alone in the world.' In contrast, the narrator of *Impressions d'Afrique* merges effortlessly into the collective; on board the *Lyncée* he quickly establishes relations with his fellow passengers, and when they separate on the quay after their return to Marseilles, it is only 'after a cordial exchange of handshakes, in which only Tancrède Boucharessas [the limbless musician] could not take part.'

The narrator presents himself as an individual (i.e. in the first person singular) only at the beginning and end of each of the book's two halves. His references to himself thus serve as a kind of frame, in a manner analogous to Roussel's self-figurations in the opening and closing lines of the poems collected in *La Vue*; but while in the poems he is wholly removed from the static scenes he contemplates, in the novel he is able to participate as an anonymous witness in the actual unfolding of each episode. André Gide, for one, has commented (in a letter to Roussel, an extract of which is included in Roussel's *cahier de critiques*) on the almost delirious sense of abandon *Impressions d'Afrique* permits, as if one were entering a unique, all-encompassing, living medium:

On a certain day of leisure I leafed at random through the book . . . Immediately I let myself go, carried out of my depth by the Gulf Stream of your fantasy . . . 'Then, like a sleepwalker, Fogar arose and entered the sea.' How many times since, like Fogar, have I plunged into your dense waters.

Fogar, who is barely fifteen years old, is the Emperor's eldest son; like his father, he is a born poet, but Fogar is a poet of the body rather than of words. Talou's *Jéroukka* hymns his active and terrestrial military conquests; his son, in contrast, passively yields himself to the physical poetry of the seabed. Fogar has been taught by the witch doctor Bachkou a method of inducing in himself a state of deathlike lethargy; while he is in this hypnotic trance his heartbeat and breathing are suspended and he is able to stay under water for up to half an hour. On awaking from this coma he always finds his veins obstructed by a clot of greenish blood, which he removes with the aid of a special flower:

> With one of the thorns of the stem he would open the engorged vein and draw out from it the dense clot. Then a single petal, crushed between his fingers, would furnish him with a violet liquid, a few drops of which were sufficient to heal the mortally dangerous fissure.

Fogar's submission to his ecstasy thus entails yet again the creation and healing of a rift, this time in the flesh rather than in language, as in the *procédé*, or in the body politic, as in the story of Souann and his descendants.

Fogar's solitary descent into the ocean depths clearly struck Gide as equivalent to his own experience of reading Roussel; once in the water Fogar is 'sustained by the dense element' and surrounded by wonders: 'he had simply to stretch out his hand to take possession of the most astonishing marvels.' In the course of this particular excursion Fogar collects six specimens which feature in his gala performance; despite the exotic locale in which they were discovered, they all resemble everyday domestic items – a sponge, a bit of dress-fringe, a pennant, some soap-lather, a block of gelatine and a plate. Fogar's subsequent experiments reveal that each is endowed with curious properties: the block of gelatine, for instance, when placed on a jagged surface, unfolds a feeler that divides into three prongs with suckers on their ends which rotate with a velocity that increases as the pain grows sharper. Accordingly, during his gala demonstration Fogar places this sensitive gelatine on a square of concrete set with a hundred bugle-beads and attaches three of Marius Boucharessas's green-ribboned cats to the suckers. As the beads penetrate the agonized body of the block the poor felines are whirled around at a terrifying speed, until eventually 'the cats, merged altogether, formed an unbroken circle streaked with green, from which escaped fierce mewing sounds.' The pennant, the soap-lather and the fringe are stirred into action by the green clots, for which they share a great relish and which each gobbles up greedily; the sponge is revealed to have a spectacularly violent aversion to fresh water, and the plate bulges like a dome when Fogar places it in the path of a battery-operated fan.

In *Opium* Cocteau described the world of Roussel's fiction as 'suspended from elegance, fairyland and fear'. The poetic patternings of the *procédé* radiate impartially through the text, and balancing the wondrous exhibitions of the Incomparables are the tortures inflicted on Naïr, Rul, Mossem, Gaïz-dûh and Djizmé. If the fairyland aspects of the novel prefigure the Surreal-ists' quest for the marvellous, its dispassionate accounts of ingenious methods of punishment remind one of the tortures featured in Octave Mirbeau's *Le jardin des supplices* (1899), in which all manner of ingenious forms of execution are described in detail. The most subtly painful of these involves being tied beneath a vast, gently vibrating bell; contemplating the gro-tesquely disfigured corpse of a victim of this treatment, the novel's torture-addicted heroine Clara rapturously exclaims:

No, but conceive of this prodigious fact – that the very thing that can make amorous virgins walking in the country in the evening cry with ecstasy and divine melancholy, can also make men roar with pain, and kill a miserable human carcass under the most ineffable agony. I say it's genius! Ah, what a wonderful torture!

But whereas Mirbeau's depictions of refined forms of cruelty are intended to generate outrage at the hypocrisy and pretensions of mankind, Roussel's punishments seem determined, rather, by the indifferent processes of language. The treacherous Mossem, for instance, perishes from the unendurable pain of having the text of his forged certificate of Sirdah's death inscribed on the soles of his feet with red-hot pokers. His death thus fulfils the random judgement imposed on him by the *procédé*: '1 *Plante* (plant) *à faux* (scythe); 2 *plante* (sole of the foot) *à faux* (falsity); hence the torture suffered by Mossem.'

Mossem might be said to deserve his punishment, but the executions of Djizmé and Gaïz-dûh suggest the remorselessly inhuman arbitrariness of Roussel's methods, the extent to which his games-playing resembles not only drawing-room charades, but also Borges's 'The Lottery in Babylon' or Georges Perec's Olympian community in *W*, in which the contestants are as likely to suffer forfeits, mutilations and even death as win glittering prizes.

Unnervingly, Roussel's writing makes no distinction between miraculous feats and hideous torments: each episode, amazing or appalling, fulfils a pre-existing linguistic conundrum and is accordingly radiant with its own perfect success. The condemned play their parts in the staging of their own executions as triumphantly as the Incomparables display their wonderful talents. Poor Djizmé is sentenced to die merely for having received from her lover Naïr a series of cartoons that poked fun at the Emperor, while Gaïz-dûh (the ambassador who betrayed Yaour and thus enabled Talou to win the Battle of the Tez) is rewarded by the victorious chieftain with the death penalty.

At the suggestion of the architect Chènevillot, Djizmé is connected during an electric storm to a lightning conductor attached to a pair of metal shoes. As she stretches out her arms towards Naïr, who is imprisoned on a platform across the square, the lightning strikes, converting her into a simulacrum of herself, 'a corpse with wide-open eyes and inert limbs'. Folgar's seemingly inanimate gelatinous block, pennant, soap-lather and fringe are galvanized by his experiments into revealing their livingness; Djizmé undergoes an antithetical translation from a state of vitality to the immobility of death.

The ongoing process of solving the narrative riddles generated by the *procédé* infuses Roussel's prose with a kind of Midas touch: everything is metamorphosed into aesthetic pattern, death as well as life. He lavishes his 'elegance' equally on 'fear' and 'fairyland'. The destruction of Gaïz-dûh offers perhaps the most startling example of this. In the drafts his death is a horribly messy affair: Rao, his executioner, first padlocks his lips together, then throws away the key. Shortly afterwards his head is chopped off with an ordinary axe; blood spurts from his severed neck and inundates the nearby corpse of Gretchen (the original name of Yaour). In the published version Roussel exactly reverses his previous emphasis on the condemned body's physicality and incontinence:

> With both hands Rao brandished his axe, and struck three blows on the traitor's neck. With the last blow the head rolled to the ground.
>
> The site remained unmarked by any red splashes, because of the curious wooden blade, which, as it penetrated the flesh, immediately caused the blood to congeal, and even absorbed into itself the first few drops whose spurting could not be avoided.
>
> The severed sections of the head and trunk presented the scarlet, solid appearance of certain kinds of butcher's meat.
>
> One could not help thinking, in spite of oneself, of those mannequins used by magicians, which, cleverly substituted by means of a false bottom in a piece of prop furniture, are neatly cut up on stage in slabs prepared in advance to look suitably gory. Here, the reality of the corpse rendered the compact redness, normally created by the art of the paintbrush, particularly impressive.
>
> The slaves carried away the remains of Gaïz-Dûh, together with the lightly stained axe.

The meticulously observed details and aesthetic comparisons are terrifying precisely because Roussel so clearly has no intention to shock or be sinister. The description perfectly illustrates Cocteau's maxim that, in Roussel, 'genius is the furthest extreme of the practical'. Cocteau also admits, however, the threat posed by a vision so seemingly impersonal, so indifferent to the claims of subjectivity. Gide's celebration of the delights of immersion in the Rousselian should be twinned with Cocteau's warning of the dangers involved:

> In 1918 I rejected Roussel as likely to place me under a spell from which I could see no escape. Since then I have constructed defences. I can look at him from the outside.

———

The general public for whose approbation Roussel longed had no need of Cocteau's elaborate fortifications. Although the book received a number of reviews that were by no means altogether discouraging, Roussel clearly felt it had not achieved the success it deserved.* One reader alone seemed fully sensible of its true merits:

* Roussel included a selection of these in the programme of the play. In the *Journal* Paul Reboux (who later published a pastiche of *L'Étoile au front*) declared: 'It is an extraordinary novel, breathtaking, droll, visionary; in other words, it is not a run-of-the-mill book. With a wealth of truly surprising details, M. Raymond Roussel has imagined marvellous devices, circumstances never before associated, events never previously realized. He accomplishes this without allowing you to believe these are the wanderings of a whimsical brain. Not for a moment does his logic relax, and his writing is clear, pure, precise and unflinching. He maliciously seduces us into following his developments, and with such a calm air that it is some time before one stops and says to oneself, "Ah! What . . . is it he who's gone mad . . . or me?" It is all very curious.' The most extended consideration of the book's effects came from Simon Crosmières in *La Flamme*: 'On opening M. Raymond Roussel's book, I imagined I would find an account, more or less highly coloured, of an African voyage. From the first lines, I was astonished; by the third page I was anxiously wondering if I were not suffering a hallucination; I began again from the start, reading closely, and I realized the title was a fiction, that these *Impressions d'Afrique* were but a pretext chosen by M. Raymond Roussel to give free rein to his imagination. From then on, I was gripped, and I read the book in a single night . . . M. Raymond Roussel is a disciple of Poe and of Wells, but at no moment could he be said to imitate them; his imagination, although fantastic, is extremely distinctive. And I am grateful to him, for he has provided me with the rare sensation of finding myself confronted by an original talent . . . If M. Raymond Roussel makes good on the promises held out by *Impressions d'Afrique*, I am convinced he will not fail to achieve an enviable place in contemporary literature' (Fonds Rondel, Bibliothèque de l'Arsenal, hereafter FRD, cat. no. Rf 71.821. The pagination of this and the other collections of cuttings that make up this archive is too erratic to be worth giving.)

Only Edmond Rostand, to whom I had sent a copy of the book, immediately understood it; he became a passionate enthusiast and talked of it to everyone, and even went so far as to read extracts from it aloud to his friends. He would often say to me, 'There's an extraordinary play to be made from your book.' This advice influenced me. Besides, I suffered from being misunderstood, and I thought I might perhaps more easily reach the public through the theatre than through books.

Accordingly, I adapted a play from *Impressions d'Afrique*, which I had performed first at the Théâtre Fémina, then at the Théâtre Antoine.

And so began Roussel's ruinous affair with the stage. It is hard to believe that the astute and immensely successful Rostand was offering this advice seriously. There is not a single line of dialogue in the entire novel. Many of the acts performed by the Incomparables appear inherently unstageable, and each episode involves exhaustive explanations likely to puzzle the most sophisticated of theatre audiences. Could Rostand himself have successfully dramatized, say, Bedu's *métier à aubes* – a loom (*métier*) erected on a river bank and powered by the action of the currents on its paddles (*aubes*) – or Fuxier's tableaux modelled in grapes, or Bex's gigantic magnetized high-velocity pencils? Undaunted by such difficulties, Roussel set about recasting his novel into a drama in five acts, for which he invented a Ponukéléan language, which has to be translated by the French-speaking Africans such as Sirdah, and even composed a couple of strophes of the *Jéroukka*. Roussel obviously wanted the play to include as much of the novel's abundance and detail as possible; the recently discovered typescript of the first version is prefaced by a note that the production's stage manager must have found particularly troubling:

While reading this play, it is absolutely vital to have in your hands at the same time the novel from which it is adapted, for, in the course of each act, numerous references are made to the book for the details of each setting.

A slimmed down, four-act version of Roussel's original adaptation opened to the public – after a number of private performances – at the Théâtre Fémina on the Champs Élysées on 30 September 1911. The Fémina was not a theatre to attract the critics, and the production received much less attention than the novel itself had done.

In his florid essay on Roussel collected a decade later in *Élus et appelés*, Robert de Montesquiou ponders the irresolvable contradiction in Roussel's character that impelled him to seek a popular audience for works that Montesquiou felt self-evidently belonged to the avant-garde:

> That a creator who is at once outrageous and delicate can take a proud, melancholy pleasure in composing the sort of works of which Baudelaire once observed, 'I call them famous because they are appreciated by me and by some of my friends,' nothing could be better; this denotes a character which, combined with talent, demands attention, or at the very least respect. But to believe one can arouse with such creations the interest of the devotees of M. Prévost, or the audience of plays like *Le Cœur dispose*, this strikes me as evidence of a misunderstanding so ingenuous that, of all the marvels, spells and artifices of M. Roussel, this one alone finds me stubbornly, obstinately unbelieving, and I defy him to explain himself to me.

It was this 'misunderstanding' which, on the one hand, drove Roussel to court terrible and exorbitant public humiliations, and on the other brought him to the notice of the writers and artists who were to champion his work and be influenced by his imaginative world. Marcel Duchamp, for instance, revealed in 1946:

> It was fundamentally Roussel who was responsible for my glass, *La Mariée mise à nu par ses célibataires, même* . . . This play of his [*Impressions d'Afrique*] which I saw with Apollinaire helped me greatly on one side of my expression . . . Roussel showed me the way.

It was Roussel's theatre that became the main rallying point to his cause for the Surrealists. Indeed, performances of his plays developed into major sites of vociferous, often violent conflict with exactly those bourgeois audiences he hoped to delight and amaze. The more elaborate and lavish the productions became, the more Roussel risked appearing to the general public he wooed not as a triumphant genius, but as a laughing stock; as a man singled out not by the star on his brow, but because he had too much money and no sense at all.

This first run of *Impressions d'Afrique* was to prove the least scandalous of Roussel's theatrical ventures. In the early hours of 6 October, just a week after the play had opened, Madame Roussel passed away in her recently completed villa at Biarritz, and all further performances were immediately suspended.

———

Earlier that year Madame Roussel and Raymond had shared what was to be their last holiday together, a two-month trip to Ceylon (as Sri Lanka was then called) and India. They were accompanied not only by Doctor Mattin but by Madame Roussel's female companion, her cook, her chambermaid and by Raymond's valet. It was on this voyage that Madame Roussel made special arrangements to have her coffin transported as part of her luggage. A letter dated 26 November 1910 from the agency arranging the tour assures the prospective travellers 'that it will be possible, in case of decease, to proceed to the embalming of the body which will be placed in the coffin brought along by Madame Roussel.' She further stipulated that her berth be enlarged by 1.2 metres, for which she had to pay an extra 500 francs. The trip cost, in total, some 40,000 francs. They spent two weeks in Ceylon, where they visited the Temple of the Tooth in Kandy, and returned via Bombay to arrive back in France in early March. Leiris has suggested that, in the course of his travels, Roussel was 'never duped into the role of the tourist'. The recently discovered photographs of Roussel abroad imply the opposite, or at least suggest the role of tourist greatly appealed to him, most particularly because it allowed him to outfit himself in a variety of appropriate costumes. In one from this trip he poses on the deck of the outward bound steamship, the *Barbarossa*, sporting an elegant nautical cap. Another features Roussel, his mother, a mahout and an elephant on the shore of Lake Kandy; Roussel is dressed in a dazzling tropical suit and sun-hat that exactly resemble those soon to be donned by the actors playing the whites in the stage version of *Impressions d'Afrique* (see Plates 9 and 10).

Madame Roussel returned in poor health from this trip, though without having had to make use of her portable coffin. She did not attend private or public performances of her son's theatrical début. Her final acquisition was two tiny lapdogs: a servant was dispatched to London to purchase the dogs, which must have arrived in Biarritz only days before her death at the age of sixty-four.* She was buried in the family vault at Neuilly. The following year the Galerie Georges-Petit conducted the sale of many of the paintings and objets d'art that adorned the villa at Biarritz and the grand salon of her Paris hôtel; this auction included works by Fragonard, Gainsborough, Corot, Greuze, Sir Thomas Lawrence, Hubert Robert and François-Hubert Drouais, her prized collection of Dresden figurines, and a significant selection of furniture and jewellery.

Roussel does not mention the death of either of his parents in 'Comment j'ai écrit . . .' If his father's coincided with the discovery of his vocation, his mother's enabled him to devote his share of the family's formidable resources, of which he inherited two-thirds, to realizing his dreams of success through every feasible means. Germaine, whose second marriage – to Charles Ney – was already foundering, took up residence at rue de Chaillot, while Raymond installed himself in the villa at Neuilly. Behind its closed shutters he set to work on his next novel, *Locus Solus*, named after the very similar property where its inventor-hero Martial Canterel pursues his equally astonishing researches.

––––––

The disappointments attendant upon the first production of *Impressions d'Afrique* appear not to have weakened Roussel's

* Madame Roussel had a great passion for lapdogs, and had a postcard made of herself and Raymond flanking a table on which sit a pair of tiny black and white dogs (see Plate 11). There are numerous pictures of small dogs in the collection of Roussel's photographs housed in Estampes.

conviction that the stage offered his likeliest means of winning over a recalcitrant public. A second adaptation, this time in four acts and a prologue, opened on Saturday 11 May 1912 at the Théâtre Antoine on the boulevard de Strasbourg. Roussel evidently felt the failure of the initial run had been due to lack of publicity. This second production was heralded by a massive advertising campaign. Playbills featuring major characters and a catalogue of the amazing acts on offer were plastered all over town. Roussel could not be accused of failing to forewarn prospective audiences of the extraordinary nature of his show:

> The earthworm that plays the zither . . . The one-legged Lelgoualch playing a flute made from his own tibia . . . Cats that play prisoner's base . . . The wall of dominoes evocative of priests . . . The echoing chests of the brothers Alcott . . .

Other posters depicted the torture of Mossem, and the well-known actor Dorival blacked up to perform the role of Talou, scowling and adorned with a jewelled and feathered crown. Roussel arranged for puffs to appear in the theatrical sections of papers such as the *Gaulois*, and even composed a poem in alexandrines in praise of the show's chief delights. The extracts from reviews of the novel included in the programme suggested that Roussel might fruitfully be compared with Shakespeare, Jules Verne, Edgar Allan Poe, H. G. Wells, Rabelais, Flaubert and the author of *A Thousand and One Arabian Nights*.

Such efforts ensured Roussel a response this time, but not the one he was after. In 'Comment j'ai écrit . . .' he recalls:

> It was more than just a failure – it provoked an outcry. People called me mad, they 'barracked' the actors, hurled coins at the stage and sent letters of protest to the manager. A tour made of Belgium, Holland and Northern France proved no more successful.

Theatrical performances in Paris around this time were often rowdy affairs, and would become more so when the Surrealists embarked on their programme of systematic confrontation and disruption. Roussel can be seen to have been, wholly unwittingly, both precursor and catalyst of their violations of theatrical conventions. Among the audience for this second run of *Impressions d'Afrique* were the avant-gardists Apollinaire and Picabia, who would soon be staging literary (or anti-literary) events calculated to produce exactly the tumult that greeted Roussel's play. Apollinaire's *Les Mamelles de Tirésias* (1917) and Picabia's Dada demonstrations of 1919–20 incited outrage and scandal by deliberately affronting the audience's conception of the theatre, yet neither was to create an image as legendary, or as provocative and unassimilable, as Roussel's whalebone statue on rails of calves' lights.

During the course of the tour of northern France, Belgium and Holland, Roussel decided to make his own stage début in the non-speaking role of a sailor. A photo survives as testimony to his fleeting career as a thespian (see Plate 12). He appears singularly pleased with himself: while the rest of the cast focus on Talou's coronation, Roussel gazes abstractedly, arms folded, into the distance, stage left. Although he may not yet have affected the public in the manner desired, he had at last discovered 'his way'.

CHAPTER 5

# A Solitary Place

Roussel pointedly discloses in 'Comment j'ai écrit . . .' that he set about composing his second prose novel while the theatrical version of his first was being hooted and hissed by enraged audiences and derided in the press. 'During this time,' he observes in a one-line paragraph, 'I was writing *Locus Solus*.' The connection suggests again some of the symmetries that structure his literary development: it is at the very moment when his theatrical novel and novelistic play are foundering, rather like the *Lyncée*, on both page and stage, that Roussel begins work on his most radiant celebration of the powers of his own genius. Further, the juxtaposition intimates yet another attempt to reverse the order of events in his literary initiation, in which 'la crise', the crisis of public humiliation, succeeded the solitary triumphant experience of 'la gloire'. By locating the genesis of *Locus Solus* in the furious outrage occasioned by the stage version of *Impressions d'Afrique*, Roussel refigures the relationship between disaster and success enacted in his earlier works on a different plane. Canterel requires no originating calamity like the shipwreck, or Gaspard's failure to resheathe his sword, to release him into the world of Rousselian carnival; on the contrary, the novel posits a fundamental opposition between the disaster of life and the redemptive, self-contained glories of literature.

'I carried the sun inside me,' Roussel insisted to Janet; it is the godlike Canterel who incarnates more fully than any other character Roussel's unwavering belief in his own election – and analogously, the novel appears to have assumed almost talismanic significance for its author. According to Charlotte Dufrène, he could recite the entire text from memory, as if he needed to know he literally carried 'the sun' inside himself. It is as Martial that Roussel appears in Janet's *De l'angoisse à l'extase*, the name chosen, he takes care to inform us in

'Comment j'ai écrit . . .', 'because of Martial Canterel in *Locus Solus*.' The use of this pseudonym creates a division in Janet's text that replicates the circumstances of the novel's composition: on the one hand Roussel is no more than 'a poor little invalid', his life a series of pathetic delusions and costly failures, his writings worthless ['insignifiantes']; on the other, to those initiated into his art, the alias enables Roussel to soar phoenix-like from the ashes of Janet's contumely, unnervingly confident in the power of his genius to fulfil itself on its own terms, indifferent to sneers and mockery. The pseudonym insulates Roussel from Janet's interpretation of his condition, just as he seems insulated from the débâcle of the performance of *Impressions d'Afrique* in the photograph discussed at the end of the previous chapter, or as the park of *Locus Solus* appears decisively separated from the outside world in the sketch used to illustrate the novel's serial publication (under the title *Quelques heures à Bougival*) in *Le Gaulois du Dimanche*.

The theme of separation might be said to determine the novel's structure also. Whereas the multiple interwoven narratives of *Impressions d'Afrique* are strung out across the two halves of the book, and hundreds of pages often intervene between an event's description and its explanation, in *Locus Solus* Roussel makes each chapter into a sealed compartment in which a given invention or series of experiments is fully presented and accounted for. Each chapter's narrative method is inward-looking, its energies devoted to binding its disparate elements into an intricate single unit, like a series of Chinese ivory balls contained within each other, or the freestanding diamond-shaped receptacle filled with *aqua micans* in which strikingly diverse objects, creatures and humans demonstrate the properties of the same medium. This may reflect the different stage of the *procédé* underpinning the book. Roussel tells us in 'Comment j'ai écrit . . .' that he made use almost entirely of what he calls the 'evolved' form, in which he would develop a series of images from the distortion of a random text. ('Elle commence tôt sa tournée asticote'/ 'Ailé coma . . . Saturne Elastique hotte'). If the *à* method mainly utilized in the composition of *Impressions d'Afrique* corresponds to the process of fragmentation and reconnection that divides the novel in two, the 'evolved' form deployed in *Locus Solus* appears to have resulted in discrete episodes that reveal ever more dazzling feats of assimilation.

Indeed, *Locus Solus* can be seen in a variety of ways as establishing an antithetical relationship with its predecessor. While *Impressions d'Afrique* presents, for the most part, aesthetic performances and public rituals whose roles are evenly distributed among a vast range of characters, *Locus Solus* concentrates on the all-unifying powers of a solitary scientific genius. Whereas *Impressions d'Afrique* might be described as centrifugal, propelled by the energies of dispersal, of imitation of the other, *Locus Solus* is, until its conclusion, insistently centripetal, with each seeming miracle unerringly controlled and decoded by the omnipotent Canterel. If shipwreck on the shores of black Africa enabled Roussel to develop his fracturing of language into a baroque fecundity of narrative, behind the severe gates of *Locus Solus* Canterel embodies a fantasy of mastery at its most isolated, exalted and implacable.

———

The narrator of *Locus Solus* is one of a number of guests invited by Canterel to visit the huge park surrounding his beautiful villa in Montmorency one Thursday afternoon at the beginning of April:

> Locus Solus, as the property is called, is a quiet retreat where Canterel, in perfect intellectual peace, enjoys pursuing his various fruitful labours. In this *solitary place* he is sufficiently sheltered from the turbulence of Paris – and yet can reach the capital in a quarter of an hour whenever his research requires a session at some specialist library, or when the time comes for him to make a sensational announcement to the scientific world, at some prodigiously packed lecture.

Canterel's villa includes several rooms converted into luxurious laboratories in which he pursues his experiments, aided by numerous passionate disciples and assistants about whom, however, we are given no further details. Like Roussel conducting his recondite linguistic researches within the equally opulent and fortress-like villa at Neuilly, Canterel is an independent bachelor whose vast fortune enables him to devote all his time and attention to his various projects. While clearly an amalgam of a number of fictional and actual professor heroes, such as Camille Flammarion* or Jules Verne's Doctor Moreau or Nemo, Roussel's *savant* is also Roussel's most complete figuration of his uniquely gifted self: Canterel, we are told, has an open countenance, regular features and keen eyes that sparkle with wonderful intelligence, while his warm, persuasive voice and forceful elocution make him 'one of the champions of the spoken word'.

Canterel's ingenious solutions to the problems posed by his 'continual discoveries' re-enact in the material realm of science – or pseudo-science – his creator's narrative solutions to the challenges set by the *procédé*. The therapeutic goal underlying a number of Canterel's experiments suggests, further, the high stakes involved in Roussel's language games: Roussel claimed to have 'found his way' out of the tortures of prospecting through his discovery of the *procédé*, and several episodes in *Locus Solus* dramatize a similar kind of decisive breakthrough. Lucius Egroizard in Chapter 5, for instance, has been traumatized by being forced to witness the death of his one-year-old daughter Gillette at the hands, or rather the feet, of a notorious company

---

* Camille Flammarion was an extremely popular quasi-mystical astronomer, and one of Roussel's most venerated heroes. An intriguing item of Rousseliana survives as testimony to his admiration. In the mid-1930s Dora Maar, best known as Picasso's lover and the subject of many of his paintings, purchased in a Parisian flea market a small, star-shaped glass box containing a star-shaped fragment of biscuit. A label attached declares: 'A star originating from a lunch I attended on Sunday, 29 July 1923, at the Observatory at Juvisy with Camille Flammarion presiding. Raymond Roussel.' For a time this fetishistic object was in the keeping of Georges Bataille, who wrote of it in *André Masson* (first published 1940, reprinted in *3uvres complètes*, Paris: Gallimard, 1970): '[The star] did not belong to me, but it remained in my drawer for several months, and I could not speak of it without feeling troubled. Roussel's obscure purpose appeared to be closely connected to the fact the star could be eaten; he obviously wanted to appropriate to himself this edible star in a manner more important and actual than simply by eating it. This strange object signified for me the way in which Roussel had achieved his dream of eating a heavenly star' (vol. I, p. 566). See also Masachika Tani's 'La Mort et le Temps: Raymond Roussel et Camille Flammarion', in *Europe*, no. 714, Oct. 1988, pp. 96-105.

of Kentish brigands called the Red Gang. These pitiless, drunken bandits had murdered the poor child in the most brutal of ways, trampling on her body as they danced the well-known jig 'Sir Roger de Coverly'. Egroizard, driven insane with grief, is afflicted by symptoms that reflect the bizarre circumstances of his daughter's death: he finds himself compelled to create tiny, lightweight gold models of the brigands whom he makes once more perform the fatal dance in mid-air through a judicious manipulation of hot-air currents. More alarming still, he keeps undergoing a painful capillary crisis in the course of which the twelve hairs that border his bald pate detach themselves from their roots and leap across his bare cranium, from root to root, in the pattern of movement ordained by the dance. Egroizard's cure involves allowing him to experiment with a heterogeneous array of objects that include, among many others, a thread capable of sewing itself, a holy wooden memory-aid engraved with Coptic letters, a ruler made of bacon,* a set of golden hinges and a primitive recording apparatus, all of which he combines in a series of complex operations that eventually enable him to produce a sound exactly resembling his young daughter's baby-talk. At this he bursts out:

'It's you, my Gillette . . . They haven't killed you . . . You're here . . . next to me . . . Speak, my darling.'

And between these broken phrases, the fragment of the word, which he constantly reproduced, returned again and again, like a response.

Speaking in hushed tones, Canterel led us quietly away, so as to allow this salutary crisis to run its course in peace.

The wise *maître* is confident that this recreation of a trace of the madman's beloved child is sure to prove an effective catalyst for his recovery.

Egroizard's systematic fusion of his unlikely chosen materials offers a revealing analogy to the compositional methods entailed by the 'evolved' form of the *procédé*. That his researches are

---

* Jean Ferry has suggested – surely correctly – that this ruler made of bacon must originate in a pun on *règle de l'art/règle de lard* (*Une étude sur Raymond Roussel*, Paris: Arcanes, 1953, hereafter UE, p. 147).

directed towards recreating and then endlessly replaying an imitation of the past is also characteristic of the book's disturbing overall dialectic of loss and recovery. For though none of life's random mischances can strike within the protective precincts of Canterel's utopian domain, many of the novel's episodes involve characters seeking cure, redress or at least consolation, either for violent disasters such as that suffered by Egroizard, or for the more routine attritions of time and bereavement. The novel as a whole evinces a profound melancholy, its narratives driven by an unappeasable yearning to salvage and reanimate by any means possible tokens or simulacra of the irretrievably lost. In this novel in particular, Roussel emerges as the 'dark and distorted' twin of Proust.

———

*Locus Solus*'s rigorous, almost classical elegance was achieved only after numerous reshapings. Roussel quarried its seven chapters from a vast, sprawling draft almost twice as long as the published version. This involved curtailing the further adventures of characters, such as the sybil Felicity, who appear in the final text and discarding a number of wholly new storylines. Whereas the drafts of *Impressions d'Afrique* reveal Roussel slowly discovering the resources and potential of his own prose, and allow us to trace his increasingly confident embellishment of stock situations with an extravagant 'mass of enriching details' – like those with which he transforms Shakespeare's *Romeo and Juliet* – the writing in the *Locus Solus* manuscript is remarkably polished and intricately patterned throughout.

My favourite of the episodes excised describes, among other things, the creation of a harp whose strings are made from wax tears shed by the wives of fifteen brothers, and an experiment performed on Shakespeare's second left rib. A friend of Boudet's (as Canterel is here called), one Isaac Zabulon, has learned from the papers of a biblical ancestor of a drug which, taken orally, converts a weeper's tears into wax. These wax tears, once solidified, possess strange acoustic powers, as the biblical Zabulon discovered when he fitted them to an Aeolian harp which he placed in a windy desert. He also found that if each string were made from a wax tear shed by women married to brothers, the music emitted became more intoxicating still. Together Boudet and Zabulon reconstruct this unique auditory experience, with the help of fifteen wax tears shed by the fifteen Mesdames Pelognes and a specially built wind machine. The resulting sounds induce in the listeners an unimaginable ecstasy.

This harp is then conjoined with Shakespeare's second left rib, which has just come into Boudet's possession. It was apparently plundered from the Bard's grave by the eighteenth-century English lord Albert of Dewsbury. During his travels Dewsbury came across a people in Australia who believed the soul resided in the second left rib. It was therefore this tribe's custom to remove this rib from each recently dead person, hollow it out and affix it to a stake. In times of trouble they would consult these ribs for advice, and Dewsbury is amazed to find that the sound of the wind through the bone does in fact resemble a kind of language. Accordingly, on his return to England he steals Shakespeare's second left rib in the hope of coaxing from it a new play. After various experiments he succeeds in evoking the vowels e, i and a, but then dies in a riding accident. The rib has recently been found by the tragedienne Adinolfa (who in *Impressions d'Afrique* unearthed Shakespeare's original version of *Romeo and Juliet*) in a secret cabinet in her Thames-side castle. She passes it on to Boudet, who produces the same three vowels as Dewsbury by directing currents from his wind machine through the harp and then the rib. As a final flourish, he has these vowels projected against a flower which has been grafted with the metal zinc, and on which a jeweller has engraved the three scenes which eventually appear as the bas-reliefs introducing the story of Hello and and the pink-attired dwarf Le Quillec in Chapter 1 of *Locus Solus*.*

---

* Various other instruments, such as a violin that makes everyone who hears it weep, and narratives too complicated to describe are involved in this episode. For further discussion of the manuscript of *Locus Solus*, and other Roussel drafts, see my 'Genius in Its Pure State', *London Review of Books*, vol. 19, no. 10, 22 May 1997, pp. 21–4, and Annie Angrémy's 'La malle de Roussel. Du bric-à-brac au décryptage,' BN, pp. 42–3. A section of this episode, edited by Annie Angrémy, is published in this issue, pp. 52–4.

Like this draft episode, most of Canterel's demonstrations serve as a means either of illustrating his discoveries or of exploiting them for practical purposes, however unlikely. The aerial paving beetle used to construct a mosaic of human teeth in Chapter 2, for instance, allows Canterel both to dispose of his 'embarrassing stock' of extracted molars, canines and incisors, and to demonstrate his ability to forecast every alteration in the weather affecting a particular location up to ten days in advance. This ingenious contraption consists of a modified paving implement, known as a paving beetle, attached to a small balloon. A variety of claws, chronometers, lenses, mirrors and magnets enable this hybrid machine to pick up the required tooth, then to rise into the air as its balloon reinflates with gas released by the action of the sun on a specially devised ochre paste. Once aloft, the machine is blown by the predicted breeze to its designated place in the mosaic, whereupon a valve releases air from the balloon, the beetle gently lands and the tooth is added to the picture.

Canterel's dental hoard derives from his invention of an instrument capable of removing infected teeth from the jaw without causing the least suffering to the patient. As many of these teeth are brown or yellowish, the subject of Canterel's mosaic is correspondingly murky, a subterranean scene from a Scandinavian morality tale depicting a reiter (a German cavalry officer) drowsing in a crypt. Aag, the reiter, has been immured in this makeshift dungeon after having been arrested in an attempt to abduct the wife of a rich Norwegian nobleman, Baron Skjelderup. While exploring the spacious vault he chances across a collection of fairy stories and reads 'The Tale of the Watery Globe', in which a young girl who has been turned into a bird saves her eleven evil brothers from the lethal effects of a large flying globe of water; in this supernatural tale, any living creature on whom the shadow of the globe falls instantly dies. After reading this story, Aag falls asleep and dreams of the eleven brothers fleeing from the globe, which is in turn pursued by their sister metamorphosed into a pure white dove. This dream is represented in the mosaic within a cartoon-like puff of smoke emanating from the sleeper's brain. The dove is composed of dazzling milk teeth, while bloodstained roots combine to create the reiter's crimson cloak, which is fastened by a copper buckle made from an assortment of gold caps; his boots are fashioned from teeth stained absolutely black, and even the glinting nails in their soles are accurately figured by numerous mercury fillings.

Having forecast the weather and decided on his picture, Canterel spent an entire night (with the aid of a specially designed lamp) distributing the teeth in their correct places around the empty picture space, like so many pieces of a jigsaw puzzle, each to be conveyed to its correct location by the perfectly regulated gadget as it wafts to and fro on each accurately foreseen breeze. When Canterel's guests arrive to view the ongoing spectacle, the paving beetle has been at work for seven days and the mosaic is nearing completion. While they watch, a brown smoker's tooth is added to the gloomy background, a pink root to the edge of the feather in the would-be abductor's hat, a white canine to the wingtip of the soaring dove and a blue tooth to the sleeper's breeches.

The episode can be broken down and viewed as embodying four concentric rings of narrative: the outer ring consists of a precise scientific description of the wind-powered gadget; inside that, we learn of Canterel's revolutionary method of extracting teeth; these teeth are then used to construct a mosaic based on the adventures of Aag, Baron Skjelderup and his beautiful and noble wife Christel (who eventually rescues the penitent reiter); and finally, inset within this tale is yet another, that of the eleven brothers, their bird-sister and the watery globe which Aag reads during his confinement, and of which he dreams. This enfolding of story within story within story is in marked contrast to the more linear – though interrupted – narratives of *Impressions d'Afrique*: one moves through the various interlocking layers, and then out again, until every aspect of their ultimate connection is established. The overall effect of the process is a kind of doubling of *la doublure*, the stories lining each other within each other, a series of seamless, self-referential, self-encircling narratives.

*Locus Solus* was written more or less exactly at the midpoint of Roussel's literary career, and the linked narrative strata deployed in such episodes might be described as a midpoint between the primitive self-enclosure of the *Textes-genèse*, composed some fifteen years earlier, and the derangingly complex, ever-receding patterns of wheels within wheels within wheels achieved in *Nouvelles Impressions d'Afrique* and *Documents pour servir de canevas*, Roussel's final projects. In 'Chiquenaude', one of the three *Textes-genèse* published during Roussel's lifetime, the seemingly invincible Méphisto perished on account of the *vers* (worms or verses) that ate away the lining of his magic scarlet suit. The *procédé* evolved out of Roussel's quest for a poetic prose that buried its rhymes, paradoxically, and hence became immune to such *vers*. Yet *Locus Solus*, even in its title, insists on the extravagant costs exacted by this need for self-insulation: though surrounded by numerous admirers and grateful patients, Canterel is as alone as his author in his solitary place, isolated by his invulnerable genius. If the shipwreck of *Impressions d'Afrique* is the final, culminating disaster linked to all the previous initiatory failures in earlier Roussel texts, and above all to his disappointment at the reception of *La Doublure*, Canterel's imperturbable sovereignty marks the beginning of the second half of his career, in which no such catastrophes are required to license entry into the legendary paradise of *la gloire*. 'He peoples emptiness,' observed Cocteau. 'Roussel never sees anyone. He finds material only within himself. He even invents historical anecdotes. He operates his automatons without the slightest outside help.' Canterel's self-sufficiency might be taken as signifying the release into the Rousselian text of *vers* that have the opposite effect of the worms that bring down Méphisto. Rather than destroying its lining they multiply it – indeed, convert it into a fabric that develops ever nearer Roussel's aesthetic ideal of the purely self-sufficient, which was interpreted by Janet as a kind of displaced religion. Roussel's 'entirely imaginary combinations,' Janet argues, anticipate

> a world beyond that of humanity. True ecstasy, which involves fixity and complete disinterestedness, and forms of life and happiness altogether beyond ordinary human experience, must inevitably take a more religious form and lead to a holy life, a life in God, a life of God.

The sinister aspects of the God-like Canterel's determination to produce strange 'combinations' – but literal rather than imaginary ones – emerge most clearly in his creation of Bertha, the child-flower, who fulfils his dreams of fertilizing a woman with pollen. In this draft episode the scientist persuades a Texan woman, Catherine Seyeux, who has already given birth to forty-five children, to allow herself to be impregnated with the pollen of an unnamed flower; the result is the alarming hybrid Bertha, whose body is 'half-human, half-vegetal':

> Her skin, of an unheard-of delicacy and transparency, exactly resembled the petal of a flower, and was an entirely even rose colour all over. Within this incredible epidermis ran an equally strange network of veins, whose greenish hue contained hints of a tincture similar to that found in certain flowers. The skin was so completely diaphanous that it was possible to see through it the various organs of the body.

Similar, though less abhorrent, kinds of bizarre grafting and physical modification occur throughout the published version as well: the sea-horses who run the chariot race in the highly oxygenated *aqua micans* in Chapter 3 have to be fitted with surgical setons to allow them to expel excess air; the Siamese cat Không-Dêk-Lèn is depilated by a special cream so that his whole body can be electrically charged and thus deliver a current strong enough to activate the decayed remnants of Danton's head; the cock Mopsus has the entire alphabet stamped on the membrane of his throat to allow him to cough letters in blood; Felicity's tropical bird, the iriselle, has a gold plate to which water is magnetically attracted affixed to her powerful, blade-like tail.

Canterel's physiological experiments culminate in his discovery of a means of reanimating the dead. The book's long central chapter describes a large refrigerated glass enclosure divided into eight compartments in which eight corpses, under the effect of Canterel's related preparations *vitalium* and *resurrectine*, are compelled to re-enact the most crucial moments of their lives. The compartments are fitted out like stage sets, with exact reproductions of the décor and furniture of the site where the action originally occurred, and the parts played in it by others are taken by well wrapped-up assistants, or by the bereaved themselves. Young Hubert Scellos, for instance, fell victim to typhoid when only seven. His distraught mother contemplates suicide, and is only deterred by 'the cruel joy of seeing a deceptive life momentarily unstiffen her son's corpse.' Revitalized by Canterel's elixir, Hubert Scellos performs once more a poem by Ronsard he had learnt by heart and recited for his mother on her last birthday before his death. In this case the set consists only of a chair, on which poor Madame Scellos sits, swathed against the cold, with her son on her lap, lost in a bitter-sweet 'illusory happiness'.

The other reconstructed scenarios are much more convoluted. In the first, for instance, the poet Gérard Lauwerys smears the face of a statue of the infant Jesus with a pink ointment, then weaves together the filaments he has garnered from some thrown-away pear cores to create an imitation child's bonnet with which he adorns the stone Christ, whom he then tucks up in bed. We later learn the reason for these actions: Gérard and his two-year-old son Florent have been kidnapped by the Italian bandit Grocco, who demands 50,000 francs as ransom. Unable to raise such a vast amount, Gérard determines at least to save his son; he bribes one of his jailers to spirit off young Florent, but is worried lest the other jailer notice the child is missing from his prison cell, which happens to be converted from a ruined chapel. The pink-faced, pear filament-bonneted statue serves as an effective dummy. While awaiting his death, though deprived of pen and paper, Gérard manages to inscribe a poem, with the aid of some gold powder (obtained by rubbing a medallion against an iron bar) and the stalk of a rose, on the flyleaves of an encyclopaedia of the mythology of the underworld.

In the event, his wife Clotilde succeeds in raising the required sum, and Gérard is released, only to die some fifteen years later of a renal infection. Clotilde and the now youthful Florent sob with emotion as they witness the momentarily resurrected poet performing once more his daring sleight of hand and ingeniously composing what he imagined would be his final work.

As the hybrids of *Locus Solus* take a stage further the cross-dressing and other kinds of miscegenation figured in *Impressions d'Afrique*, so these ghoulish recreations of the key events in an individual's life can be seen as developing on a more complex plane the earlier novel's obsession with imitation. Artistes such as Bob Boucharessas afforded 'a complete illusion of reality' by mimicking the sound of a train or the pop of a champagne cork, but the revivified corpses of *Locus Solus* find themselves imitating their own lives without knowing it. In the case of the third tableau, which features the actor Lauze, the relationship between experience and its representation or recreation becomes more entangled still, for Lauze performs once more a scene from the play *Roland de Mendebourg* in which he starred to great acclaim numerous times. The sculptor Jerjeck in the fifth tableau also returns to a particular incident from his artistic career, and under the influence of Canterel's potent infusions produces one of his trademark figurines of a pierrot, modelled, according to his custom – using tools fashioned from hardened bread – in a black waxy substance exuded by a strange plant won in a school competition from his botany teacher. The resultant statue proves indistinguishable from that produced during the relevant minutes of the sculptor's life.

━━━━━

The pane of glass separating the entranced onlookers from the dead, who are unwittingly transformed into actors in the spectacle of their own lives, calls to mind the window Roussel had inserted into his mother's coffin so he could observe her features to the very last. The reanimated corpses are perhaps the most striking illustration of the fetishism that structured Roussel's life and pervades his writings. In 'Nanon' (a reworking of the *Texte-genèse* 'Les Anneaux du gros serpent à sonettes'), published in *Le Gaulois du Dimanche* in 1907, he even has the narrator receive a sonnet entitled 'Fétichisme' from the poet Sylvestre, who only writes sonnets and who also plays on the archaic wind instrument known as a serpent; the narrator has just rescued his friend from the clutches of a rattlesnake (*un serpent à sonnettes*). All his life Sylvestre has cherished two gold earrings that belonged to his dead childhood sweetheart, and two curls of her golden hair that he clipped from her head on her deathbed. These he now hands over with two sonnets, each apostrophizing the different treasures he is yielding up; by insistently using words that could refer to either ('boucles', 'cercles d'or'), these double poems on two pairs of totemic relics establish a provocative link between word-play and fetishism. This link is made still more explicit in Canterel's painstakingly accurate pageants of the dead: each corpse is equipped with the necessary props (if possible, those used in the original action; if not, perfect simulacra), setting and extras, and then instilled with factitious life.

These mini-dramas are thus a kind of literal recovery of lost time, but whereas Marcel's flood of memories are prompted by chance occurrences – the taste of the madeleine dipped in tea, the unevenness of the paving stones in the Guermantes' courtyard, the sound of a spoon chiming on a plate – Canterel's two fluids enable him to reanimate these particular scenes from the past scientifically and at will. They replicate as well the fusion of the contingent and the deterministic inherent in the *procédé*: Roussel's random scraps of language throw up a heterogeneous assortment of elements which are then connected with a narrative that is normally a version of some common fable. As Michel Leiris first pointed out, Roussel's stories normally derive from the most popular sources – melodrama, newspaper serials, operettas, vaudeville, fairy tales – and for all their freakishness, in their own way participate in what Leiris called the 'common stock' of myths and legends. Canterel's reanimated corpses illustrate with particular clarity the synthesis of the pre-existing and the dizzyingly improbable which underlies all Roussel's fiction.

By bequeathing his *procédé* to future writers, Roussel perhaps hoped he would be preserved in a fetishized limbo rather like Canterel's ice-house: the future writers he imagined fruitfully exploiting his method would be the means whereby, like Jerjeck, he could continue creating works of art after his own death. His posthumous disclosure of the *procédé* is prefigured in several episodes in the novel. François-Jules Cortier, for instance, secretes the confession of his murder and necrophiliac violation of his adopted daughter in the bejewelled gold model of a playbill commemorating the hundredth performance of a comedy that was the greatest success of his authorial career.

François-Jules hopes to palliate the heinousness of his crime by contriving a series of clues which will make use of items reflecting credit on himself. This involves inscribing on to a skull, with which his real daughter was playing just before she perished in a fire many years before, a formula encrypted in Norse runes, which direct the investigator to an entry about the Cortier family in a guide to the great families of France, which finally leads to the playbill in which the confession is hidden. This communication from beyond the grave is unearthed not once, but twice: first his son, François-Charles, discovers and follows the trail to his father's confession – which, after adding his own coda, he restores to its niche before shooting himself. Canterel is in turn led to the runic skull, the entry in the peerage and the jewelled playbill by the actions of the reanimated corpse of François-Charles, and is thus able both to clear up the mystery of his suicide and to procure the release from jail of the Cortiers' servant, Thierry Foucqueteau, wrongly convicted of Cortier *père*'s dreadful crime several years before.

The novel's final demonstration is the result of a similar double bequeathing. In Chapter 7 Canterel presents as the climax to the day's proceedings the repertoire of a young fortune-teller called Noël, who was raised by the ex-opera singer turned wandering minstrel Vascody. During his brief career on the stage – interrupted by an accident to his larynx – Vascody had sung to powerful effect the lead in Count Ruolz-Montchal's opera *The Vendetta*. Ruolz-Montchal is one of the historical personages in Roussel's work who is not invented, and the names and dates of the operas mentioned in the episode are accurate. He died in 1887 in Neuilly, a neighbour of the Roussels, and he and young Raymond may even have met. A polymath like Canterel, he dabbled in medicine and literature and enjoyed two successful careers, as a composer and as a chemist. When Ruolz and Vascody meet up decades later, on the eve of the Count's death, he presents the penniless busker with the fruits of his latest, indeed final, chemical experiment: Vascody's inheritance consists of four tiny scrolls of metal tracery, which, when heated in a mica box, expand into a wonderfully filmy metallic gauze. On three occasions Vascody earns excellent sums, on which he survives for a number of years, by exhibiting the startling distension of one of Ruolz's scrolls, and then selling the metal lace produced. The last scroll he wills to his protégé Noël, who, handsomely remunerated by Canterel, heats the minute cylinder with glowing charcoals placed beneath the mica box, and creates the final example of Ruolz's metallic lace – for the Count, the day after receiving Vascody, succumbed to a heart condition without divulging the secret behind his invention.

The extraordinary elegiac power latent in this episode derives from the uniqueness of the scroll whose secret potential Noël now releases, in the process explaining its provenance and relation to the story of his life. Most of the inventions expounded during the day end up as inductions into a world of infinite repetition: *resurrectine* and *vitalium* compel the corpses endlessly to re-enact their chosen scenes; Lucius Egroizard tirelessly replays the echo of his child's voice; in Chapter 3 Roussel describes seven scenes modelled in seven bottle-imps that continuously rise and fall in the *aqua micans*-filled diamond, each narrative reperformed ad infinitum; Danton's head may be reactivated by the hairless cat, Không-dêk-lèn, at will. Noël's expansion of his metal scroll, on the other hand, is inherently unrepeatable, and serves as prologue to the exhaustion of Canterel's mysteries. At the conclusion of the experiment the guests gaze in wonder at the intricate tracery and shimmering patterns of this 'marvellous piece of work'. Meanwhile Noël packs up his various carefully itemized accoutrements, loads them on to his cock Mopsus and departs alone, though not before receiving 'an unsolicited round of silver coins and friendly words':

> Then Canterel, announcing that all the secrets of his park were now known to us, took the path back to the villa, where we were all soon united at a cheerful dinner.

Like the cordial handshakes exchanged between all except Tancrède Boucharessas at the end of *Impressions d'Afrique*, this cheerful dinner presages its opposite, the dispersal of the temporarily united host and guests to each one's private 'lieu solitaire.'

Although printed by Lemerre in October 1913,* it was not until
the following year that copies of *Locus Solus* went on sale in
bookshops, where most of them remained, alas, gathering dust.
Nor did the novel receive much critical attention until eight
years later, when Pierre Frondaie's lavishly funded adaptation
for the stage recreated the kind of public interest in Roussel's
work aroused by the stage version of *Impressions d'Afrique*. It
was in January 1914, however, that Robert de Montesquiou's
account of Roussel's fiction and person first appeared in the
magazine *Gil Blas*. The legendary Montesquiou is probably
better known now for the characters he is said to have inspired,
such as Huysmans's Des Esseintes or Proust's Baron de Charlus,
than for his own writings. His florid, self-consious, extravagant
dandyism contrasts interestingly with Roussel's fastidious reticence. His article in *Gil Blas* concludes with a description of a
visit he had paid to Roussel some time the previous year:

> I found a young man who was very polite, very gracious
> and gentle in manner, wearing grey shoes, like Spinoza, and
> buttons of arborized agate.

Roussel has him admire a blue cedar which he has recently had
planted in his garden, and which was so large it had to be
hoisted over the gate, at enormous expense. During the ensuing

---

* Roussel spared no expense on the book's production. He had a number of
copies printed on Japanese vellum and one on parchment. He also had the
printers devise an entirely new typographical character, a sort of semicircle
used as an accent in the name of the Siamese cat, Không-dêk-lèn (here
denoted by a circumflex). The novel's *date d'achevée d'imprimer* was 24
October 1913 but, oddly, it began appearing as a serial in *Le Gaulois du
Dimanche* almost a month and half later (it ran from 6/7 December 1913 to
28/29 March 1914) under the title *Quelques heures à Bougival*. The hero in
this version is called Daniel Saron. The title *Locus Solus* and the name Martial
Canterel appear only on the final set of proofs, but these were still corrected
long before the serial commenced. In a postcard to Robert de Montesquiou
dated 16 May 1914, Roussel explained why he wanted his novel to appear
first as a serial: 'Alas, since my books don't sell, the only means I have of
procuring a few readers for them is by publishing them in a newspaper. I
don't have much choice with books of this sort ... No one wants them'
(Département de Manuscrits, Bibliothèque Nationale, Robert de
Montesquiou, *Lettres reçues*). The fact that the serial had a different title from
the published novel could hardly have helped sales.

months Roussel and Montesquiou exchanged postcards and gifts, but Montesquiou seems soon to have grown tired of Roussel's mixture of unctuous flattery and extreme reserve. In his autobiography *Les Pas effacés*, published in 1923, two years after Montesquiou's death, he characterizes Roussel as 'pas très sympathique':

> but how could he be? His soul must be constructed like one of his characters, who create mosaics made out of teeth and force galvanized corpses to perform dramas. Something chilly – or should I say pneumatic [an allusion to the aerial pile driver] – emanates from his mere presence.

His roman à clef, *La Trépidation* – also published posthumously, in 1922, but written in 1914 – contains a rather acerbic caricature of Russell, as he is here called: Russell clenches his teeth, perpetrates a couple of appalling puns and, despite the sumptuous luxuries of his 'Villa Sola' and its gardens, keeps false-modestly apologizing for its inadequacies.*

More than twenty years older than Roussel, Montesquiou was in no danger of having to participate in the war that broke out in the autumn of 1914, though even he was forced into certain sacrifices: 'I offer my Palais Rose to destiny,' he is said to have exclaimed when his villa at Vésinet was commandeered by the army. Since his initial national service Roussel had spent two further short periods as a reserve in the French army, in 1911 and 1913. At thirty-seven, however, he was not required to take part in active combat at the front line; instead, he found himself assigned to the 13th Vincennes artillery regiment, based in Châlons. The exact nature of his duties is unclear. Eugène Leiris, according to Michel, had to send him a military knapsack,

---

* For a full account of their correspondence and relationship, see FC, pp. 179–89 and 217–20. Montesquiou's pique may have been partially the result of a horticultural gaffe committed by the younger dandy. One of Montesquiou's gifts to Roussel was a rare shrub (Latin name *Pittosporum*) which has to be carefully cultivated in a greenhouse. Roussel, however, initially had the delicate bush planted in his windswept garden at Biarritz. Montesquiou appears to have been deeply affronted when he learned of his precious specimen's fate, and although Roussel instantly rectified the error, no correspondence survives between the autumn of 1914 and Roussel's return from his trip around the world in 1921, the year of Montesquiou's death.

for Roussel had left for his service 'carrying only his cane and gloves'. He hardly ever spoke directly of his war years, though a number of anecdotes have filtered into the public domain. To Roger Vitrac, the Surrealist playwright, he revealed in 1928 that he acted as a chauffeur during his military service, yet when Leiris asked Dufrène to confirm this, she expostulated, 'Him! Drive? He couldn't even open a bottle!' He also briefly mentioned his experience of being shelled. 'We were heavily bombarded,' he recounted to Vitrac, and then pointed out a 'very curious' coincidence: 'Could you tell me why Rheims, which was the most bombarded of towns, has the largest cellars in the world?'

In 1933, shortly after Roussel's death, Robert Desnos wrote of an encounter between Private Roussel and his editor, Désiré Lemerre*, in the course of the war. Roussel was counting petrol cans:

> The cataclysm stupefied him. His highly logical mind could not conceive of such an enterprise. When asked what had most struck him in the course of those tragic years, he answered – and it was a profound thing to say – 'I have never seen so many men.'

Among those killed first in the conflict was Roussel's nephew, Robert de Breteuil, Germaine's only child by her first husband. Roussel, apparently, had hopes even many months later that Robert, who was just twenty, had somehow survived: in early January 1915 he wrote to Eugène Leiris asking him to forward news of his nephew as soon as possible. Despite his comparison of his state while composing *La Doublure* with that of Napoleon in 1811, Roussel evidently had no personal military ambition. He remained a soldier of the 'deuxième classe' throughout his four years of mobilization.

In July 1918 he was hospitalized for scarlet fever, and produced certificates from two doctors describing his long-standing disorders. A Jean-Charles Roux of boulevard Raspail related treating Roussel in 1911–12 (the years of his mother's death and

---

* Alphonse Lemerre had died in 1912. Désiré, his son, succeeded him as head of the firm.

the two runs of *Impressions d'Afrique*) 'for dyspeptic disorders, whose symptoms are repeated bilious attacks which involve considerable weight loss, and an aggravation of nervous disorders from which the patient has suffered for a long time.' In a letter dated 27 July Pierre Janet tells a similar tale: he records seeing Roussel 'in the years preceding the war and on several occasions in recent years, during his periods of leave. For a long time now the patient has shown signs of serious neuropathic disorders, mental depression, obsessions and distressing phobias in relation to food.' By the time Roussel was fit to return to the war zone, the armistice had been signed.

Whatever the nature of Roussel's actual involvement in the carnage, it is interesting to note that the years 1914–15 proved a decisive watershed in his literary evolution. On completing *Locus Solus* he embarked on a third prose novel to be called *L'Allée aux lucioles*, the text mentioned in 'Comment j'ai écrit...' as 'mainly concerned with Voltaire and a site filled with fireflies'; the composition of this work, he further informs us, was 'interrupted by mobilization in 1914'. This interruption turned out to signal the end of Roussel's career as a novelist, though he returned to prose fiction in the highly compressed *Documents* begun during the last years of his life. Aside from the twelve months he set aside to write his two plays, from 1915 to 1928 Roussed devoted himself entirely to poetry. The war is not mentioned explicitly in *Nouvelles Impressions d'Afrique*,* which would not be published until 1932, a generation after hostilities commenced, but Roussel's instruction to his illustrator Zo for the twenty-seventh engraving (see Appendix 3) requests the following military scene: 'A truce bearer with his eyes blindfolded (an officer) escorted by two soldiers in uniforms different from his. No other people.' It is worth bearing in mind the poem's distant origins in Roussel's own years in uniform; however unwittingly, its disjunctions and disintegrations effec-

---

* In a footnote in Canto III, however, we learn that the horse is nobler than the mule: 'au lieu du bât,/C'est la mitraille, lui, qui, par devant, le blesse' (instead of the pack-saddle,/It is the machine-gun that wounds him, from in front), NIA, p. 65.

tively enact the radical break-up of a coherent world view, as John Ashbery has eloquently suggested:

> In *Nouvelles Impressions* the unconscious seems to have broken through the myths in which Roussel had carefully encased it: it is no longer the imaginary world but the real one, and it is exploding around us like a fireworks factory, in one last dazzling orgy of light and sound.

It is impossible to know whether it was the 'dazzling orgy of light and sound' produced by relentless shelling that turned Roussel from the 'carefully encased' myths of his fiction to the explosive poetics of *Nouvelles Impressions*. He was undoubtedly committed to prose narrative throughout 1914, for in December of that year he asked Eugène Leiris to store in his office safe a copy of the text that has come to be known as *Flio*, and which was unearthed by Leiris's son Michel and published in *Bizarre* in 1964. *Flio* may be the draft of an episode destined for *L'Allée aux lucioles*, though it seems more likely that Roussel had already abandoned Voltaire and his fireflies and it represents the start of a wholly separate novel.

The typescript of *L'Allée aux lucioles* was discovered in the Bedel warehouse boxes, tucked into a copy of the newspaper *La Liberté* dated 21 May 1914. Its title alludes to a particular avenue at Frederick II's summer palace in Sans-Souci where the philosopher-king enjoyed spending his evenings in conversation with the finest spirits of the age:

> There, installed on rustic seats, Frederick and his guests chatted for hours, while all around them thousands of living sparks constantly blazed and faded – the fireflies who flew from branch to branch of the boughs that surrounded the walk. The king never tired of admiring this enchanting spectacle.

We reach this magical site, however, by typically circuitous means. The novel's framing evokes both the gala of the Incomparables and Canterel's park at Locus Solus. The rich bibliophile Flavier has died leaving a will that stipulates his vast library, château and grounds should be inherited by whoever wins a very loosely defined competition: each aspirant must present the results of some personal research undertaken in any field whatsoever. The novel opens with a description of the large sandy arena where this contest is to take place. As after his mother's death Roussel maintained the villa at Neuilly exactly as she left it, so the victor must agree to preserve Flavier's extensive property in Seine-et-Marne in its precise original condition. Nine of Flavier's friends are to act as judges, but in the event the only contestant we learn of is a certain Pierre Lannoy, a second-hand bookseller who has acquired a copy of Lavoisier's *L'Allée aux lucioles*, in which the prodigious young inventor relates his experiences as one of Frederick II's guests at Sans-Souci in the summer of 1769.

As in *Locus Solus*, many of the experiments and episodes dovetail together to form increasingly complex narrative cycles. Lavoisier, for instance, has developed a kind of non-melting ice that proves perfect for keeping wine cool in hot weather without the risk of diluting it. Since Voltaire is among the guests staying with Frederick, by way of compliment Lavoisier models this ice into little figurines that allude to a new chapter of *Candide* in which the adolescent Pangloss, then a chorister, is seduced by a ravishing Marquise. She prosecutes the affair under the watchful eyes of her jealous husband by dressing the fresh-faced philosopher in women's clothes and claiming he is Amanda, the daughter of a poor relation; as part of his transvestite disguise, like Claude/Carmichaël, Talou and Yaour before him, Pangloss adopts not only female attire, but 'a luxurious woman's wig'. During their idyll the lovers take part in a play staged at the country house that requires him to cross-dress further still, since his character decides to personify Ceres in Springtime at a costume ball; accordingly, Lavoisier's tiny ice figurine is modelled to resemble the young philosopher in the costume of the vernal goddess of April. And like numerous earlier Roussel protagonists, Pangloss is eventually undone by an insufficient *doublure*: the Marquise's jealous husband notices that the wig he wears as Ceres in April is insufficiently elevated from his skull, given Amanda's seemingly luxuriant head of hair. He should, Roussel notes, have placed the theatrical wig *on top* of that assumed for his disguise, whereas he in fact substitutes one for the other. His suspicions aroused by the 'complete absence of this cranial padding', the Marquis slips from the audience and pounces on the adulterous couple embracing back-stage. As punishment Pangloss is condemned to spend the night in a huge vat of manure, an experience which forces him to consider the vicissitudes of experience – indeed, proves crucial in his intellectual development. It is while pondering the properties of manure, immersed in his tub of it, that he evolves his famous philosophy of life, that all is for the best in the best of all possible worlds.

Sipping their ingeniously cooled wine, Frederick and his guests engage in a complex game that makes use of special dice, in each of which twenty-one fireflies are enclosed, and of the manual that determines the timetable operated by Spanish boatmen on the Ebro. Episodes still further inset include an attempt by Don Juan to seduce an abbess, a cure for baldness and the invention of a weightless cloth called *lin d'Icare*, after the very light fabric supposedly worn by the mythological airman.

The manuscript contains no indications as to why Roussel broke off this compelling series of fictions and began, in the pages dispatched to Leiris senior at the end of the year, yet another scenario featuring a white man *parmi les noirs*. *Flio* survives in a much rougher draft than *L'Allée aux lucioles*, and may even have been dictated. Although the name Flio figures a number of times amid the endlessly revised nomenclature of Roussel's manuscripts,* he doesn't in fact appear in this episode that seems to bear his name – for *Flio* may just be a truncation of *Folio*. The progress of the story is also somewhat uncertain, for Roussel changes his mind about a number of matters as it proceeds. Two main narrative strands emerge, tentatively intertwined. The first involves a two-volume poetic work composed at one stage by R . . . , but then attributed to the main character Crosmel, describing the two kinds of statue observed by the poet everywhere in the island of B . . . off the coast of South

---

* In the manuscripts of *Impressions d'Afrique* the name is that originally allotted to Naïr. It is applied to four different characters in the drafts of *Locus Solus*: a young shepherd, an astrologer, the blood-spitting cock who ends up as Mopsus and the powerful bird Asnorius who nearly succeeds in strangling Alexander the Great in one of the bottle-imp scenarios described in Chapter 3.

West Africa. Half these statues are provided with loincloths, and half are naked. It transpires that at one time the inhabitants of B . . . devoted themselves entirely to the worship of their god and goddess of love; no one worked and half the population perished in a famine. A violent reaction against the life of sensual indulgence set in, and the survivors not only mended their ways and began worshipping their god and goddess of labour, but many of the men took the drastic measure of castrating themselves, which again threatened the population with extinction. Hence a decree was issued to the fetish-loving B . . . iens obliging each statue of a loinclothed god or goddess of work to be balanced by an unloinclothed god or goddess of love. In turn the visiting poet produces two collections of poetry, one devoted to the statues of work, the other to the statues of love. When published on his return, these volumes prove wildly successful, and he finds himself haloed by 'a sudden glory'.

Like Flavier in *L'Allée aux lucioles*, Crosmel is a fervent bibliophile, as indeed is his daughter E . . ., who suffers from a peculiar mental weakness: she cannot help believing all the stories she reads, however outlandish. When Han . . ., the son of a recently deceased close friend, joins Crosmel and his daughter's household, she falls in love with him, convinced he is the young prince in a Scandinavian fairy tale who, in the course of the story, is metamorphosed by an evil fairy into a white bear. Han . . . dies in a skating accident, and in desperation Crosmel procures a polar bear and persuades his daughter that the animal is the young prince under the fairy's spell. The typescript breaks off before the narrative fully unfolds, but it seems likely, as Jean Ferry first conjectured, that E . . . was to discover Crosmel's second volume of poems inspired by the unloinclothed statues, and suffer some kind of fatal collapse.

*Flio* thus signals a return to the dualistic colour-coding of *Impressions d'Afrique*: the white polar bear and the black naked statues of B . . .'s divinities of love represent a radical antithesis between the pure fantasies of romance and the imperatives of the flesh. Whereas in *L'Allée aux lucioles* Roussel appears to revel in the delights of highly refined artifice, in *Flio* poor E . . .'s credulity leads her to fall in love with a polar bear. *L'Allée aux lucioles*, even in its unfinished state, seems Roussel's most self-

delighting text: Lavoisier's cunning inventions are not, like Canterel's, shadowed by death and dispersal, but serve as a means
of heightening pleasure. The episodes spin beyond the reach of
the obscure dread that subliminally haunts so much of Roussel's
work. In *Flio* the familiar divisions and oppositions reappear.
The perfect equilibrium between naked and decent statues is
described as symbolic of 'LA CLE DU BONHEUR' (the key to
happiness), a phrase that evokes Roussel's personal quest for
'serenity', which also involved alternating between radical
abstemiousness and indulgence, rather as the inhabitants of
B . . . swing between hard labour and sensuality. Leiris offers an
interesting example of what Janet called Roussel's 'phobias in
relation to food':

> The idea that the act of eating is harmful to one's 'serenity'
> also led him, during one period, to fast for several days on
> end, a fast he would break by going to Rumpelmeyer's and
> devouring a vast quantity of cakes (in line with his taste
> for childish foods: marshmallows, milk, bread pudding,
> racahout).

For whatever reasons, neither *Flio* nor *L'Allée aux lucioles* succeeded in imparting to their author the key to aesthetic
happiness, and the following year he started working on the
poem that would absorb nearly all his creative energies between
1915 and his death.

━━━━━━

Yet Roussel had by no means lost faith in the two works of
fiction he had already published. In September 1918 he had
Lemerre issue a volume entitled *Pages choisies*, made up of a
selection of episodes from *Impressions d'Afrique* and *Locus
Solus*, and the following year he opened negotiations with Pierre
Frondaie, one of the period's most successful adaptors of novels
for the stage.* Frondaie, it was agreed in a contract signed on 27

---

* Pierre Frondaie was the pen-name of René Fraudet (1884–1948). His
numerous plays and adaptations include *Montmartre* (1910), *L'Homme qui
assassina* (1913), *Aphrodite* (after the novel by Pierre Louÿs, 1914) and
*L'Insoumise* (1922).

December 1919, would produce a stage version of *Impressions d'Afrique*:

> Since the philosophical character of the novel is so unusual, M. Frondaie is anxious to make sure that, whatever the outcome, he will receive due payment for the work he undertakes.

Frondaie demanded 50,000 francs and the first 15,000 francs of profits from the show; after that, the spoils would be shared equally between novelist and playwright. This contract was superseded by a later agreement which stipulated that Frondaie receive a flat fee of 75,000 francs. The arrangement also states that M. Frondaie would have 'the right to substitute for *Impressions d'Afrique* another novel by M. Raymond Roussel entitled *Locus Solus*.'

In his pursuit of popular acclaim Roussel can seem like a stubborn salesman offering his product in every possible size and shape, but refusing ever to accept the unsuitability of the product itself for his target audience. By hiring Frondaie, who had enjoyed hits with adaptations of Pierre Louÿs, Anatole France and Maurice Barrès, Roussel seems to have believed that the 'caractère philosophique' of his vision would at last assume a form that would prove irresistibly appealing to a vast public. As his shrewd negotiations show, Frondaie clearly harboured doubts about the project's box-office potential from the start, but, like Lemerre, was more than happy to indulge a rich eccentric on such royal terms. Eventually Frondaie decided to adapt *Locus Solus*, and Roussel departed on his voyage around the world convinced he would be returning to fame – or at least some sort of dividend on the fortune he was about to spend wooing the admirers he had imagined, with such confidence, swarming to worship him in *Mon Âme*, written almost a quarter of a century earlier.

———

Roussel's renown as a traveller depends more on what he did not do than on what he did. He alludes to his voyage around the globe by way of India, Australia, New Zealand, the Pacific

Archipelagoes, China, Japan and America in 'Comment j'ai écrit . . .', only to insist that none of his experiences of these countries had any influence on his writings.

Conversely, the travels themselves seem inspired more by favoured literary precedents than an interest in other countries. His visit to Loti's Tahiti was evidently the climax of the journey, but its overall lineaments surely derive from Jules Verne:

> 'But the trunks,' said Passepartout, unconsciously swaying his head from side to side.
>
> 'No trunks. Just a travelling bag. Put in two woollen shirts and three pairs of stockings, and the same for yourself. We shall buy what we require on the way.'

On his similar *tour du monde* Roussel travelled even lighter than Phileas Fogg, without a servant and with just one bag containing a few possessions that he replaced when necessary. It was also a journey, if not to the centre of the earth or Captain Hatteras's North Pole, then to an equivalent sort of antipodean realm in which familiar landmarks are reversed and familiar reality is parodied. From Melbourne he sent a postcard to Charlotte Dufrène:

> Near here there are two bathing resorts which are called Brighton and Menton. It's well worth the trouble of coming so far to make excursions to Brighton and Menton, which is what I've done.

In Tahiti he delighted in the inverted symmetries, to which Loti refers in his novel on a number of occasions, between its capital Papeete and Paris. 'In Papeete', he wrote to Dufrène, 'I live on the rue de Rivoli, which is exactly upside down the one in Paris. If my rue de Rivoli lacks a Rumpelmeyer, in compensation here one eats astonishing fruits.'

Other attractions he treated more cursorily: when Dufrène inquired if he'd been struck by the sunsets in the South Seas, he replied that he'd been working in his cabin and had not had time to notice them. On arriving in Peking he made a brief tour of the city and then retreated to his hotel, where he spent the rest of his stay struggling with *Nouvelles Impressions d'Afrique*.

The additional work sessions on the boat were undertaken so

that Roussel could get ahead with his long poem – itself in essence a sort of pseudo-travelogue – and thus feel at liberty to indulge his Loti-mania in Tahiti with a clear conscience. *Le Mariage de Loti* (1880) was one of the naval officer-turned-author Julien Viaud's most popular works. Although Viaud had used the pseudonym of Pierre Loti both as a pen-name* and as the name of the hero in his previous book *Aziyadé* – his first, published in 1879 and set during the blockade of Constantinople in 1876 – it is in *Le Mariage de Loti* that the name is formally assumed. In the book's opening scene the English naval officer Harry Grant, who has just arrived in Tahiti, ceremonially adopts the alias that would make his creator famous:

> Loti was baptized on 25 January 1872, at the age of twenty-two years and eleven days. When the deed was done, it was about one in the afternoon by London and Paris time. On the other side, and the other way up, of the earthly globe, in the gardens of Queen Pomare, where the event took place, it was almost midnight. In Europe it was a cold and dismal winter's day. On the other side, in the queen's gardens, it was a calm, languorous, enervating summer's night.

In this inverted tropical setting, and under his new name, Loti proceeds to enjoy an idyllic romance with a young Tahitian called Rarahu. Eventually Grant's naval duties compel him to return to England, and he later learns Rarahu has died. As in *Aziyadé*, Loti deliberately blurs the distinctions between fiction and autobiography, deftly allowing the reader to imagine the hero's amorous adventures are a minimally transposed version of Viaud's own.

Roussel's visit to Tahiti was thus a pilgrimage to the primary site of Viaud's metamorphosis into Loti. Just as Roussel was convinced Loti must have experienced *une gloire* similar to his own, so he was sure that Viaud was transformed into Loti by a geographical equivalent of the *procédé*'s turning of language inside out. Tahiti's antipodean relationship to Paris makes it a looking-glass world in which things run backwards: the water-

---

* This was for practical reasons: French naval officers were not allowed to publish under their own names.

fall of Fataoua, by which Loti and Rarahu meet, tumbles 'en sens inverse', in the opposite direction to those of Hyde Park and the bois de Boulogne. This inversion once accomplished, every location, act and character is transformed into legend: Viaud becomes Loti or Mata Reva, and even the descendants of those he wrote about are endowed with mythical status in Roussel's eyes. He piously visited the pool of Fataoua, obtained a copy of the supposed original of Rarahu's death certificate and searched out the tombs of her children. He introduced himself to the grandchildren of the Queen Pomare who features in Loti's text, and later sent them lavishly dedicated copies of his books (see Plates 15 and 16). On his return to Paris he attempted to interest the Master in his various relics (which included what Roussel believed was a photograph of Rarahu five years before her death) and documents relative to the novel's characters, but was rebuffed by Mauberger, Loti's secretary. The following year Loti died, and Roussel, 'overwhelmed by the dreadful news,' sent his condolences to Mauberger, and tried to arrange to meet with him in Paris to reminisce about the 'Grand Disparu'.

If, for his fanatical admirer, Loti's novel converted Tahiti into an 'île de rêves' similar to the 'pays de rêves' Raoul discovered on his boat trip with Jeanne in 'Sur le Nil', Roussel himself took pride in achieving the diametrical opposite: by excluding all details of his travels from his writings, he was able to maintain his ideal of perfect independence. Not only was his fortune, like Canterel's, 'exempt de charges' (free from all commitments), but his imagination, he felt, owed no debt to the world around him. Democratic America, however, seems to have affronted Roussel's sense of his inviolable uniqueness. Janet reports him complaining:

> On arrival in New York, I want to take a bath, and the idea of this gives me a certain pleasure. I learn that there are three thousand bathrooms in the hotel, and that three thousand travellers can take a bath at the same time; my pleasure disappears. It's impossible to enjoy good fortune unless one enjoys it alone; the happiness of others makes one suffer.

The next time he travelled extensively it would be in his luxurious, custom-built *roulotte*, a vehicle that provoked attention and excited admiration wherever it went.

# CHAPTER 6

# Nous sommes la claque et vous êtes la joue

Roussel returned to Paris in the spring of 1921. Despite an initial deadline of December 1920, Pierre Frondaie had made little progress with his adaptation of *Locus Solus*, which would not, in the event, receive its infamous première until December 1922.

Frondaie originally intended to call the play *Le Mystère de 'Locus Solus'*, and to concentrate on the final story of Chapter IV, in which François-Jules Cortier (or Cartier as Frondaie spells his name throughout) murders his adopted daughter Andrée Aparicio. Two drafts of the opening act of this first version have been recovered. Frondaie evidently planned to develop Roussel's novel into a slightly wacky detective story in which Canterel would feature as a sort of scientific Sherlock Holmes. The wrongful imprisonment and ultimate release of Thierry Foucqueteau were to provide the play's dramatic suspense. Frondaie's first act is a standard courtroom scene: despite his and his mother's stauch testimonies to his innocence, poor Thierry is condemned to a life behind bars. Canterel (his name is also misspelt throughout as Cantarel) witnesses the trial from the gallery, and hints to his friend Noussel that one of his ongoing experiments, which allows the dead to speak, should enable him to get to the truth of the matter.

It seems likely that Roussel was unhappy with Frondaie's decision to concentrate on a single episode, for he wanted to set before the public a theatrical extravaganza that would realize on stage as many of the wonders of Canterel's park as was feasible. It is not clear to what extent performances followed the various parts of the script found among Frondaie's and Roussel's papers: the programme notes and accounts and reviews of the play suggest that this text was in turn extensively modified, and further drastic alterations were made even in the course of its two-week run.*

It is impossible, also, to gauge accurately how much influence Roussel had on the evolution of Frondaie's adaptation. Frondaie, though not just a hack, was a writer unlikely to respond sensitively to the *esprit Rousselien*, and Roussel had no right to be surprised when Frondaie's version turned out to be a travesty of the original. 'Why does the play make people laugh?' a review of 13 December recorded Roussel lamenting: 'The novel is sad. I don't understand anything, I don't understand anything.' Frondaie's approach is perhaps best summed up by an article puffing the show in *Le Cri de Paris* just before it opened:

> *Locus Solus* is at once a fairy play, a light comedy and a satirical comedy. One of the actors suggests it offers a delightful mix of *Ubu roi* and *Caligari*. The action takes place in the present in a cubic country, and its sets, it seems, will prove truly astounding.

Frondaie added his own mock-Rousselian episodes to those adapted from the novel: a catalogue of scenes made by a critic who attended the opening on 8 December includes a ballet of skeletons and a scene in which fish are desalinated and then taught to sing; the play climaxed, not with the low-key dinner of the original, but with a spectacular set-piece in which Canterel ascends on a rope into the heavens. A spread bet, Frondaie obviously realized, would be his best policy; accordingly, the play filters Roussel's troubling inventions through a mesh of

* Two draft versions of *Le Mystère de 'Locus Solus'* and the four-act 'version definitive' are published in *Épaves* (pp. 93–261). Another version was discovered among Roussel's papers (FR, cat. no. 4489). Programmes, publicity material and newspaper reviews of all Roussel's plays are collated in a series of fragile albums in the Fonds Rondel in the Bibliothèque Nationale de l'Arsenal. A number include M. Rondel's own ticket to the play in question. Material relating to the production and reception of Roussel's plays derives mainly from this archive. François Caradec includes a wide range of extracts from reviews in his section 'Locus Solus au Théâtre Antoine' (pp. 220–47). See also Andrew Thomson's 'Selections from the critical writings about Roussel's theatre', AT4, pp. 13–24, and John Ashbery's 'Les versions scéniques d'*Impressions d'Afrique* et de *Locus Solus*' in BZ, pp. 19–25.

low-level farce, sub-Jarry burlesque and pastiche-Surrealist song and dance routines.

Yet watered down, bastardized Roussel was to prove no more assimilable than the real thing. Roussel had paid lavishly to secure the services of many of the contemporary theatre's best-known names: Signoret, the actor who played the part of Canterel, received 13,000 francs for a mere ten performances, and the bill for costumes alone came to 50,000 francs. The critics, however, were unimpressed; indeed, many deplored above all this criminal waste of theatrical funds and talent.

> Is our eccentric author quite sure he can find no more
> agreeable way of disposing of the vast sums which he
> delights in lavishing on the stage? ... Has he never heard
> talk of social misery, of poor people burdened with large
> families, or of the distress of our students, of the desolate
> lives of those out of work?

Roussel's munificence was felt to have a corrupting effect on the Parisian theatre in general. 'How awful to see so much money wasted, and even worse, a theatre monopolized in this way in mid-season, especially when talented authors find it so difficult these days to get their work presented to the public,' grieved André Antoine in an article published during the first week of the run. 'I demand the creation of a police for theatrical morals to prevent the repeat of such scandals,' fulminated a particularly outraged malcontent a few days later. Signoret and his fellow actors came under heavy fire for accepting their lucrative roles in this play, described by the critic Pierre Veber as 'a dismal fantasy, conceived in a madhouse': 'a rich lunatic,' he protested

> is free to roam at large, and even to hire a theatre and have
> his play puffed in the papers. No one brings a straitjacket for
> him ... But do you want to hear my opinion of those who
> shamelessly exploit the insanity of the unfortunate wretch?
> No, decidedly, I'd better not tell you.

In their final contract Roussel and Frondaie had agreed that Roussel should appear as sole author of the piece. Most in the theatrical world knew of Frondaie's collaboration, but it was on Roussel that they vented their spleen, mainly, one suspects, on account of his legendary wealth. The play itself appears to have anticipated these attacks. In his 1928 article on Roussel, Roger Vitrac alludes to a scene (not to be found in the surviving drafts) in which Canterel has witnessed the suicide of an impoverished young poet. 'Ah,' he exclaims, 'if I were poor I would be a genius! But I am rich!'

Vitrac was one of the 'group of very lively partisans,' as they are described in 'Comment j'ai écrit . . .', who rallied to Roussel's cause. They first made their support known to the unwitting proto-Surrealist on the night of the private première. The invited audience gradually grew more and more restive: some began to heckle, and during the third act took to pelting the stage with coins and hooting and whistling so loudly the actors could no longer be heard. When Signoret reproved them from on stage, they barracked him. Vitrac, Leiris, Breton, Aragon and their Surrealist confrères responded by hurling abuse at Roussel's detractors. Vitrac relates that Pierre Frondaie was among those mocking Roussel, and was stupefied to learn the Surrealists were seriously championing his work. The perfomance ended amidst general confusion, and the next day it was announced the run was suspended until Monday the 11th. Though resolutely indifferent to their movement, Roussel was grateful to the Surrealists for their vociferous support. The day after the première, he sent Michel Leiris a copy of *Locus Solus* inscribed 'to my most passionate supporter at yesterday's première of *Locus Solus*, with gratitude and affection.' Nevertheless, he agreed the play needed radical surgery: when it reopened three days later, Act III and one of the ballets had been cut. The Surrealists were dismayed to find the evening's entertainment now began with a short patriotic two-hander entitled *La Guerre en pantoufles*, which they at once proceeded to shout down. The police were called and Breton and his wife taken to the local station to explain themselves: no charges were preferred. Breton evidently had hopes of recruiting Roussel for the Surrealist cause. The following day he forwarded a copy of *Champs magnétiques* (1920) with a dedication thanking Roussel for his play, 'the *only* show at which it was given I should be present'.

The eight further performances of *Locus Solus* provoked scenes as rowdy as those disrupting the private and the public premières. The General Association of Students issued a vehement protest in December's issue of *L'Université de Paris* condemning Roussel's vanity and wantonness:

> Great numbers of students live in real poverty, and, for want of a few francs, cannot afford to eat properly. A certain person, who no doubt thinks himself an intellectual, has found a million francs to stage a completely inept play – *Locus Solus* ... To spend so much money at this time on a spectacle of this kind is like throwing a piece of bread into the gutter.

Pierre Frondaie seems to have believed after the third performance on the Tuesday that the run should be abandoned altogether, but Roussel insisted the show go on. Even ridicule and scandal might serve to win him new converts. He had the novel readvertised with a quotation from the recently deceased Robert de Montesquiou and a subheading proclaiming 'It is this book which is the original source of *Locus Solus*, the drama currently being performed at the Théâtre Antoine.' And in fact a couple of critics, including Édouard Dujardin, whose *Les Lauriers sont coupés* (1887) was to be championed by Joyce as the first novel ever to make use of internal monologue, took the trouble to compare the adaptation with the original. In a piece published in *Revue de l'Époque* in May 1923 Dujardin wrote:

> Having seen the play, I wanted to read the novel; my surprise was immense. In the novel there is no trace of the buffoonery which had enchanted me in the play; at bottom, it was the same mind at work; but what in the drama was pushed to the point of farce, is developed in the novel with a tranquil, wholly untroubled seriousness that is quite stupefying. And this mind is like that of Villiers de L'Isle-Adam or that of Edgar Allan Poe: an idea of logical order, normally of a scientific kind, is driven to its furthest reaches with a hallucinating accuracy of detail.

Dujardin also offered an interesting explanation for the ill-will aroused by Roussel's generosity. Roussel, he explained

is not an adroit millionaire: not only does he not know how

to defend himself, but he enables others to exploit him at will; he allows ridiculous publicity to go out under his name; through sheer simplicity (that is clear) and without being aware of it (that is less clear) he makes a display of himself. I mean, one can sense the money, the piles of money, circulating all around his work. It is precisely his clumsy naïvety which, in my opinion, pleads in his favour, but it exasperates the masses . . .

Yet Roussel, ever optimistic, drew quite other lessons from his savaging by 'la foule': it was the fact that both *Impressions d'Afrique* and *Locus Solus* derived from novels that was the sticking point:

> Thinking that the incomprehension of the public was perhaps due to the fact that so far I had only staged adaptations of books, I decided to compose a work especially for the theatre.

According to Roger Vitrac, Roussel insisted that Signoret accentuate particular speeches, such as Canterel's reflections on his wealth after the suicide of the young poet. Roussel also, Vitrac claims, had a small platinum fork especially designed and manufactured to serve as Canterel's magnetic tooth-removing instrument. Whether such stories are true or not, Roussel clearly identified with his fictional hero and sanctioned the eliding of Canterel with himself in the publicity article (probably written by Frondaie but signed CANTAREL) with which the show was relaunched after its inauspicious private première: 'Good public! You thought me dead. Did you not know I have the secret of "resurrectine"? The pen, even that of the critics, cannot kill me.' After conceding that the theatre may be too limited to embody his creations successfully, he urges the curious to procure 'the novel I have published under my pseudonym, Raymond Roussel; there you will find not only these inventions, but a thousand other unexpected ones.'

In the months preceding the production of *Locus Solus*, Roussel was working on his own 'unexpected invention'. This was a method of insulation based on the non-conductivity of a vacuum. On 18 September 1922 he applied for a patent at the Office National de la Propriété Industrielle:

> The present invention concerns a means for increasing the comfort of houses and vehicles. The method [*procédé*] consists of the following:
>
> In constructing a house, to install in the walls, roof, floorboards, ceiling, partitions and doors hollow metal plaques in the interior of which a vacuum has been created . . .

Windows are to be replaced with two panes of glass with a vacuum sandwiched between. In houses already built, these metal sheets are to be used to line [*doubler*] the walls and ceiling, floorboards and roof – and, Roussel suggests, they can equally be fitted to all kinds of vehicles, such as cars, railway coaches, boats and aeroplanes.

This patent was duly issued, and then amended several times over the ensuing years. Roussel also had constructed in one of the garages in the grounds of his villa at Neuilly a three and a half cubic metre building whose walls were insulated with this revolutionary vacuum. When eventually obliged to sell the property in 1931, Roussel had the purchaser officially informed of the building's secret inner lining:

> this little building is full of tubes of glass which, if demolished, could explode if special precautions are not taken.

Here again Roussel's genius tends, as Cocteau observed, to 'the furthest extreme of the practical'. Rousselian practicality, however, could fulfil itself only in a glass-encased void like that insulating the walls of his little building from fluctuations in temperatures. Roussel was to be made gradually aware over the next decade that the money he spent trying to reach an audience large enough to satisfy the promise of his early visions, was precisely that money which had hitherto insulated him from the world, and so made his art possible. The logic of this paradox required him to bankrupt himself publishing, staging and advertising works that no one wanted, while at least subliminally aware all along that his approaching insolvency would signal the end of his literary and physical life. Perhaps he hoped his vacuum insulation would turn into the material eqivalent of his first writing experience, the single blow of the pickaxe that opened up a whole mine. The imaginative symbolism grows dizzying: was this *procédé* for a physical, yet empty, *doublure* intended to reverse the losses incurred by Roussel's pursuit of the multitudes, whose admiration alone could redeem the failure of his first published work (*La Doublure*), and of his punningly lined fictions inspired by his 'procédé très special'? Needless to say, Roussel did not put this particular *equation de faits* to the test, for, despite his officially sanctioned patent, he never attempted to induce the public to buy his one practical invention.

━━━━

Defending his decision to accept the role of Çahoud in Roussel's next theatrical venture, the actor Callamand outlined some of the difficulties posed by the piece: 'The text is so tightly written that it took more than a month of work to learn it, for it allows no room for ad-libbing or approximation.' It was therefore only just that the author should reward his actors with 'cachets intéressants' (substantial fees). Roussel, he insisted, 'has a very personal conception of the theatre,' and while the play may have outraged audiences, no one could object to its language: *L'Étoile au front*, he points out, is written 'in a French that is irreproachable, and is free from all coarseness'.

In 'Comment j'ai écrit . . .' Roussel refers to 'several sheets that explain very clearly how I wrote *L'Étoile au front* and *La Poussière de soleils*.' These worksheets were not, however, among the papers recovered from the warehouse. In his post-humous memoir Roussel offers only one example of the workings of the *procédé* in *L'Étoile au front*: 'the words *singulier* (singular) and *pluriel* (plural) gave me *Saint Jules* and *pelure* (skin)' and an episode in which the beneficent pope Saint Jules saves a young boy from freezing to death by lending him the hide that covers Jesus's crib from a life-size nativity scene constructed in the Vatican grounds.

But if the *procédé* served to generate the stories to be told in

Roussel's play, it could not help him to develop dramatic techniques capable of enacting the marvels it created. In his CANTAREL-signed publicity article for the reopening of *Locus Solus*, Frondaie subtly implied that Roussel's art was in fact fundamentally incompatible with the stage: 'the means of the theatre', he has the *savant* acknowledge, 'are too limited to realize properly the products of my imagination, and reduce me to describing them to you, whereas you wish to see them fully embodied on stage.' Roussel's yearning to see his inventions performed, in the teeth of all difficulties, was perhaps the ultimate source of his decision to present theatrical versions of his two novels. Yet no amount of free-spending on platinum props and the like could dramatize his fiction vividly enough to convince a sceptical audience of his genius. The failure of both projects led Roussel to search for a different way of using stage and actors to communicate the stories produced by his linguistic experiments: rather than attempting to exploit the theatre's limited resources more judiciously, Roussel opted, to all intents and purposes, to ignore them altogether.

*L'Étoile au front* consists more or less entirely of anecdotes; these anecdotes are not so much told by the characters as distributed evenly among them. Most are connected to some unusual artwork or object or apocryphal literary text. In Act II, Scene III, for instance, Geneviève is explaining to her uncle Trézel and her fiancé Claude, how the young Milton, when only sixteen, fell in love with his tubercular near neighbour Maud de Perly. One spring day he spied her stretched out on a chaise-longue in a room opening on to her garden, about to eat a raw egg for her lunch:

TRÉZEL: A rich and light food suitable for her condition.
GENEVIÈVE: She pierced one end of the egg with the point of a knife, then forced herself to swallow the egg's contents . . .
CLAUDE: No doubt, alas, it was duty rather than pleasure which motivated her.
GENEVIÈVE: Her irksome task over, she was for a moment encumbered with the shell, which, now mere refuse, could not be put back with the rest of her meal, for fear it might

arouse her disgust and cause her to lose what little appetite she had.

CLAUDE: On the other hand, it is hard to stir when one is stretched out and feeble.

GENEVIÈVE: So in the end she threw the bothersome egg-casing out of the window, where it disappeared into a clump of shrubs.

CLAUDE: How carefully Milton must have noted the spot where it fell!

TRÉZEL: What a treasure for him, this shell against which he had seen his beloved doggedly fix her lips!

GENEVIÈVE: So, the following night, he made use of an improvised knotted rope hung from his window to climb down to the garden – then, armed with the precious empty egg, he swiftly reascended . . .

The ardent poet then composes a sonnet which he copies out on to the shell, meaning to declare his feelings to the invalid by presenting it to her. Maud, however, dies the very next day. This precious testament to his youthful amour was piously preserved by Milton's dutiful daughters, and has now come into the hands of the antique dealer Joussac, who in fact arrives with it the moment the story ends. Trézel (who is as wealthy as Canterel) at once purchases the tenderly inscribed shell and adds it to his extraordinary collection of rarities.

Shared-out narratives of this sort occupy most of the play's three acts. The first act is set in the drawing-room of Trézel's spacious villa at Marly, where he lives with Geneviève, his twenty-year-old niece, Claude, his pupil and Geneviève's intended, and the sixteen-year-old Indian twins Zéoug and Leidjé. Many years before, while visiting his plantations in Pondicherry, Trézel had been approached by a frantic Indian woman, who begged him to save her two daughters, otherwise destined to become human sacrifices to the god Shiva. Trézel spirited the threatened twins to France, and brought also one of his servants on the plantation, the half-Indian and half-French Meljah. In Act I Meljah secretly meets her former sweetheart Çahoud, who has come to France on a double mission: he hopes to persuade Meljah to return to India and marry him, and he has entered into a contract with the high priest of Shiva to pursue and murder the absconded twins.

This potentially suspenseful plot is no sooner outlined than it melts away: by the end of Act I Meljah has agreed to return with Çahoud to India on condition he abandon his projected assassination of the twins, and that is the last we see of them. Zéoug and Leidjé are dispatched to a safe house, and also disappear from the play. Whereas the interactions between black and white are imaginatively crucial in 'Parmi les Noirs', *Impressions d'Afrique* and *Flio*, the Orientalist sub-plot – except that it is the only plot the play has to offer – serves merely as a vague distraction in *L'Étoile au front*, a quickly resolved prelude to its relentless pageant of objects and anecdotes.

Not all of the items introducing each secret history are inherently valuable. 'You will excuse my frankness?' the antiquary Joussac asks his client in Act II, Scene IV:

TRÉZEL: Absolutely.

JOUSSAC: Well then, how could an amateur collector as refined as yourself keep preserved in glass this wretched yellow butterfly with its wholly ordinary ocelli, which is hardly worthy of the most shabby collection?

TRÉZEL: However wretched, I would not exchange it for the rarest of specimens.

CLAUDE: And everyone here treats this fragile paperweight with care and respect . . .

GENEVIÈVE: . . . so we tremble to see you handle it so casually.

This humdrum butterfly, it emerges, inadvertently caused the death of a famous industrialist, and led to the disinheritance of his illegitimate son. 'Ugh! Yet another mite! . . .' grumbles Geneviève in Act I, Scene III: 'They come from this old stuffed pigeon . . . I must persuade my tutor to throw it out . . .':

CLAUDE: Throw it out! . . . but that's impossible! . . . a historic bird! . . .

GENEVIÈVE: Historic? . . .

The mite-ridden preserved pigeon turns out to have played a

crucial role in warning various anarchists in Tsarist Russia of an imminent crackdown.

Whereas nearly all the inventions and performances staged in the theatrical versions of *Impressions d'Afrique* and *Locus Solus* involved, in their various improbable ways, some kind of action – a worm playing the zither, seahorses running a chariot race, the dead coming back to life – in *L'Étoile au front* every narrative depends on some lifeless relic, or immobile artwork, or the memory of a passage in a book. In this the play resembles the poems collected in *La Vue*, each based on a tiny picture: both poems and drama make fetishism their structural *donnée*, the primary ground of their endlessly unspooling descriptions and stories. The images inspiring the poems, however, are all mechanically produced, and therefore infinitely repeatable. The collectors Trézel and Joussac, on the other hand, are interested only in items that are unique and irreplaceable. Should two of these rare curios be brought into some kind of conjunction, their value is mutually enhanced. In Act I, Scene II, for instance, Trézel produces for the admiration of Geneviève and Claude a Racine letter in which he relates to his lover, the Countess de Mirval, his plans to write a play about a third-century Corsican tightrope walker; this manuscript is scrolled up and tied, most appropriately, with a fragment of the wire on which the legendary Blondin, the most famous nineteenth-century tight-rope artist, first crossed the Niagara Falls. When this double treasure appears at auction, Trézel has to fight off particularly fierce bidding from rival collectors to secure it.

But while the objects whose origins the characters describe are made precious by their dazzling singularity, the characters themselves are more or less indistinguishable from each other. Although Roussel takes care in his list of dramatis personae to give their ages and signal the Indianness of Çahoud, Meljah, Zéoug and Leidjé, they all speak in exactly the same manner. Even the scene in which Çahoud and Meljah meet in secret to resolve their future is taken up mainly, not with the dilemma confronting them, but with discussion of a bas-relief by the sculptor Carpeaux. The characters function almost as a Greek chorus: they don't so much interact as succeed each other, like participants in a complex game of verbal tag. The anecdotes they tell never serve as clues to inner feelings or private motivations, but are presented instead as emerging from some collective pool of narrative. As in *Locus Solus* and *Impressions d'Afrique*, each story is told for itself, and for itself alone.

And yet the play's title alludes directly to Roussel's sense of his personal uniqueness: 'Whatever you may think, there are some who are predestined! As the poet says: "*et voilà qu'on se sent une brûlure au front . . . L'étoile que l'on porte au front resplendissante.*" ' Roussel's theory of artistic election is attributed in the play to the psychographer Boissenin; his chef d'œuvre 'revolves around a poetic image: that of *the star on the forehead*', the sublime mark of genius with which all great creators are endowed. Among the many examples Boissenin adduces in support of his thesis is the moujik Roudnitski, who, despite his humble origins, developed into a universally celebrated sculptor. Trézel owns the carving which made Roudnitski's name: it depicts the martyrdom of Bihorel, a thirteenth-century scientist whose theory of the body's instinctive reflexes was condemned as heretical by the Inquisition. So sure was Bihorel of the truth of his researches that even while being burned at the stake he broke off a smouldering twig and courageously traced a diagram irrefutably illustrating his innovative ideas.

The episode neatly balances the different kinds of fame awaiting those gifted with a star on the forehead. Roussel desperately hoped that he, like his semi-namesake Roudnitski, would receive his due from his contemporaries. Whereas, as Roussel saw it, even Wagner died before receiving sufficient public acclaim, Roussel himself was determined to make every effort to ensure his own efforts were properly appreciated during his own lifetime. Yet by obtruding his work so insistently on the public's attention, Roussel also courted the fate of the defiant Bihorel, whose prescient discoveries are only acknowledged by future generations. 'Such energy is expressed in the martyr's face as he finishes his diagram in the midst of the triumphant flames!' observes Joussac while contemplating the statue, which is now part of a fountain in Trézel's garden. Roussel would have to draw on similar reserves of self-belief to survive the theatrical martyrdom his play was preparing for him.

Roussel's cast again included a number of highly respected actors who would be pilloried in the press as mercenaries demeaning their profession in return for Roussel's lavish pay packets. There was no question this time, however, of Roussel's recouping his expenses from box-office receipts. *L'Étoile au front* was performed at the Théâtre du Vaudeville on three successive afternoons (5–7 May 1924) to non-paying, invited audiences. Roussel issued his invitations freely, even reserving a large block of seats for members of the General Association of Students, which had denounced *Locus Solus* two years earlier. Perhaps he genuinely hoped this new play would win them over, but an advance publicity notice also suggests he was fully prepared for these performances to be another battle 'between the "advanced", who praise the author of *Locus Solus* to the skies, and the traditionalists who are still shocked by his audacities.' The 'advanced' attending the première included André Breton, Michel Leiris, Robert Desnos and Roger Vitrac, who by this stage of the Surrealist revolution were all inured to riotous confrontations with the bourgeoisie. In 'Comment j'ai écrit . . .' Roussel recalls:

> Another tumult, another battle, but this time my supporters were far more numerous. During the third act the furore reached such a pitch that the curtain had to be lowered, and was only raised again after a considerable interval.
>
> During the second act, one of my opponents cried out to those who were applauding, 'Hardi la claque' [Go to it, you hired band of clappers], to which Robert Desnos replied: 'Nous sommes la claque et vous êtes la joue' [We are the hired band of clappers/the slap, and you are the cheek]. This witticism caught on, and was quoted in various papers. (It's amusing to note that by inverting the l and the j one obtains 'Nous sommes la claque et vous êtes jaloux' [We are the hired band of clappers/the slap, and you are jealous], a phrase which no doubt contained more than a grain of truth.)

Roussel was so pleased with Desnos's punning riposte that he commissioned Zo (the artist responsible for the illustrations to *Nouvelles Impressions d'Afrique*) to paint a diptych featuring on one side the battle raging in the auditorium during the first

1 Many years of perfect bliss: Roussel aged three, on a swan.

2 In Turkish costume, pretending to smoke a pipe.

3 Dressed as a chambermaid.

4 As an eighteenth-century Marquis.

5 In the grip of *la gloire*: Roussel in October 1896, aged nineteen, in the midst of composing *La Doublure*. A month before his death he stipulated that this picture should be used as a frontispiece to all posthumous editions of his work.

An unlikely soldier: Roussel in 1900, in the uniform of the Versailles Engineers.

7  In gleaming spats, amusing a tiny dog.

With Charlotte Dufrène, who is sporting a rather Rousselian *chapeau mouette*, in 1911.

9  The trip to India: Rousel aboard the outward-bound steamship, the *Barbarossa*.

10  With his mother and an elephant on the shores of Lake Kandy.

I Mother and son with a pair of ekinese in Monte Carlo, shortly efore Madame Roussel's death in )ctober 1911.

12 On stage as a *matelot* in *Impressions d'Afrique*.

3 In a Basque beret.

14 Posing with a miner's pickaxe and lantern in Berchtesgaden: 'With one blow of the pickaxe,' Roussel explained to a sceptical Janet, 'I had opened up an entire seam of marvels.'

15 Homage to Loti: Roussel in Tahiti at the supposed grave of one of Rarahu's children in 1920.

With the descendants of Queen Pomare: Roussel remained in correspondence with members of the Tahitian Royal Family for the rest of his life.

The *roulotte*.

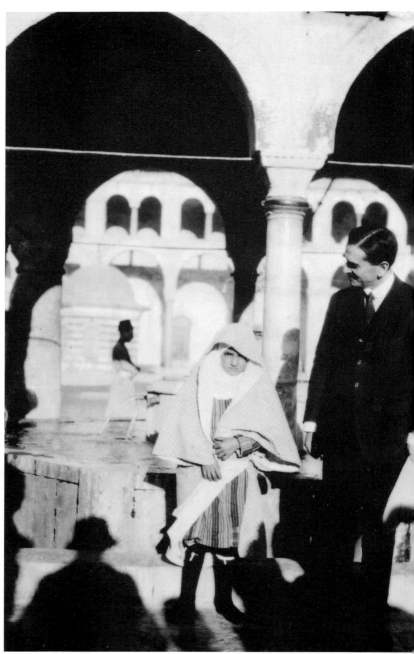

18  The trip to the Middle East: Roussel outside a mosque in Damascus with a young Syrian girl in 1927.

night of Victor Hugo's *Hernani*, and on the other the similar scenes that disrupted the première of *L'Étoile au front*. A bronze plaque inscribed with Desnos's jest was affixed to the bottom of the frame.

Desnos seems to have been the most vociferous of the claque this particular evening. His wife Youki pieced together his memories of the occasion into a lively account included in her memoir *Les Confidences de Youki*:

> After a while the atmosphere had become stormy. Up above, people were booing. Desnos stood up: 'Shut up, you idiot!'
>
> The society women whom Roussel had invited were as distressed by the play as by the attitude of the public: 'Ah, the ill-bred hooligan! What a horror!'
>
> The booers were more direct: 'Idiot yourself!' . . .
>
> There followed a scrum, as in rugby . . . Robert was thrown to the ground, and on hands and knees managed to escape from the auditorium by crawling between the combatants' legs.
>
> Thérèse [Desnos's partner at the time] followed him. Once outside, they took up positions on the pavement facing the theatre and awaited the end of the struggle. The safety curtain had been lowered, the police called and the auditorium evacuated.

The reviews in the theatrical papers concentrated far more on disturbances of this sort than on the peculiarities of Roussel's play. As had happened during renditions of *Locus Solus*, the audience threw coins at the stage and yelled abuse at the actors, some of whom responded in kind, while others seem to have sided with the spectators and began sending up the play they were being paid so handsomely to perform. The critics who did address the drama came to a more or less unanimous conclusion, as Roussel ruefully noted in 'Comment j'ai écrit . . .':

> This time again the critics savaged me, and, as always, talked of madness and hoaxes. They called the play 'L'Araignée sous le front' ['The spider under the forehead'] and journalists interviewed my actors to find out if I composed my plays in all seriousness, or if my aim was to poke fun at everyone.

He also regretted his generosity to the students whom he had tried to appease by offering them free tickets. He claims that, far from being grateful, they planned to waylay him after the show so as to harangue him yet further.

'It was an appalling scandal,' recalled Roussel's nephew Michel Ney: 'They threw baked apples at him . . .' Ney attended the première with his mother, who was horrified to witness the family name brought into such disrepute. It was a scandal which Roussel had, wittingly or not, himself engineered by inviting both his supporters and his detractors to the same performance. Indeed, his commission to Zo suggests he was coming to accept that his work was inherently scandalous, and might only achieve wide-scale acceptance after first arousing furious debates and bitter public conflicts. But Roussel was not yet ready to concede that his writings would for ever be caviare to the general. Soon after this production of his first play, Philippe Soupault met Roussel and assured him of the esteem of the Surrealists:

> He was, he told me politely, flattered, but that wasn't the audience he was after, for he did not believe in what was called then – and he used the term himself – the avant-garde.

Not until towards the end of his life would Roussel begin to reposition his work as destined, like Bihorel's theories of the reflexes, to be appreciated properly only by later ages. By all accounts Roussel was the least confrontational of men, and quite unable to thrive, as the Surrealists did, on opposition and antagonism; even on social occasions he took elaborate precautions 'to avoid all dangerous conversations', which caused him acute distress. The lack of drama in his plays may be related to this fear of conflict, although, ironically, this was precisely the aspect of Roussel's theatre which so provoked the audiences who attended his plays. It is interesting, however, that he chose to conclude his final *Cahier de citations*, that appended to *Nouvelles Impressions d'Afrique* (1932), with a defiantly aggressive remark overheard in the course of a performance of *L'Étoile au front*:

> You think yourselves shrewd, but you are idiots.

Philippe Soupault was the first of the Surrealists to promote Roussel's work in print. In 1920 he published a whimsical article in the Surrealists' house magazine *Littérature* celebrating the 'absolute uselessness' of Roussel's writings. Soupault met Roussel a number of times, but was never able to persuade him to talk about his books. Instead he discoursed about either music or the novels of Jules Verne. Benjamin Péret was similarly thwarted when he attempted to arrange an interview with Roussel in autumn 1924. His approaches were all answered by Pierre Leiris, Roussel's business manager and Michel's older brother. Péret, nevertheless, decided to publish Leiris's correspondence in the first issue of *La Révolution surréaliste*:

16 October 1924
Monsieur,

M. Raymond Roussel received your letter. At the moment he is away from home, but he asked me to receive you in his stead, at least if you would like this.
Should you do so, I would then pass on to him our conversation.
Please accept, Monsieur, my very best wishes.
Pierre Leiris

28 October 1924
Monsieur,

Rather than have a conversation with me, it would no doubt suit you better if M. Raymond Roussel wrote to you.
He has just telephoned me from London to suggest this. If you write to him at Neuilly, your letter will then be sent on to him in London.
Please allow me, Monsieur, to wish you all the very best.
Pierre Leiris

10 November 1924
Monsieur,

M. Raymond Roussel telephoned me this morning from London. He thanks you for your kind letter, but finds himself unable to respond to your questions on the subject of Surrealism, for he does not class himself as belonging to any school.

Furthermore, he is somewhat specialized in his reading, and he does not know Jarry's work sufficiently well to deliver a serious judgement of it. As for the questions you ask in relation to his own work, he fears that in replying to these he would be attributing to his writings an exaggerated importance which might be interpreted as vanity.

He would like to thank you, nevertheless, for your friendly and flattering approach.

Please allow me, Monsieur, to wish you all the very best.

Pierre Leiris

As these letters show, Roussel was anxious to maintain his distance from the Surrealist movement, and the avant-garde as a whole. Robert Desnos was another who vainly attempted to breach Roussel's formidable defences. After the première of *L'Étoile au front*, he wrote to Roussel extolling his play for its fidelity to life:

> Let me tell you at once how much I admire your concept of human destiny and the strange coincidences which surround it . . . Your play is magnificently poetic, and those there who did not understand it are perhaps at this very moment reperforming it unconsciously beside some meagre fire or at a table in a brasserie.

Having his work praised for its empirical truthfulness must have come as something of a surprise to Roussel, who took so much pride in its exclusion of the real. In the spring of the following year, when *L'Étoile au front* was published by Lemerre, Roussel dispatched a copy to Desnos with an inscription reminding him of the first night and of his devastating *bon mot*:

> to Robert Desnos – who, at the première of *L'Étoile au front*, when one of my adversaries cried out 'Hardi la claque!', so wittily launched the famous jest: 'Nous sommes la claque et vous êtes la joue!'

Desnos replied in a letter that again combined lavish compliments and sophisticated literary criticism:

> I admire the astonishing genius which enables you to evoke fate and restrained pathos in the manner that is characteristic of your works. What is marvellous is that, on reading, the emotion emerges as if sublimated, but as intensely as during the performance ... with you the full style is perfectly adequate to your rigorous thought, and this is due, I think, to a perfect understanding of poetic regions unknown to the vulgar.

Further, he published an article in *La Revue européenne* in which he declared Roussel's genius 'unquestionable':

> The star to whose mysterious influence he refers is revealed in the eyes of this extraordinary astronomer, and with each of his utterances new constellations are born.

Delighted to be appraised in such terms, Roussel invited Desnos to visit him at Neuilly one evening. Roussel received his admirer in a manner that was 'extremely affable', but refused to be drawn into discussing his work:

> Whatever efforts I made, the conversation was kept strictly on an impersonal level, the style in which one discusses the weather. This was in spite of the very precise questions I asked him, to which he responded, moreover, with equal precision.

Though Desnos and Roussel continued to correspond over the following years, Desnos came to realize that it was futile to expect disclosures from a man fundamentally isolated from all around him:

> I knew him ... as much as one could know a man who never allowed anyone to penetrate into his inner life.

━━━━━━

By the end of his voyage around the world in 1920–21, Roussel had packed and unpacked his single bag so often that he developed a phobia about luggage altogether.

Accordingly he had constructed a sumptuous *automobile rou-lotte* that would make suitcases redundant. Roussel's *roulotte* was thirty feet long and eight feet wide; its living quarters consisted of a sitting room, a bedroom, a study, a bathroom and a small dormitory for the three domestics (two chauffeurs and a valet) who would accompany Roussel on his travels. It was equipped with electric heating, a paraffin stove and a paraffin hot water system. Its interior was elegantly finished in dark woods and luxuriously furnished. Other features mentioned in admiring accounts of Roussel's *maison roulante* include a state-of-the-art braking system, a Fichet safe and a radio capable of receiving all the major European stations.

This house on wheels was exhibited at the 1925 Salon de l'auto in Paris, and was written up several times in Parisian papers over the next couple of years. The authors of these articles invariably drew comparisons between Roussel's literary and touristic experiments. 'As can be seen,' enthused an anonymous columnist in *Le Matin*, 'the great poet of *Locus Solus* is no less an innovator in the domain of reality than in the domain of dreams.' The *Revue du Touring-Club de France* devoted a detailed feature to the spectacular caravan devised by the author whose work 'is acclaimed by distinguished minds' as that of a genius. *L'Illustration* – the paper that had declared *La Doublure* 'unintelligible' – praised Roussel as an experimenter 'in matters of tourism, as he is so boldly in matters of literature'.

Roussel was so pleased with his new method of transport that he had a set of postcards made up, which he would hand out as souvenirs to those impressed by the *roulotte* (see Plate 17). In December 1926 he journeyed to Rome, where he tried to interest both Mussolini and the Pope (Pius XI) in his revolutionary vehicle, with some success. He wrote back to Charlotte Dufrène:

Mussolini came and spent a long time visiting the *roulotte* (see Plate 17); he is very simple and very kind. I also had a long audience with the Pope, to whom I showed some photos of the *roulotte* and who kept them (Mussolini also, so now I have none left).

The Pope had apparently wished to inspect the *roulotte* in person, but since, as Roussel lamented to Vitrac,

he was not able to leave the Vatican, and I couldn't decently
– but I wonder why – have my *roulotte* driven in, he sent
someone: the Papal Nuncio, who left absolutely amazed.

Yet if on the one hand the *roulotte* was conceived as a means
of attracting attention, it was also, paradoxically, another of
Roussel's stratagems for insulating himself from the world.
Vitrac also records the following conversation on the subject:

'It's very pleasant,' he confided to me. 'I stop where I want,
leave when I want – it's truly a land-yacht. And I can be
alone.'
  'Alone,' I said. 'But all the people . . .'
  'Yes, that's true, but it's possible to avoid the villages . . .'

He spent his time on the road with the curtains closed, immersed
in his daily ration of Loti or Verne, indifferent to the landscapes
through which he was passing. The *roulotte* lessened still further
the danger of details from his voyages seeping into his writings;
Roussel's house on wheels allowed him to travel, almost literally,
without travelling at all.

One of the major difficulties posed by Roussel's theatre is the
relentless concision of his style. Although *L'Étoile au front* consists almost entirely of anecdotes irrelevant to its soon-
abandoned plot, these digressions are delivered by the characters
in a manner so terse as to verge on the elliptical. Leiris recalls
praising Roussel for the precision and brevity of the language
deployed in the play; deeply gratified, Roussel responded, 'I
forced myself to write each story with as few words as possible.'
His second play, *La Poussière de soleils*, creates a different kind
of balance between the forces of compression and prolixity.
Indeed, like *Impressions d'Afrique* and *Locus Solus*, Roussel's
two plays can be seen as forming an antithetical diptych.
Whereas the anecdotes in *L'Étoile au front* first distract from,
and then wholly stand in for, its absconded main action, in *La
Poussière de soleils* Roussel goes to an opposite extreme: here
the inset tales are structured as a series of clues in a treasure
hunt, and hence made synonymous with the play's central plot,
whose progress depends wholly upon them. So while the teeming
narratives in Roussel's first play are connected, to a maddening

extent, by the merely tangential, in his second each anecdote is a link in a predetermined chain that will eventually lead Julien Blache and his assistants to his uncle's secret cache of gems. The excess of arbitrary story-telling in *L'Étoile au front* finally resolves itself into the single symbolic image of the star blazoned on the forehead of the uniquely gifted; in *La Poussière de soleils*, on the other hand, the stories narrowly succeed each other with unremitting logic, only to open out suddenly at the play's conclusion, after the treasure has been found, into a dizzying vista of the immeasurability of the universe:

> JACQUES: Look up there at that nebula. Do you know what it might be compared to?
> SOLANGE: No.
> JACQUES: To an immense cloud of dust, composed of millions of particles, each of which might be a sun serving as the centre of a whirling system of worlds! . . . Of these millions of suns, many are – much, much more than ours – vast, fiercely burning, bright, powerful! . . . And each of these millions of suns is the pivot of some universe! . . . And from here we see these millions of suns all together in the form of a cloud of dust . . .

*La Poussière de soleils* is set in French Guyana. The enormously wealthy misanthrope Guillaume Blache has died intestate; his sole heir, his nephew Julien (a retired colonel), arrives to claim his inheritance. Guillaume Blache's views of humanity had soured after his wife and son perished in an epidemic ten years before. Distraught, Blache cut himself off from the world, realized all his assets and purchased a vast stock of precious stones which he buried one night in a well shaft in the Estyne Caves. When he needed cash, he'd extract a single gem from his trove, sell it and then live off the proceeds. With the approach of death, Blache – like François-Jules Cortier – found himself unable to decide whether or not to make public his secret; again like Cortier, he eventually resolved to devise an elaborate string of clues that would lead a cunning investigator to his carefully hidden deposit.

Meanwhile Julien's daughter Solange has fallen in love with a lawyer's clerk called Jacques. Jacques is an orphan, but by the end of the play has discovered he is in fact the son of an illustrious Brazilian general, and, what's more, the legal inheritor of an extensive estate in his father's homeland. A third plot involves the scheming of an evil fence called Zuméranaz, who sends spies to keep track of Blache's sleuthing, in the hope of nabbing the loot for himself. Zuméranaz eventually does get his hands on the casket of jewels, but is surprised by Blache and his cohorts before he has time to dispose of them.

The play is arranged in twenty-four tableaux (abridged to twenty-one in performance), each representing an exotic Guyanan locale. Roussel was so concerned that these tableaux should succeed each other as efficiently as possible that he offered the stagehands a bonus of two francs each for every second they shaved off a scene change. Roussel seems to have felt that the backdrops to each scene were an integral part of the play, for he had seventeen of them reproduced as illustrations when *La Poussière de soleils* was published by Lemerre the following year. These generic theatrical landscapes contrast strangely with the characteristically Rousselian freaks, artefacts and memorabilia that make possible the progress of the quest.

Within the play, a similar contrast is effected between the childlike device of the treasure hunt and the recondite nature of Guillaume Blache's extremely challenging clues. As in *L'Étoile au front*, the characters are all staggeringly erudite and never puzzled for more than a second or two by Blache's obscure puns and allusions. Indeed, although the play's labyrinthine trail initially seems an attempt to generate some kind of suspense, the characters solve each conundrum so effortlessly that in the end the plot of *La Poussière de soleils* turns out to be as uncompromisingly undramatic as that of its predecessor.

The play was advertised, like *L'Étoile au front*, as a potentially crucial battleground between Roussel's admirers and his foes:

Those who are for him are so fanatically; those who are against are so equally passionately. The former consider him one of the most innovative intellects of all time, as a sort of literary Richard Wagner; to the latter, however, he is either a hoaxer or a madman. Will *La Poussière de soleils* open the eyes of the benighted?

The play received three private matinée performances at the Théâtre de la Porte-Saint-Martin on 2, 3 and 5 February 1926. Roussel had hired the theatre at double its normal price, and made his usual generous arrangements with the cast of twenty-four. The day before the opening he handed out envelopes containing a ten per cent bonus with which they were to purchase some souvenir to commemorate the production. Although besieged with requests for tickets, Roussel later complained in 'Comment j'ai écrit . . .' that many of those attending the performance were drawn more by the promise of scandal than a genuine curiosity about the play itself:

> There was enormous demand for places at the première, at which there was a huge crowd. Many only came in the expectation of being present at a stormy performance, wishing to play their parts in the disturbance. Nevertheless, the show passed off calmly. At one moment, however, when some hostile barracking broke out, one of my supporters cried, 'Silence the idiots!'
>
> The play was not understood, and – with a few exceptions – the reviews were execrable.

With no scandal to report on, the critics took to decrying the absence of just those aspects of Roussel's theatre they had previously derided. The public, observed Pierre Veber on 4 February, 'has been deceived':

> They came with the intention of kicking up a row, of protesting. They had to give that up, for the work was quite unexceptional; we are a long way from rails made of calves' lights and a one-legged man playing a flute made of his own tibia.

On the other side of the barricades, the Surrealists were also disappointed that Roussel's new play failed to provide them with a suitable occasion to do battle with the bourgeoisie. 'During the interval,' reported *Aux Écoutes*, 'the Surrealists, Cubists and Dadaists, who had come in the hope of a good ruckus, could not hide their disappointment.' In 'Fronton-Virage' Breton recalls discussing his initial response to *La Poussière de soleils* with Louis Aragon:

We had no difficulty agreeing on the desperately dull character of the action that Roussel, in skimping less than ever on the scenery, seemed nevertheless to have done his utmost to make interesting. In this respect, the play as such has undeniably fewer qualities than *Locus Solus* and *L'Étoile au front*, which, from a conventional theatrical standpoint, were already hardly defensible.

For the more discerning Desnos, in contrast, the play's deployment of a single, all-cohering plot signalled Roussel's laudable determination not to repeat himself. On receiving a copy of the Lemerre edition he wrote to thank Roussel:

> The style is less involved than that of your previous books; in my opinion it represents both a desire for renewal and another incursion into the domain of the unknown which you alone are exploring.

———

Roussel arranged a longer run of fifteen performances of the play in January 1927. It opened on the 12th at the Théâtre de la Renaissance, with a cast largely drawn from that of the previous year. Most accounts suggest that this production did not pass off as peacefully as its predecessor. According to Leiris, it was during a particularly stormy performance in the course of this run that Roussel fled the theatre while the show was still in progress, never to return. In 'Comment j'ai écrit . . .' he records this, his final engagement with the theatre, as a mixture of humiliation and triumph:

> While the curtain was falling, people shouted sarcastically, 'Author! . . . Author! . . .' And yet, at each of my shows, I saw new faces rallying to my cause.

The reviews imply, however, that the Parisian theatre-going public was beginning to tire of the controversy altogether. Roussel's plays had achieved a *succès de scandale* of sorts, and in avant-garde circles a *succès d'estime*, but they would never achieve the only success Roussel cared for, the kind enjoyed by the initiator of his dramatic career some fifteen years earlier, Edmond Rostand.

And yet, although they disappointed their author by failing to satisfy his yearning for universal acclaim, Roussel's plays are intriguing for precisely the reasons they were unable to win over a popular audience. Their fascination resides in the disjunction they reveal between the richly textured poetry of the *procédé*-inspired episodes related by the characters and the deadpan banality of the theatrical means used to convey these narratives. In 'Fronton-Virage' André Breton complained that *La Poussière de soleils* was fissured by 'a certain disproportion between the seen and the mentally assimilated'; it is surely this disproportion which constitutes the most striking originality of Roussel's theatre. What we see on stage, whether it is a butterfly in a paperweight or a manuscript tied with wire, a pigeon full of mites or a skull engraved with a sonnet, exists only in relation to the story that explains its provenance or significance; as soon as this has been fully disclosed, the object is discarded and the play moves on. With their proliferating narratives, the plays come to resemble the bewilderingly infinite galaxies of space evoked by Jacques at the conclusion of *La Poussière de soleils*. Their indifference to matters of plot and characterization further exacerbates the sense of helplessness they create. The stories dissolve into each other like patterns in a kaleidoscope, leaving only a baffled awareness of endless possible combinations of words and narrative connections. It is the clash between the interminable processes of language and the confinements of the stage that creates the peculiar tension underlying Roussel's hypnotic, unnerving plays. For, despite their evasion of the primary requirements of drama, *L'Étoile au front* and *La Poussière de soleils* are still, as John Ashbery has noted, 'theatrical in a curious way.' The shared-out speeches result in a 'lilting and oddly dramatic language' that creates its own unique kinds of resonance:

> The anecdotes cast on the characters who tell them an
> unearthly glimmer that is like a new kind of
> characterization. And these stories, cut up and distributed

among the speakers, somehow propel us breathlessly forward. The plays are among the strangest and most exciting in modern literature.

# CHAPTER 7

# In Parenthesis

Despite the admiration of the Pope and Mussolini, of gossip columnists and car enthusiasts, Roussel's voyage to Rome and back in December 1926 was the last long journey he made in the *roulotte*. Throughout the 1920s Roussel's enormous expenses had been steadily encroaching on the capital he had inherited from his parents. Yearly Pierre Leiris presented him with ever more worrying sets of figures, but Roussel was not easily persuaded to retrench. His villa in Neuilly, for instance, was maintained by sixteen employees: a chef, a governess, a maître d'hôtel, two foot servants, a washerwoman, three chauffeurs, three gardeners, three cooks and a valet de chambre.

One of the under-cooks, André Guillot, who later became a celebrated chef, was employed in Roussel's household from October 1926 until spring 1927. In his memoirs, *La Grande cuisine bourgeoise*, Guillot records in considerable detail the peculiarities of Roussel's dining habits and the inflexible, lavish routines of his Neuilly establishment. Rather than be served at intervals during the day, Roussel ordered his various meals be compressed into a single marathon sitting. This would begin at 12.30 with seasonal fruits, followed by a bowl of tea, coffee or hot chocolate (specially imported from Switzerland) in which floated halves of small, freshly cooked brioche. He would then be offered some cheese, normally Bondon de Neufchâtel. On his completion of breakfast, around 1.15, lunch would immediately begin: a plate of shellfish, followed by a helping of fish or pasta, then a choice of two entrées with garnishings, a sorbet or a spoom (sorbet mixed with champagne) to cleanse the palate, then a roast meat dish, vegetables, a salad, followed by a second helping of fruit. Lunch over, a selection of teatime cakes would be served: éclairs, cream horns, almond gâteau, ice-cream laced with spun sugar. Towards late afternoon the big meal of the day, Roussel's early dinner, would be brought to table: this would customarily include a choice of two soups, a serving of fish, a garnished entrée, followed by a roast of some kind, vegetables, and concluded with a sweet dessert. The meal, or rather series of meals, would end some five hours after it began. There seems no doubt that this elaborate ritual was Roussel's way of preserving the luxurious culinary traditions established by his mother; given his 'phobias in relation to food,' it also seems likely – as Guillot suggests – that most of these elaborate dishes ended up being consumed by his enormous establishment below stairs.*

In July 1927 Roussel embarked on the last trip mentioned in the travel section of 'Comment j'ai écrit . . .' – to the Near and Middle East. The *roulotte* had been disposed of† and Roussel travelled mainly by chauffeur-driven car, accompanied by an interpreter. His first stop was Constantinople and the supposed tomb of Loti's heroine Aziyadé. Roussel reverently gathered a rose from the spot, which he had preserved in a glass case mounted on red velvet, with an engraved label affixed to the base proclaiming 'CETTE ROSE A ÉTÉ CUEILLIE PAR MOI SUR

---

* Guillot also includes a couple of sample menus from October and November 1926, which are reproduced in Appendix 2. Roussel may not – indeed, could not possibly – have eaten all his Escoffier-trained cook, M. Masclet, set before him, but he was, according to Guillot, extremely fastidious about the preparations of each dish: the spun sugar with which desserts were adorned had to be slightly warm when it arrived at table, or else he sent it back. 'Ah,' Guillot exclaims, 'those *voiles en sucre filé*! My hands are still, forty-seven years later, scarred by the burns made by heating that sugar, which had to be done so quickly. On the one hand the *voile* (literally veil) had to be warm; on the other, it would not have done to keep M. Roussel waiting'. It was stipulated also that none of the vegetables should bear the slightest trace of the knife with which they had been cut: the least serration, and they too were returned. It was, Guillot observes, 'an extraordinary household, on account of the diversity of the preparations that had to be accomplished, and the exceptionally high quality of the dishes served and the care taken in their execution'. He reports himself, however, as being somewhat relieved to be dismissed for some minor infraction of protocol at the end of his term of probation.
† It was sold in late 1926. Nothing is known of its new owners or subsequent history.

LA TOMBE D'AZIYADÉ. Raymond ROUSSEL.'* His subsequent
itinerary included Palestine, Syria, Lebanon, Iraq and Iran. In
Jerusalem he had his photograph taken at another legendary
site, in the Dome of the Ascension on the stone from which
Jesus was reputedly assumed into heaven. From Isfahan he sent
back a postcard to Charlotte Dufrène, dated according to the
Muslim calendar in the year 1346 since the Hegira:

> On my way to Tehran I spent a night in Ecbatane, which
> was the capital in the time of Darius and Xerxes. I made an
> excursion to the Caspian Sea, the kingdom of caviare. I was
> hoping to eat some extra-fresh, but it was not yet the season,
> and that which I was served was a bit salty. If there I was
> too early for the caviare, here in Isfahan I am too late for
> the roses. Persia is very curious, but very uncomfortable. It
> would be easy to believe it is AD1346 rather than 1346
> since the Hegira.

Roussel's complaint about the country's backwardness may well
relate to the threat it posed to a special course of hair treatment
he was following at this time. Six months previously Roussel
had turned fifty, and had become obsessed by the fear that his
dark brown hair might soon be turning white. Therefore, as
Charlotte Dufrène explained to Leiris,

> on the advice of a respected doctor, he would, twice a week,
> heat each part of his hair with a hot-air dryer until he could
> feel his hair almost burning. Remarking that, if he missed a
> single application, he would have to abandon the entire
> treatment, having broken the 'series', he found himself
> forced, while travelling in regions where he could not use the
> appliance, which he'd always carry with him, to make use
> of preheated saucepans; on one occasion, unable to get
> hold of a saucepan, he used a sheet of hot metal, under
> which he had to kneel.

* Like the glass star enclosing the fragment of biscuit gathered from the table
of Camille Flammarion, this fetishistic trophy ended up for sale in a Parisian
flea market, where it was purchased by the Romanian painter Jacques Hérold.
A picture of it is reproduced in DG, p. 35.

Hair-loss and ageing feature a number of times in the poem on which Roussel had already been working for twelve years, and which was slowly nearing completion:

> ((((pendant notre hiver notre tignasse essaime,
> Tels les rayons plantés dans le soleil vernal
> S'en vont quand il se change en soleil hivernal;))))

((((during our winter our head of hair emigrates,/ As the furrows of seeds planted in the spring sun/ Disappear when that sun is changed to a winter one:))))

he points out, within four sets of brackets, in Canto III. The last parenthetical interruption in the whole poem, in Canto IV, also concludes with a meditation on the inevitability of physical decay:

> chez l'homme,
> Le feu d'œil s'éteint à l'âge où dent par dent
> Et cheveu par cheveu, sans choc, sans accident,
> Par l'action du temps, sa tête se déleste;))))

with man,/ The fire in the eye is extinguished at the age when tooth by tooth/ And hair by hair, without shock or accident,/ Simply through the action of time, the head sheds its load;))))

Whether or not as a result of his painful-sounding applications of heat to the scalp, Roussel's hair did not in the event turn white, or even grey, during the six years of his life remaining.

———

On his return, Roussel seems reluctantly to have begun to acknowledge his approaching ruin. He was forced to relinquish the majority of the staff employed at Neuilly in preparation for the sale of the property. His methods of economizing could not, however, be called stringent. In spring 1928 he took up residence in Room 303 at the Ritz, where he ran up a stupefying series of laundry bills and miscellaneous expenses.* After three months of this makeshift existence, Roussel arranged to occupy the second floor of his sister Germaine's hôtel on rue Quentin-

---

* One month he spent almost a thousand francs on fruit alone (FR, cat no. 4510, f. 260).

Bauchart. This was to be his base in Paris until his departure for Palermo in June 1933, and it was here he left his archive of personal and literary papers that were boxed up and deposited after his death in the Bedel warehouse.

Soon after Roussel effected this transfer, Germaine, who was separated but not divorced from her second husband, Charles Ney, inherited the title of Princess of Moscow, following the death of Ney's older brother Napoléon. Roussel sets forth in detail the magnificence of his brother-in-law's connections in 'Comment j'ai écrit . . .', despite the fact that by the time the essay was composed, in 1932, Germaine was dead and Ney had remarried.* Strangely, Roussel doesn't mention an elevation in his own status granted earlier the same year: on 14 February Roussel was notified that he had been elected a chevalier of the Légion d'Honneur, and the following month he received his official award. The news cannot have come as a complete surprise, for Roussel's correspondence with the august body reveals he had recently made them a voluntary donation of 50,000 francs. These dubious honours were accorded Roussel just as his life entered its protracted endgame, to borrow a metaphor from chess – to which he would soon be devoting much of his attention. Though he continued furiously adding footnotes and further examples to the proofs of *Nouvelles Impressions d'Afrique*, which he had poor Eugène Vallée, the foreman at Lemerre's printing house, recompose time and again between the first set of galleys (dated 27 September 1927) and the last (dated 30 June 1931), Roussel also started to experiment with other possible means of recovering the euphoria of *la gloire*. He began with alcohol, but soon moved on to drugs, principally barbiturates, prescribed by doctors at the time for cases of neurasthenia. By autumn 1928 Roussel had become addicted enough to need treatment at a clinic in Switzerland. Later in the year he began an eight-month residence at a detoxification centre

---

* Leiris speculates in his notebook that it may have been the distant connection to France's first emperor which appealed to Roussel in the families with whom he claimed kin: 'He mentions only those connected to Napoleon (identification with Napoleon?)' (R & CO, p. 102).

in Saint-Cloud, near Paris. There he met Jean Cocteau, who was attempting to wean himself from a dependence on opium.

Cocteau was particularly struck by Roussel's resemblance to another literary invalid: 'He had the hair, the moustache, the gait of Proust,' he recalled in an interview in 1951. In his memoir *Opium* (1930), Cocteau provides no indications as to the kind of relationship he established with Roussel during their time at Saint-Cloud, but we know they exchanged letters subsequently, though none have yet come to light. Roussel includes (as well as an extract from *Opium*) some praise from a Cocteau missive in his final *cahier de critiques*: '*Locus Solus* is a prodigious feat, a book which discourages one from writing; Roussel, you dominate us all.' And in *Opium* Cocteau refers to a postscript added to a recent letter received from Roussel, in which he alludes to some cryptic lines from Cocteau's 1921 play *Les Mariés de la Tour Eiffel*:

FIRST LOUDSPEAKER: But this telegram is dead.
SECOND LOUDSPEAKER: It's just because it's dead that everyone understands it.

This quotation, Cocteau adds, 'proves that Roussel is not unaware of what he is or of what is due to him.'

Yet although Roussel may well have known what was due to him, his writings consistently avoided fitting into the kinds of category that would have allowed his work to be placed and assessed with confidence. 'Is Raymond Roussel mad?' inquired the critic Georges Pioch in a review of *L'Étoile au front*. 'Or is he possessed of such luminous powers that we cannot bear the glare?' And if Roussel's writings as a whole somehow sidestep the criteria by which literature is normally judged, his final completed work, *Nouvelles Impressions d'Afrique*, develops the business of sidestepping into a pure yet bewildering end in itself: within twenty-four lines of the first poem one has been forced to broach five sets of brackets and been plunged into the first of many rhymed footnotes. Unlike his earlier writings, *Nouvelles Impressions d'Afrique* signals its strangeness as defiantly as Mallarmé's *Coup de dés*, to which both Michel Leiris and John Ashbery have compared it.

In 'Comment j'ai écrit . . .' Roussel presents a rather puzzling account of the poem's tortured genesis. *Nouvelles Impressions d'Afrique*, he informs us, was begun in 1915 and was to be a series of descriptions of two tiny images:

> It concerned a tiny pair of opera-glasses to be worn as a pendant, each of whose lenses, two millimetres in diameter and meant to be held very close to the eye, contained a photograph on glass – one of the bazaars of Cairo, the other of a quay in Luxor.
>
> I made a description in verse of these two photographs. (It was, in short, an exact sequel to my poem *La Vue*.)
>
> Having completed this initial work, I took up the poem again from the beginning to polish the verses. But at the end of a certain time I realized that an entire lifetime would not be sufficient for this polishing, and I abandoned my task. This had in all taken me five years of work. If the manuscript could be retrieved from among my papers, it might perhaps prove interesting, such as it is, at least to certain of my readers.

Aside from a very brief fragment dating from 1906 set in an Egyptian bazaar, nothing of this sort has been recovered. On the other hand, throughout the First World War Roussel consistently dispatched envelopes containing work in progress to Eugène Leiris for safekeeping. Most of these envelopes have gone missing or were found empty, but in one the manuscript of *Flio* was deposited, and two, numbered 13 and 14 and dated 12 November 1916 and 2 March 1917, contained manuscript drafts of *Nouvelles Impressions d'Afrique*. Contrary to expectations, these drafts did not concern two photographs imprisoned in miniature opera-glasses, but proved to be passages from Canto I and Canto II of the so-called second version of *Nouvelles Impressions d'Afrique*. On 6 March Roussel sent Leiris a typed draft of Canto I, which is reproduced in facsimile in the miscellaneous collection of Roussel's writings, *Épaves* (1972). This is simply a not yet fully expanded version of the canto as eventually published. One line is slightly altered, and Roussel has not yet begun introducing multiple brackets or footnotes as a means of demarcating the various parentheses, but this and the other early drafts reveal that the methodology of the poem was established from the outset, rather than in 1920, as Roussel claims in 'Comment j'ai écrit . . .'

The poem's inching progress in the years after the war can be partially deduced from the almost 160 worksheets discovered among Roussel's papers in 1989. These obsessively worked pages suggest that Roussel was not exaggerating when he referred in 'Comment j'ai écrit . . .' to the unique difficulties posed by the poem's eccentric procedures and 'the immense amount of time demanded by composition of this kind of verse'. In this, the poem is starkly opposed to Roussel's earlier verse works, from *La Doublure* to *Les Noces*, which demonstrate an almost compulsive facility with alexandrines. And although Roussel firmly insists in his essay that *Nouvelles Impressions*, like *La Doublure* and *La Vue*, makes no use at all of the *procédé*, its deployment of brackets and footnotes to create a poetics of systematic self-enclosure, of relentless bifurcation, is in many ways analogous to the double-dealing methodology under-pinning his fiction. Confusingly, many of these worksheets also include instances of the 'evolved' method of the *procédé* in action. On one page, for instance, Roussel deforms a line from Canto II of the poem:

À prendre l'appareil qui trouvé par Franklin
(To take the apparatus which discovered by Franklin)

becomes

Arpent drelin spirale guilledou guipure frugal
(Acre tinkle spiral night-haunts pillow-lace frugal)

and is then subjected to three further lines of phonetic modifi-cation. These word games do not appear to have affected the composition of *Nouvelles Impressions* itself. More likely, even as he worked on his final long poem, Roussel was gathering materials on which to base episodes of the *procédé*-inspired prose work that was to be his next project, just as he had earlier used lines from *La Vue* as source material for *Locus Solus*. For instance, the words *Europe* and *cubaine* in a list derived from the line 'Comme si choisissant la seconde opportune' (As if choosing the opportune second) (also from Canto II) clearly helped determine the narrative of 'À la Havane', which is set in

Cuba, and features a passionate Europhile and a Dresden figurine of 'L'Enlèvement d'Europe.'*

At the foot of some of these draft pages Roussel provides details of his punishing work schedule: eleven hours on Saturday, eight on Sunday, nine and a quarter on Monday, ten and a quarter on Tuesday, twelve and a half on Wednesday . . . Here again we have evidence of Roussel's similarity to the *prédestiné* mentioned by Boissenin, who might easily have lived an idle life, but instead 'gives to the world a strange example of relentless hard work and manly fortitude'. The poem was eventually delivered to the printers in 1928, but then expanded yet further with each fresh set of proofs. In his correspondence with Roussel the print foreman had to ask him to destroy all outdated galleys to avoid confusing different states of the text.†

Roussel's calculation in 'Comment j'ai écrit . . .' that the poem took seven years to write is thus extremely doubtful. If we assume it was begun in 1915 and finished in 1931, and extract the two periods of six months during which he wrote *L'Étoile au front* and *La Poussière de soleils*, the period of its composition ends up as roughly fifteen years – which is thirty times what it took Roussel to write his first long poem, *La Doublure*, which is well over four times as long as *Nouvelles Impressions d'Afrique*. For by the end of these fifteen years of 'mâle persévérance' Roussel had completed a poem that occupied a mere fifty-nine pages.

Accordingly he decided to include with it fifty-nine illustrations and the text of his first poem, *Mon Âme*, slightly altered and retitled as *L'Âme de Victor Hugo*. He also decreed that the verso of each page in the book should be left blank. Thus, when finally published in 1932, *Nouvelles Impressions d'Afrique* appeared as an imposing volume almost as thick as *Locus Solus*,

---

* The figurine mentioned in the story appears to be a memory of, or an allusion to, one of Madame Roussel's Dresden statuettes, also entitled 'L'Enlèvement d'Europe' (either the rape of Europa or the triumph of Europe), which fetched 1,500 francs at auction. A picture of it is reproduced in AT4, p. 92.
† Like Proust, Roussel used proof sheets as an integral part of his compositional process, regardless of expense. 'The important thing is to get as close as possible to perfection,' he wrote in a letter to M. Vallée, urging him to make sure the parentheses were accurately distributed (R & Co, p. 206).

or as its supposed precursor *Impressions d'Afrique*. And intriguingly, as J.B. Brunius first pointed out in an essay in 1938, the entire text of the poem can be read without the book's pages having to be cut; it was the illustrations which were printed on the pages that had to be prised open, like some secret visual parenthesis, or yet one more inner mystery prepared for Rousselian initiates. In a further self-referential conceit, one of these illustrations is actually of a reader peering between the uncut pages of a book poised vertically on his desk (see Appendix 3 for this and other Zo illustrations referred to).

———

*Nouvelles Impressions d'Afrique* consists of four cantos, of 228, 642, 172 and 232 lines respectively. Each begins innocuously enough, as a description of a location in Egypt. Canto I, for instance, opens with the poet contemplating the house in Damiette where France's Louis IX was imprisoned in the thirteenth century:

> Sans doute à réfléchir, à compter cela porte,
> D'être avisé que là, derrière cette porte,
> Fut trois mois prisonnier le roi saint! . . . Louis neuf! . . .
> Combien le fait, pourtant, paraît tangible et neuf
> En ce pays jonché de croulantes merveilles,
> Telles qu'on n'en sait point ici-bas de plus vieilles!
> Elles présentes, tout semble dater d'hier:

No doubt to reflect, to take cognizance of this truth has an impact,/ To be informed that there, behind that door,/ The saintly king was for three months a prisoner! . . . Louis the ninth! . . ./ How this fact, however, seems tangible and new/ In this country strewn with crumbling marvels,/ That are so old that no one knows of any on earth that are older!/ In their presence, everything seems to date from yesterday:

Roussel then proceeds to illustrate this trite reflection. His first example of something which, in comparison with the relics of ancient Egypt, seems new is that of an old name of which the bearer is so proud,

Que de mémoire, à fond, il sait sans une faute . . .
 – Racines, troncs, rameaux, branches collatérales –
L'état de ses aïeux;

That in his memory he knows absolutely, without a single
mistake . . ./ – Including roots, parent stocks, subdivisions,
collateral branches – / The condition of his ancestors;

But between the first line quoted above – the poem's ninth –
and the second – the poem's 225th – Roussel interposes a parenthesis: the bearer of the illustrious pedigree knows his family
ancestry 'sans une faute'

(Comme sait l'occupant, dans une maison haute,
D'un clair logis donnant sur le dernier palier
 – Photographe quelconque habile à pallier
Pattes d'oie et boutons par de fins stratagèmes – . . .
L'avis roulant sur l'art de mouvoir l'ascenseur:)

(Just as knows the occupant, in a tall building,/ Of a bright flat
which gives on to the top landing/ – Some photographer who is
skilful at palliating/ Crow's feet and spots by clever stratagems
– . . ./ The notice, always in motion, on the means of operating
the lift [i.e. because he spends so long each day going up and down
in it]:)

Only, between the fourth line quoted above – the poem's thirteenth – and the fifth – the poem's 224th – Roussel introduces
further subsidiary considerations. The photographer's skill in
erasing crow's feet and spots from his pictures inspires an
address to the art of doctoring photographs:

((Pouvoir du retoucheur! lorsque arborant ses gemmes . . .
Se fait prendre en famille une beauté qui, mûre,
N'entend plus sur ses pas monter aucun murmure,
De mère, sur la plaque, elle se change en sœur;))

((Power of retouching! when, sporting her jewels . . ./ A beauty has
her photograph taken with her family, but, now mature, one who/
No longer hears appreciative murmurs follow her footsteps,/ On
the photographic plate she changes from being a mother to a
sister;))

But between the first line quoted above – the poem's fourteenth

– and the second – the poem's 221st – Roussel is drawn to consider how each person, when having a photo taken, dresses up and strikes a pose that expresses their sense of themselves: the fencer is pictured wearing his protective vest, the poet holding a pen, the rich woman displays a huge jewel on her breast, the traveller to the North Pole appears in an Eskimo outfit, and so on and so on.

There is no denying that the method deployed in these poems presents formidable difficulties to the reader. In Canto II 625 lines and some eighteen interruptions separate the opening sentence from its conclusion. It is impossible to hold so many incomplete trains of thought suspended in the brain simultaneously: one is best off skipping to the conclusion as soon as the first bracket arrives, and then working one's way towards the middle of the poem from both ends. Also, it must be said that the occasions or justifications that Roussel establishes for each new parenthesis are often tendentious in the extreme. In Canto I, for instance, he describes the person having his photo taken as wondering if his breathing will make the image fuzzy:

> – Se demandant, pour peu qu'en respirant il bouge,
> Si sur la gélatine, à la lumière rouge,
> Dans le révélateur il apparaîtra flou, –

Wondering, even if only by breathing he moves,/ If on the gelatine, in the red light,/ In the developing fluid he will appear blurred, –

at which a fourth bracket opens and we are presented with a series of equivalent states and images of wondering, all in apposition to this initial act of speculation:

> ((((Tels se demandent: –...

Such also wonder: a penniless fop who has just married a rich woman wonders if he is any different from a thief; someone who has just arrived in Nice wonders if it's warm enough to wear linen; an animal-tamer being eaten by one of his wild beasts wonders if, a year on, his widow will still be dressed strictly in black ... Indeed, Roussel offers us in total fifty-four examples of quandaries, not all of them focused on human beings: the thermometer 'ailleurs placé que sous l'aisselle' (placed somewhere other than the armpit [i.e. in the rectum]) wonders how far away it is from the next stool; a wall battered by a window shutter during windy weather is puzzled to know what fault it has committed to deserve such treatment (a scene Roussel chose for one of Zo's illustrations); a flower on which someone who has dined on asparagus has just urinated wonders if its scent will ever return.

The rhymed footnotes are linked to the text by similarly tangential means. The description of the newly arrived visitor to Nice gives rise to a forty-five-line footnote based on the premise that, because people who spend the winter in Nice always claim it's warm there even if it's snowing, it's as pointless to give one of the city's winter sojourners an overcoat as it is to give an emetic to a novice at sea during a hurricane (he won't want it because he's already vomiting), or an aphrodisiac to a man being hung (he won't need it because he'll already have an erection), or a pair of bellows to someone struggling to put out a hearth fire suddenly out of control, or a hammer to someone who takes a long-pressed flower from a book (depicted in Zo's fourth picture), or a brush-stroke the wrong way up the spine of a dog who is growling and about to attack.

The poem's methodology can be seen as embodying yet again the equation between compression and prolixity which so out-raged audiences of *L'Étoile au front*. Each illustrative vignette is presented in bewilderingly concise terms, and yet, in relation to the poem's ostensible overall purpose (in this case to describe the house where Louis IX was imprisoned), is wholly irrelevant. A mind-boggling density and intricacy of detail is marshalled by Roussel in the service of wholly banal or self-evident propo-sitions. Most of Canto II is taken up with comparisons of things that look the same but are different sizes. The 'hook' here derives from the image of a man eavesdropping on people talking derogatorily about him: even when thus confronted with his faults, they still appear small to him, as if he were under some spell and liable to confound

> l'appareil qui, trouvé par Franklin,
> Sans danger dans un puits fait se perdre la foudre
> Pour un fil gris passé dans une aiguille à coudre;

– Pour ceux dont s'orne un bras arrivé d'officier
Au ciel trois jumeaux blancs astres d'artificier;

the apparatus which, discovered by Franklin,/ Makes lightning disappear without danger into a hole [i.e. a lightning conductor]/ For a grey thread passed into the eye of a sewing needle;/ – For the stars which ornament the arm of someone made an officer/ The three twin stars in the sky of a firework-maker;

Roussel provides some two hundred further illustrations of large things being mistaken for small: a white house with blue shutters for a Roquefort cheese; an alligator by a sun-umbrella in a colonial park for a lizard by a mushroom; an eyelash for the horn of a chamois; a stalactite in a cave reddened by the setting sun for the inflamed uvula in the throat of someone suffering from a bad cough; snow falling on a pile of red eggs on a windless day for sugar being sprinkled on strawberries. Although most of these outlandish comparisons are only two or three lines long, they often convey an extraordinary wealth of information:

pour celle qu'à l'ampoule
L'épingle arrache à point, la fuite qu'au désert
Le fer d'un traitre extorque à l'outre;

for that which from a blister/ The pin releases through a hole, [the water] running away in the desert/ Which the sword of a traitor releases from a goat-skin;

We are not only offered the visual resemblance between the pricked blister and the punctured goat-skin (see illustration 20), both leaking liquid, but an entire mini-scenario of desert treachery.

un lac de sang surgi
Dans un quartier suspect, pour le crachat perfide
D'un phtisique;

a lake of blood that appears/ In a dangerous district, for the treacherous spittle/ Of a consumptive;

The first half creates in a mere nine words a thumbnail sketch of a murder in a dangerous city slum; a low-life genre scene reminiscent of that described so elaborately in Roussel's early fragment beginning 'Quel est donc dans un coin . . .' The six words of the second half of the equation, on the other hand, plangently evoke the horror of a consumptive whose bloody sputum betrays him, in both senses of the word.

Michel Leiris has likened Roussel's use of parentheses in the poem to the way in which his stories are often embedded within each other in his novels:

> Here occurs again, but transposed on to the plane of poetry, the technique of stories with multiple drawers that is so common in the work of Roussel; but this time, the drawers operate within the sentences themselves (and not within the narrative), as if Roussel had decided to use these parentheses as a means of making language disintegrate.

But if the brackets continually rupture the progress of a particular line of argument, they also serve as forms of connection, almost as a synapse or railway points that enable the poem to cross into whole new regions of proliferative analogy and illustration. Roussel seems to want to suspend language rather than destroy it, to complicate and delay its drive towards conclusion. Metaphor begets metaphor begets metaphor, until language seems turned wholly inside out, the richness of its inner linings all but obliterating awareness of the encasing literal scenarios. The series of comparisons that make up the bulk of Canto II have to be tracked back through layer after layer of figuration if one wants to connect them to the poem's original pretext; which in this case is a reflection on the fact that when Napoleon fought the Battle of the Pyramids, he had not yet adopted the famous overcoat and hat that he took to wearing in later years.

And however long and involved the diversions, each poem does, in the end, fulfil its initial premise. Just as each episode in the fiction eventually binds together the elements provided by the *procédé*, so each of the interrupted syntactic units is returned to and completed, and its opening sentence is at long last closed. While the poems do not, as Roussel insists in 'Comment j'ai écrit . . .', make use of the *procédé* itself, their structure can be seen as embodying a very similar kind of linguistic experiment and as gratifying the same urge to dramatize patterns of distortion, dispersal and reintegration.

The poems in fact allude on several occasions to Roussel's earlier texts. In Canto II, as part of a list of things that have got smaller in some way, he refers to the performance by Kalj and Méisdehl, both aged between seven and eight, of scenes from the original script of *Romeo and Juliet* (discovered by the tragedienne Adinolfa) in *Impressions d'Afrique*. In the same canto, as an example of things that look alike but are of different sizes, he includes a reference to the watery aerial globe that terrifies the wicked brothers in the story read by the reiter in the crypt in *Locus Solus*. This example again demonstrates the poem's formidable powers of compression:

> la boule aquatique et nue
> D'un dentaire effrayant recoin, pour l'abreuvoir
> D'un serin sobre;

the unsupported watery globe/ Of a frightening dental nook, for the drinking-ball/ Of an abstemious canary;

Finally, in Canto III Roussel dilates at length on the *Impressions* of a bogus travel writer who publishes books on foreign countries without ever visiting them. This 'faux explorateur' (false explorer) is the antithesis of the globetrotting Roussel, whose two volumes of pseudo-*Impressions* deliberately confound the reader's expectations.

Roussel also makes a series of coded references to the plight of the man of genius scorned by his contemporaries. 'La gloire a l'horreur du teint frais' (Glory abhors a fresh complexion), he reminds us in a footnote prompted by the image of the young poet wondering for how much longer he will have to pay for the publication of his books. A second footnote attached to the following line declares that only ageing artists are famous, as only old oak-trees are flourishing and shady. In a footnote in Canto IV, in a catalogue of things for which one has to wait, Roussel goes further and suggests that only the dead are allowed to be famous:

sommité disparue
Seule est en droit d'avoir sa statue et sa rue, –*

only an important person who has died/ Has the right to a statue
and to name a street, –

A couple of pages later, as the poem nears its conclusion, Roussel
adverts again to the young artist's conviction of his own greatness, and the rhapsodies to which these give rise:

le saint feu du génie
(((((Qui rend l'élu touché par lui si vaniteux
Qu'il trouve au firmament les vrais astres piteux
Auprès de l'astre neuf qui sur son front rayonne
Et songe à devenir le maître que crayonne
Quiconque a pour métier l'art caricatural . . .

the holy fire of genius/ (((((Which renders the elect touched by it so
vain/ That he finds the real stars in the sky wretched/ In
comparison with the new star which shines on his forehead/ And
he thinks of becoming a master who is drawn/ By anyone who
has the job of being a caricaturist . . .

But the fire of genius is evoked in this instance as an example
of things that are extinguished, and the enraptured ephebe's
visions of glory are interrupted by the conclusion of the parenthesis:

le sainte feu du génie
((((( . . . )))))
S'éteint quand l'âge rend son détenteur gaga . . .

the holy fire of genius/ ((((( . . . )))))/ Is extinguished when age
renders its possessor gaga . . .

With hindsight, the poem can even be seen as almost disclosing
the workings of the *procédé*: a long footnote in Canto IV takes

* When Roussel eventually sold his property at Neuilly – for 11,550,000
francs (FR, cat. no. 4509, f. 150), although the previous year he had received
an offer of 17 million francs – he had a clause inserted into the contract
stipulating that if ever the land should be developed and a road built through
it, that road should be called avenue Raymond-Roussel. Alas, no such avenue
exists among the network of co-operatives built during the 1950s on the plot
occupied by 25 boulevard Richard-Wallace.

as its theme 'Combien change de force un mot suivant les cas!' (How a word is forced to change according to circumstances!) and produces twenty examples of double meanings.

Yet despite these allusions to his earlier writings and future revelation, and its wholly original format, *Nouvelles Impressions d'Afrique* is a disturbingly impersonal poem; if the *procédé* enabled Roussel to create, in Leiris's words, 'authentic myths' that seem to plumb the remote depths of the collective unconscious, the eccentric methodology deployed in *Nouvelles Impressions* similarly allows Roussel to represent the world's diversity with a panoramic detachment. The straitjacket of its form results in a curious freedom and objectivity: the examples, many metaphors and syntactic constructions removed from their long-lost origins, take on a vitality of their own. Furthermore, they never come to seem deliberately dreamed up to illustrate the strangeness of existence, in the manner, for instance, of Lautréamont's famous image of an umbrella and a sewing machine on a dissecting table. Roussel's conjunctions are as likely to be banal as surreal, and serve as evidence only in relation to a series of truisms: that, for instance, we are all sometimes in need of help ('(((Besoin d'aide! ô besoin sublime, universel!' (Need of help! O sublime, universal need!)), or that one can get used to anything ('((((Se fait-on pas à tout? deux jours après la tonte,/ Le mouton aguerri ne ressent plus le frais . . .' (Does one not get used to everything? Two days after the shearing,/ The inured sheep no longer resents the cold . . .)), or that the cross appears in many contexts, as the Southern Cross in the night sky, figuratively (we all have our cross to bear), in Christian ceremonies, when a waiter about to carve sharpens his knife (see illustration 40).

There appears, moreover, to be some kind of antithetical relation between the cerebral intricacy of the poem's form and the range and frankness of its contents. The exigencies of its parenthetical structure can make it seem like a fiendish *casse-tête*, the linguistic equivalent of a problem in chess or mathematics. The mental gymnastics demanded for its composition appear, however, to have released or licensed in Roussel an opposite impulse: an urge to represent bodily impurities, discharges and waste products. Roussel, we know from Charlotte

Dufrène, was extremely fastidious in all matters of hygiene, and would spend two hours on his toilette before venturing forth in the evening. His bills during his stay at the Ritz reveal that he consigned as many as twenty-five handkerchiefs a week to the hotel laundry. To make sure he never wore a suit or overcoat too often, he took the precaution of having a small square of material sewn into the lining, on which he kept a tally of its use: after the item had been worn fifteen times it was passed on to his valet. This obsession with filth emerges in the text of *Nouvelles Impressions d'Afrique* in a startling series of scatological images. Among the examples adduced in Canto II, for instance, of things that look alike but are different sizes, one finds:

> – le jour du blanchisseur,
> Un drap qu'ont de leur pourpre enrichi des menstrues,
> Pour un mouchoir à sang nasal . . .

– on the day of the laundry,/ A sheet which menstrual discharges have enriched with their crimson,/ For a handkerchief stained with blood from the nose . . .

> – Quand d'un bas on l'expulse, un œuf à repriser,
> Pour ce qui d'une chèvre, avec retard, clôture
> L'allègement . . .

– When it is expelled from a stocking, a darning egg,/ For that with which a goat eventually terminates/ The alleviation [of its bowels] . . .

> – pour ce qu'orneé
> De clous une semelle a dans la crotte empreint,
> Un solitaire sans billes . . .

– for that which, ornamented/ With nails, a boot-sole has imprinted in a horse-dropping,/ A solitaire board without pegs . . .

In the same Canto, in a long list of absurd propositions to which a determined flatterer would agree, Roussel introduces the outrageous claim

> Qu'outre-Manche à certains essuyages intimes,
> En aveugle accomplis, jamais ne sert le *Times* . . .

That on the other side of the Channel, for certain intimate wipings/
Accomplished without looking, *The Times* is never used . . .

In a footnote in Canto III Roussel advises us that one way to
recognize a drunkard is by the clearness of his 'horizontal jet
fort' (strong horizontal jet of urine), and in the catalogue of
various quandaries in Canto I Roussel includes a shirt wondering
what purgative its owner took that morning, a bird wondering
about which picnicker's plate to deposit its droppings on and
these reflections attributed to the sole of a shoe:

> – Quand, poisseuse, elle a l'heur de puer, la semelle,
> Si de son sort chanceux jalouse est sa jumelle . . .

> – When, all sticky [with shit], a shoe-sole has the good luck to
> stink,/ If the other sole is jealous of her fortunate fate . . .

'What sluice-gates burst in him, allowing these malodorous jets
to break forth,' Jean Ferry muses in the first of his two studies
of the poem. This eruption of the forbidden seems connected to
its opposite, the sublimation of his physical existence inherent
in Roussel's experience of *la gloire*. In his state of elation the
young Roussel refused to eat, or even acknowledge his body,
standing immobile for hours on end, pen in hand, absorbed like
the young poet at the end of Canto IV in visions of his future
greatness. Food disturbed the 'sérénité' of these raptures, and
yet the transformations accomplished by the *procédé* can seem
almost analogous to the alimentary processes: words and sentences are absorbed, broken down, then reconfigured into
wholly new linguistic matter. At the same time the *procédé*
allowed Roussel to conceal his investigation into each word's
dark underside or double meaning, to hold back the secret stages
by which his miraculous fictions were produced. In *Nouvelles
Impressions d'Afrique*, on the other hand, Roussel fuses the
surface of the poem with its complex methodology; we are
forced to negotiate the brackets as readers just as Roussel was
when writing it, whereas without 'Comment j'ai écrit . . .' the
*procédé* might have remained hidden forever. In practice each
canto comes to resemble a peculiar journey to the centre of
language, as we penetrate ever more figurative strata, and then

return as the brackets complete themselves, eventually emerging (to adapt a line of Robert Frost's) not far from our going forth.

By refusing to disguise its workings – indeed, by making the reader submit to them also – the poem explicitly enacts the sort of fragmentation and reconstitution of language performed in private by the *procédé*. The poem's scatology is consistent with its frankness about its parenthetical procedures, which are as 'special', to use Roussel's term from 'Comment j'ai écrit . . .', as the *procédé* itself. This is why *Nouvelles Impressions* has seemed to such as Ashbery, who considers it 'Roussel's master-piece', a fuller transcription of the various levels of experience than his earlier works: 'It all adds up', he writes, 'to a tumultuous impression of reality which keeps swiping at one like the sails of a windmill.' And it was perhaps the poem's inability to conceal its – or the body's – inner operations that was the source of Roussel's anxiety about the polishing of such verses, a task for which an entire lifetime would not suffice.

Oddly, then, this poem which is more or less all lining – if we treat the parentheses as so many layers of discourse encased by the outer surface of a single circumambient sentence – is also the least mediated, the work most open to the multiple contingencies of existence. In the context of his overall career, it is also like the final sentence of one of his *Textes-genèse*, in which all the story's opening words recur, subtly changed by only one letter and thus all given different meanings. It was surely for this reason that Roussel decided to conclude the volume, the last published during his lifetime, with *Mon Âme*, slightly altered and printed as *L'Âme de Victor Hugo*; though the words are almost the same as when it first appeared in *Le Gaulois* in 1897, its import is now wholly different. The complexity of the technique of *Nouvelles Impressions* can be seen as the last in the series of experiments with the word with which Roussel attempted to recover the 'sensation of moral sunlight' of *la gloire*, which he ended up having to attribute to Victor Hugo instead. Analogously, in *Nouvelles Impressions* the primary act of sublime revelation is reversed into its opposite, the scato-logical, and his sense of election transposed into a wholly generalized commonality. Roussel refers to himself only once in

*Nouvelles Impressions d'Afrique*, in the first line of the last canto:

> Rasant le Nil, je vois fuir deux rives couvertes
> De fleurs, d'ailes, d'éclairs, de riches plantes vertes . . .

Skimming over the surface of the Nile, I see recede two banks covered/ With flowers, wings, flashes of brightness, rich green plants . . .

As Raoul discovered his 'pays de rêves' on the Nile in the early fragment discussed in Chapter 4, so Roussel figures himself in the same location and at what can be seen as an equivalent moment of metamorphosis. But if Raoul found himself transformed into his gender opposite, the chanteuse Claude, Roussel's subjectivity is briefly glimpsed only to merge once more with the anonymous collective who dominate the poem:

> Dont une suffirait à vingt de nos salons
> (Doux salons où sitôt . . . etc

Of which one would suffice for twenty of our salons/ (Sweet salons where as soon . . . etc

The sense of disintegration noted by critics such as Leiris and Ashbery is thus another inversion: the sovereign I of *la gloire*, who believed he was about to illuminate the entire universe, undergoes a correspondingly absolute annihilation, his lyric self wholly diffused amid the poem's multiple, parallel lines of discourse, and the self-sufficient metaphors of which they are mainly comprised. It is as if the industrious work-force imagined in *Mon Âme* as eagerly carrying out the poet's instructions had overthrown the factory-owner and set up in business for themselves. Rather than irradiating all around him, Roussel resembles his Pascalian astronomer, who, in the list in Canto IV of people (and animals) getting used to things,

> Se fait aux profondeurs du grand vide céleste
> Où la lumière court sans jamais le franchir . . .

Gets used to the depths of the vast empty void/ Where light runs without ever exceeding its limits . . .

---

This image corresponds with the last of the illustrations commissioned by Roussel and executed by Henri A. Zo, the artist who had seven years earlier produced the diptych contrasting the first night of *Hernani* with the première of *L'Étoile au front*. This time, however, Zo had no idea from whom his assignment derived. Roussel employed a detective agency, Agence Goron, to act as an intermediary between himself and his chosen illustrator. Zo thus received a set of anonymous but extremely specific instructions for fifty-nine prints, but was not permitted, until after publication, to read the poem they were to embellish. Since Roussel had had previous dealings with Zo, and could, anyway, have looked up his address in the Paris telephone directory, it seems likely he made use of the Agence Goron as a means of preserving the work's neutral impersonality. 'These are not the pictures I would have made if I had known I was illustrating Raymond Roussel!' the artist later complained when he found out to what use his illustrations had been put. In a letter of 17 October 1932 he remonstrated with his secretive employer:

> Please allow me to tell you that I bitterly regret the fact you wanted this collaboration to be shrouded in such an impenetrable mystery . . . my illustrations . . . would have been more in harmony with your work if I'd been able to read the text, or had the honour of knowing the personality of the poet.

It was clearly the prospect of this sort of interaction that Roussel went to such lengths to avoid.

Zo also complained that Roussel's precise descriptions of the scenes required left him little room for manoeuvre – and hence his illustrations 'lack liberty, lack fantasy'. Roussel's directions to Zo were indeed unequivocal:

> 43. A parrot on its perch seeming to talk to a passer-by. No other people.

> 51. An elegantly dressed man pointing the barrel of a revolver to his temple, his finger on the trigger.

53. A portrait (unnamed) of Amerigo Vespucci. You might base the picture on that in the *Nouveau Larousse illustré*.*

59. A section of starry sky without any earthly landscape as if seen from some vantage point in space and giving the impression of infinity.

Each scene relates to a line that occurs on the preceding page of text in the Lemerre edition, but there is no knowing what principles of selection ultimately determined Roussel's choice of images. Possibly, as Leiris has argued, they construct a deliberate pattern in relation to certain themes, such as fire, ecstasy, fortune and so on, but they can also be viewed in the overall context of the poem as taking one step further its compulsion to embody the merely figurative, as if metaphors piled on metaphors, far from distancing one from actuality, lead to the heart of the real. Illustration number 33, for instance, relates to a comparison in Canto II between green beans falling from a plate and the slats of a Venetian blind being lowered at evening. Roussel stipulates the image be of a woman 'lowering the Venetian blind of a window. The blind is already half-closed, the slats almost horizontal.' Liberated from the other half of the comparison, the woman assumes an identity and independence of her own, though we remain at the same time subliminally aware of the sequence of parentheses that ultimately link this Mariana-figure to Napoleon's hat and overcoat, and the site of the Battle of the Pyramids. Indeed, the poignancy of the illustrations lies in their unawareness, not just of their own banality, but of the ties that bind them to the rest of the poem. For if on the one hand they appear free-standing and autonomous, on the other we know they have merely been thrown up by the exigencies of the poem's form. They again enact the illusion and defeat of subjectivity which underlies Roussel's relentlessly disruptive yet all-connecting poetics of suspension.

———

In his review of *Nouvelles Impressions d'Afrique* published in 1933, Salvador Dalí argued that the poems 'make us witness

---

* Zo's illustration is indeed very close to that in the dictionary suggested.

conflicts that are the most obscure, the most impenetrable that have ever been produced.' Though at enormous cost, the poem's form does succeed in containing these conflicts within its multiple parentheses, yet the warning delivered (too late) to Belshazzar, which Roussel chose as the topic for Zo's penultimate illustration – 'mene, mene, tekel, upharsin' (numbered, numbered, weighed, divided) – can seem, with hindsight, to point to his own impending dissolution. On 22 May 1930 Roussel's sister Germaine died at the age of fifty-six, after being operated upon for a brain tumour. Roussel's only remaining blood-relation was his nephew Michel Ney, who became his sole inheritor. Roussel continued to rent the second floor of the house on rue Quentin-Bauchart, but he began also to frequent a seedy residence at 75 rue Pigalle, attracted, according to Charlotte Dufrène, by the homosexuals and drug-users who inhabited the district. 'He had a second life which few people knew about,' reflected Michel Ney on his uncle in his interview of 1962. 'He had a double personality.' The sale of the villa at Neuilly was finally completed on 30 June 1931, and Roussel would use the money to finance the indulgences of his last years and the publication of his two final books, *Nouvelles Impressions d'Afrique* and *Comment j'ai écrit certains de mes livres*.

Germaine was buried in the Ney family tomb in the east section of Père Lachaise rather than with her relatives in the Roussel grave at Neuilly. The following autumn Roussel turned his mind to his own burial arrangements. He too shunned the company of his immediate family at Neuilly, and decided his remains should rest, like Germaine's, in Père Lachaise. In November 1931 he acquired in perpetuity a veritable catacomb containing thirty-two divisions which, in an addition to his will dated 22 May 1932, he made available to the Ney family and its various collateral branches. Roussel evidently hoped to unite himself in death with his ex-brother-in-law's illustrious Napoleonic connections; as yet none of Ney's descendants or relations have taken advantage of this offer, and Roussel remains alone in his vast mausoleum.

He also entered into negotiations with a firm specializing in funerary statuary for a monument to adorn his tomb. Roussel wanted this to consist of a sculpture of himself based on the picture taken in Milan in 1896, when he was nineteen and in the midst of composing *La Doublure*. The statue was to be posed before serried ranks of books in a well-stocked library, and an artist produced a couple of designs for his approval. Roussel died, perhaps fortunately, before this grandiose tribute to his *gloire* could be executed, and his grave is marked by a large coffin-shaped slab bearing the puzzling legend FAMILLE R. ROUSSEL in relief, and inscribed in smaller letters on one of its many side panels with his full name and dates.*

———

Roussel also set about assembling materials for his final volume of miscellaneous writings, *Comment j'ai écrit certains de mes livres*. The title essay was delivered to Lemerre on 16 April 1932, on the strict understanding it was to be kept secret until the whole collection appeared posthumously. Roussel decided to include in this book a range of material that he felt pertinent to a full understanding of his literary career. It seems, however, that he was in no mood to delve into his own archive in search of copies of texts that he wanted reprinted; hence Lemerre – no doubt on Roussel's instruction – commissioned the versatile Agence Goron to retrieve copies of four items that appeared in *Le Gaulois du Dimanche* between 1904 and 1908: 'Nanon', 'Une Page du Folk-lore Breton', 'L'Inconsolable' and *Têtes de Carton du Carnaval de Nice*. Roussel's publishers would have had less difficulty obtaining a copy-text for *Chiquenaude*, for thirty-two years on this *plaquette* had still not sold out. Eugène Vallée himself purchased Pierre Janet's *De l'angoisse à l'extase*, from which he copied out the relevant pages on Martial from Volume I, but for some reason omitted Janet's subsequent discussion of Roussel's case in other parts of the work. And, as further evidence of the exceptional nature of his gifts, Roussel chose to reprint a number of documents relating to his recent discovery of 'La Formule Raymond-

---

* Roussel's grave is in the 89th division, near the corner formed by avenue Circulaire and avenue Carette. It is not far from that of Oscar Wilde. A map and directions explaining the easiest way of locating it are included in BZ, p. 159.

Roussel', a means of deploying knight and bishop that infallibly leads to checkmate.

The book also allows us to contrast the origins and the conclusion of the workings of the *procédé*. Taken together, and in the context of his sudden interest in chess, Roussel's *Textes-genèse* (of which he includes seventeen) come to seem like a series of classic openings, and his *Documents pour servir de canevas* as six swift, ruthless endgames.

Roussel seems to have been uncertain about whether or not to publish his final prose work, particularly its introductory section entitled *À la Havane*. In 'Comment j'ai écrit . . .' he alludes specifically to this episode, which was, he explains, composed with the aid of the *procédé* and typeset by Lemerre's printers, whose address he then gives in the hope, one imagines, that a *roussellâtre* might rescue it from oblivion. A footnote, however, informs us that this fragment has since been destroyed, and in a letter of 15 January 1932 to Vallée which was inadvertently used as a preface to the six documents published in the volume, Roussel declares:

> If I die before I finish this work, and someone wants to publish it even in its incomplete state, I would like the opening suppressed so it begins with the PREMIER DOCUMENT; the initials should be replaced by names arrived at by completing the blanks, and this overall title should be used: *Documents pour servir de canevas.*

The proofs of *À la Havane* were eventually unearthed by Ashbery in the course of his Roussel researches, and published in *L'Arc* in 1962. Roussel probably resolved to exclude it because none of the six documents really connect with the frame this introductory episode establishes. It concerns a set of twins passionately devoted to each other, A . . . and his sister M . . ., who live in Havana. A . . . is sickly, for M . . . absorbed 'many vital essences' in their mother's womb, much to her brother's detriment. Nevertheless, we are given two elaborate examples of A . . .'s courage and authority as a schoolboy, and when he dies at the age of twenty his sister resolves to commemorate his short life by founding a club in honour of A . . .'s ardent love of all things European. Each member is to furnish a historical episode illustrating the superiority of the Old World to the New, and M . . . eventually receives 'a sheaf of arguments for her cause: the thirty documents which follow'.

But the six recessive narratives published in *Comment j'ai écrit* . . . bear little or no relation to this project: though for the most part set in Europe, they could not be said to demonstrate its superiority to America, which is barely mentioned, and a number involve wholly fictitious countries such as Eisnark or Belotina. All they prove is the infinite powers of self-complication inherent in Roussel's conception of literature. In these final fictions he seems to be attempting to unite the narrative fecundity of his *procédé*-inspired novels with the structured, parenthetical layering of *Nouvelles Impressions d'Afrique*. The first document, for instance, contains nine interconnected story-lines enclosed within each other: the initial narrative, which features a young peasant girl Eda, evicted from her home for spurning the advances of a rich landowning lord, slides into a second about a young vagabond, Romé, who falls in love with Eda while watching her sleep, but flees for fear of being disappointed by her eyes when she wakes up, taking with him a lock of her hair and three bluebells; to save himself from aimless despair he joins a recently founded religious order, the Grey Crosses, whose origins in a miraculous tale about Mary Magdalen are then recounted . . . The document proceeds through six further narrative strata and then begins its gradational return to Romé's love for Eda and the churlish lord of the opening sentence. Romé is murdered by the ex-lover of one of his converts, and with his dying words avows his love of Eda to his companion, Fircine, who in turn delivers the lock of hair and bluebells to Eda as proof of his devotion. When Lord de Courty hears of this he is ashamed to compare his brutish lust for Eda with Romé's pure affection, and allows her to reoccupy the cottage from which he had driven her.

The *Documents* thus radically accelerate and intensify the story-within-a-story technique of *Locus Solus*, and structurally come to resemble the poem from whose lines Roussel garnered elements for these new narratives. His prose style thoughout is so terse that each *Document*, though only a few pages long, appears to contain enough storylines for a three-decker nine-teenth-century novel. We should remember, however, that Roussel presents them as unfinished, as mere outlines to be developed further, and perhaps they are best treated as barely opened Japanese flowers that would eventually have expanded to almost unimaginable dimensions; had Roussel subjected the existing *Documents* to his famous 'mise au point' (polishing) and completed the remaining twenty-four, he would have been facing a gargantuan bill from Lemerre for some five or ten volumes – a bill he would by then have had no means of paying.

On the other hand, there can seem something powerfully expressive in the steady accumulations of savagely compressed, self-enclosing stories that make up each *Document*. For one can gaze through them, rather as through the lens set in the pen-holder of 'La Vue' or the tiny opera-glasses described in 'Comment j'ai écrit . . .', into impossibly vast regions of narrative stretching in all directions, sublimely beyond the scope of aesthetic proportion or reason. Their concision becomes itself a way of embodying the endless diversity of existence, and this concision can be seen as the inverted double of the early Roussel's obsession with exhaustively minute description: in the end their brevity creates an awareness similar to that created by the prolix precisions of *La Doublure*, *La Vue*, *La Seine* and *Les Noces*, of the immeasurability of the world, of how narrative, like descriptive, relations can never finally be said to end anywhere.

———

Roussel may himself have felt daunted by the dimensions of his final project. The *Documents* were begun in 1929 while Roussel was still working on the proofs of *Nouvelles Impressions d'Afrique*, and their eventual abandonment in fact signalled the end of his creative life. During his remaining years in Paris he composed only his literary testament and a couple of newspaper articles published in early 1933, in which he extravagantly lauded the work of various contemporary writers who have since sunk without trace, and attacked the playwright Henry Bataille (who had been dead ten years), whose every line,

Roussel forthrightly declared, 'n'est que de la boursouflure' (is mere piffle).

Roussel never formally renounced writing, and his note of 15 January 1932 to Lemerre suggests he had hopes of one day fleshing out his *Documents*: 'If I die before I finish this work . . .' He spent the rest of the year, however, dividing his time between playing chess and taking barbiturates. 'In 1932 I took up chess,' he explains in a preface in *Comment j'ai écrit . . .* to the 'Formule Raymond-Roussel': 'At the end of three and a half months I discovered the following means of achieving the extremely difficult checkmate with bishop and knight.' During this period Roussel took lessons from a teacher called Romih at the Café de la Régence at the Palais-Royal; there he met the chess master Tartakower, who wrote up Roussel's formula in the November issue of *L'Échiquier*, and in the following month's issue published his further reflections on Roussel's discovery. Roussel was obviously keen that Tartakower establish connections between his technique as a chess-player and his technique as a writer, for a footnote makes links between the concision of his formula and that of his literary style. In yet another article, which appeared in the January/February 1933 number of *Les Cahiers de l'Échiquier français* (edited at the time by François le Lionnais, who would co-found the Oulipo movement in 1960), Tartakower places Roussel in the context of a tradition of writers interested in chess, including Alexandre Dumas, Diderot, Rousseau, Voltaire and Poe:

> The chess world should celebrate the fine acquisition of the great Surrealist writer, Raymond Roussel, who, with his discovery of a simple formula for achieving the extremely complicated checkmate with bishop and knight, reveals himself also a great thinker in chess.

It was while pondering a move at the Café de la Régence that he was observed, but not approached, by his admirer Marcel Duchamp, who would likewise abandon art for chess, or at least claim to do so. 'He seemed very "strait-laced", high collar, dressed in black, very very Avenue du Bois,' Duchamp later recalled in an interview. For the nihilist, post-modernist Duchamp, chess would become a typically dandyish means of revealing the futility of aesthetic endeavour; for his more naïve precursor, on the other hand, it was clearly yet another means of attempting to recover his early conviction of artistic power. It both appealed to his 'esprit terriblement logique' (the phrase is Michel Ney's) and won him public admiration and renown. Yet after the discovery of his *formule* he appears to have lost interest in the game, and – though this may seem rather fancifully Duchampian – one cannot help wondering if his sudden enthusiasm for *échecs* wasn't an attempt to act out a buried pun: he had just composed 'Comment j'ai écrit . . .', in which he relates the successive *échecs* (failures) of all his books and plays, beginning with *La Doublure*, which is itself predicated on a dramatic *échec*, Gaspard's inability to resheathe his sword. Further, 'Comment j'ai écrit . . .' opens with a discussion of 'Parmi les Noirs', which is presented as the origin of the *procédé*, and is based on the interaction of black and white. To have his name immortalized in a *procédé* relating to *échecs* must have at least gratified Roussel's love of symmetry, and it seems no coincidence, either, that the formula he devised, within a year of his own death, was a method for achieving checkmate with a minimum number of pieces left on the board.*

———

Tartakower introduces Roussel in his third article as a 'great Surrealist writer'. *Nouvelles Impressions d'Afrique* went on sale in November 1932, accompanied by a *cahier de critiques* containing some seventy-five responses to his work, of which only about ten derived from writers associated with the Surrealist movement, yet Roussel seems to have accepted by this stage that it was they who were most likely to achieve for him the 'little posthumous fame' that he speaks of in the last paragraph of 'Comment j'ai écrit . . .' Certainly it was only the Surrealists who responded positively to the publication of Roussel's final poem. On receiving a dedicated copy Robert Desnos wrote back to Roussel:

* It is perhaps worth pointing out that the thirty-two divisions of Roussel's tomb may also be a cryptic allusion to the thirty-two squares of half a chessboard.

My stupefaction in the face of such a regeneration of poetry cannot really be called astonishment. My admiration for you had prepared me for such a disconcerting work . . . These are poems which are made more for eternity than for popularity.

In another letter, of 5 December, he assured Roussel that it was one of the few important books published during the last twenty years. Salvador Dalí was equally enthusiastic. He discusses Roussel's poem in characteristically frantic language in the sixth issue of *Surréalisme au Service de la Révolution*, published on 15 May 1933:

This, of all the books of our era, is the most 'ungraspably poetic', and consequently the one which contains most for the future.

He goes on to argue that Roussel's startling conjunctions prove the irresistible power of the irrational, and reflect his own pursuit of a 'paranoiac' art. Dalí even commends Roussel's decision to have the book illustrated by Zo:

It is by systematic and endlessly repeated use of this associative mechanism, designed to make 'valuable' a content which is, with regard to its choice of compound elements, obsessive and delirious, that *Nouvelles Impressions d'Afrique* presents itself to us as a dreamed journey of new paranoiac phenomena.

The choice of illustrations testifies yet again to the genius of Raymond Roussel.

And Raymond Queneau (the other co-founder, with Le Lionnais, of Oulipo) published in the January 1933 issue of *La Critique Sociale* a more general celebration of Roussel's imagination, 'which unites the delirium of the mathematician with the reason of the poet'. Indeed, Queneau claims almost divine powers for Roussel, who, he argues, 'creates works with a power, an originality, a verve to which, hitherto, God the Father believed he had exclusive rights.'

Unsurprisingly, *Nouvelles Impressions d'Afrique* excited no such rhapsodies in the popular press. Roussel attempted to boost interest with a publicity article he had placed in three papers in early December in which he claimed that, ten years after the scandal of the theatrical production of *Locus Solus*, his genius was at last widely recognized:

Today, the greatest authors and the greatest critics have both proclaimed the genius – yet a genius powerfully tempered by classicism – of Raymond Roussel, and all the young literati consider his monumental œuvre as an inexhaustible well at which entire generations of writers will drink often and deeply.

He chose, bizarrely, to have this article illustrated with a picture of himself painted by Madeleine Lemaire when he was about four, as if readers were to discern the predestined powers of the adult artist in the features of the child. This final act of self-promotion prompted a couple of spoofs and sneers about 'rails en mou de veau', but otherwise newspapers and general public alike responded to *Nouvelles Impressions d'Afrique* very much as they had to the publication of *La Doublure* thirty-five years earlier, by ignoring it altogether.

So it was to the Surrealists that Roussel turned when considering how best to ensure his legacy to the future. On 20 January 1933 he deposited with his lawyer the testament in which he asks that copies of his two posthumous works, *Comment j'ai écrit . . .* and *Documents pour servir de canevas* (which for reasons of economy, Lemerre ended up printing as one) be sent to his Surrealist supporters, as well as a number of other writers such as Gide and Élie Richard who had championed his work. He took steps to have a copy of the title essay dispatched to the group in case the original disappeared, though eventually neither letter nor manuscript were posted. *Faute de mieux*, Roussel at last consented to be aligned with a movement he had never been interested in or understood, but whose members had consistently – and often physically – defended his work, and had praised his genius in terms even Roussel considered sufficiently superlative.

Michel Leiris was the last person associated with the group to visit Roussel before his departure for Palermo in June 1933. He had just returned from his first ethnographic expedition to

Africa, to which Roussel, despite the rapidly deteriorating state of his finances, had handsomely contributed. Armed with his own *impressions d'Afrique*, Leiris returned in February 1933 and left this description of his final encounter with Roussel. He had shaved his moustache, but looked, as always, 'handsome and elegant, but a bit heavier, somewhat slumped, and he spoke as if from a great distance':

> He had not seen me for about two years, and he asked a long series of questions about my parents and my family relations. A melancholy reflection (with a smile) on life: 'It goes faster and faster!' After I had taken my leave, he accompanied me into the anteroom, and we stood talking for a long time (this was one of his customs – out of timidity? fear of looking as if he were showing you the door? fear of finding himself alone? – he would keep you with him long after saying goodbye). During the same visit, when I asked him if he was still writing, he replied, '*C'est tellement difficile!*'

━━━━━

Roussel left Paris for Palermo in a chauffeur-driven car with Charlotte Dufrène on 1 June 1933. On arrival several days later, they checked in at the Grande Albergo e delle Palme, where Richard Wagner – with whom Roussel compares himself in *De l'angoisse à l'extase*, and who features in one of the bottle-imp episodes in *Locus Solus* – had composed *Parsival* just over fifty years earlier. It was assumed they were lover and mistress, for they occupied adjoining rooms, connected by an internal door. During his stay Roussel ate only one meal a day, which he had served in his room at lunchtime. In the afternoons he would be assisted by his hotel valet, Orlando, and his chauffeur (who has not been identified) into the back seat of his car and have himself driven at random through the streets of Palermo. In the evenings he would swallow quantities of one of nine kinds of barbiturate in the hope of recovering the euphoria of his youth.

In the middle of the month Roussel persuaded Dufrène to return to Paris to obtain fresh supplies of drugs, which she smuggled into the country under the mattress of her sleeping-car couchette. His first overdose occurred while she was away. On 16 June the hotel doctor, Michele Lombardo, was summoned to Roussel's room: he found him completely unconscious, surrounded by assorted empty bottles of pills. Lombardo performed a blood-letting and injected Roussel with glucose. By the time of Dufrène's return a few days later, he had wholly recovered, but refused to abandon his nightly intoxications. He would grow angry whenever she attempted to persuade him to moderate his intake: 'Cut, cut, but give me my drug!' he expostulated during a period of privation, 'meaning by that', Dufrène explained to Leiris, 'that he would rather have his arms and legs cut off than be deprived of his barbiturates.' Lombardo advised her to keep a record of the drugs and quantities consumed by Roussel, and the effects he experienced. Her catalogue was confiscated by the police after Roussel's death and preserved with their records. Soneryl emerges as Roussel's drug of choice, regularly procuring him 'formidable euphorie', 'bonne euphorie' and 'euphorie très grande'. Neurinase inspired on one occasion 'euphorie toute la journée', but it was after emptying a bottle of this particular barbiturate that Roussel attacked himself with a razor on the night of 1 July. That afternoon, on returning from his outing in the car, Roussel offered his hotel valet a hundred francs to slit his wrists for him. Horrified, Orlando refused, but next morning found Roussel bleeding in his bath, having himself opened the veins in his left wrist, and clumsily hacked at his throat and other parts of his body. 'How easy it is to open one's veins,' he exclaimed when the valet arrived in response to Roussel's call for help: 'It's nothing at all.' Doctor Lombardo dressed these self-inflicted wounds, and stitched up the gash in Roussel's lower arm. He also added his pleas to those of Charlotte Dufrène that Roussel seek treatment for his addiction, and eventually he was persuaded to enrol in the Binswanger detoxification clinic in Kreutzlingen. He and Dufrène were to leave for Switzerland on 16 July.

━━━━━

It is not clear, and will never be known, whether Roussel deliberately planned to kill himself three days before their agreed date of departure. During the previous weeks he seems, like Cleopatra, to have 'pursued conclusions infinite/Of easy ways to die'. He had Dufrène write to a servant at rue Quentin-Bauchart asking him to send on a certain box containing a revolver, perhaps one of those with which Roussel had previously won numerous pistol-shooting prizes. He also told her he would not have the courage of the 'suicide riche' of *Nouvelles Impressions d'Afrique*, and she would have to pull the trigger. Dufrène, like Orlando, refused, despite the ever-larger sums with which he offered to reward her. Money had failed to persuade the public to confer on his work the acclaim that might have made his life bearable, and it now failed in his irresolute search for a means of ending his existence.

On the afternoon of the 13th Roussel returned from his drive in a state of complete exhaustion. Orlando and the chauffeur had to carry him from the car to the lift, from the lift to his room. He was suffering from lack of food and from long-term narcotics poisoning. That evening Palermo was celebrating on two accounts: it was the festival of Santa Rosalia, and Mussolini – to whom Roussel had recently sent a copy of *Nouvelles Impressions d'Afrique* – had decreed that the whole of Italy should commemorate the completion of a successful transatlantic crossing by a squadron of his burgeoning air force. From seven in the evening until late at night a vast crowd surged through the streets around Roussel's hotel, and the sky was ablaze with fireworks. It is tempting to imagine that the pandemonium may have reminded him of the flames, the noise and the turbulent crowds of *Mon Âme*:

> Mais voilà que, de la campagne,
> De tous côtés mon peuple accourt,
> Venant des champs, de la montagne,
> Au bruit du canon qui rend sourd.
>
> Chacun, en voyant que je gagne
> Le gouffre, laisse son labour
> Ou ses troupeaux – et m'accompagne,
> Augmentant la foule alentour.

(lines 153–60)

But look, from the country,/ From all sides, how my people flock,/
Coming from the fields, from the mountains,/ At the ear-splitting
sound of the cannon.

Each one, on seeing me reach/ The gulf, leaves his work/ Or his herds
– and accompanies me/ Swelling the crowd all around.

Roussel had in prospect only three more nights of the artificial
exaltation to which his early visions had ultimately led. The
previous evening he had swallowed a bottle of Veriane and
enjoyed only a partial sleep and a 'disordered euphoria'. He had
already informed Charlotte Dufrène of his intention to take the
more effective Soneryl that evening, which she duly noted down
in advance in her diary of Roussel's drug use. During his states
of intoxication Roussel had developed a fear of falling out of
bed, and accordingly had his mattress laid on the floor; on this
particular night it was positioned against the internal door that
connected his room with that of Dufrène. At around eleven
o'clock, after the festivities had subsided, she inquired through
the partition if Roussel was in pain, but he brusquely responded
that she was not to worry herself.

The inquest decided that Roussel died between midnight and
2 a.m. His body was not discovered until eleven the following
morning. The Italian authorities were eager to file their report
as soon as possible, so the matter could be hushed up: suicide,
even by a neurasthenic Frenchman, was seen as an affront to
the brave new world of Mussolini's Italy. The valet, Orlando,
later recalled that Roussel had ejaculated, perhaps during his
death throes, like the hanged man of *Nouvelles Impressions
d'Afrique*, who 'pendant l'ivresse, avant le serrement complet'
(during the intoxication, before complete constriction) has no
need of an aphrodisiac. He confided this detail to the Sicilian
novelist Leonardo Sciascia, whose 1971 article, 'Atti relativi alla
morte di Raymond Roussel,' reproduces the coroner's and police
reports and the depositions of the various witnesses. Perhaps to
help extricate herself from a potentially difficult situation,
Dufrène rather exaggerated her employer's reputation in his
home country, informing the police that 'in France he is considered a genius'. The investigators may have been impressed,
but in their haste failed to connect the pale, scarred corpse of

the writer with twelve volumes of a book entitled *Locus Solus* which they found in his room, and in their report attributed to one Armand Roussel.

They also failed to include Roussel's chauffeur among those required to testify at the inquest. He was staying at a nearby hotel, and seems to have disappeared as soon as he heard of Roussel's death. Michel Ney later claimed that Roussel's driver had immediately returned to Paris and tried to blackmail him, without of course disclosing details of the threatened revelations. The authorities were surely right, however, to conclude that 'in this affair any responsibility of a third party can be excluded'. Although unable or unwilling to take his own life deliberately, Roussel was aware when he left Paris that he was unlikely to return alive. He had resigned from the various clubs to which he belonged, and willed certain of his books to the Bibliothèque Nationale. On 9 March he had left with his lawyer an envelope to be opened immediately after his death containing the following instructions:

I absolutely insist that a long incision is made in the vein of my wrist so there is no risk of my being buried alive.

There was to be no danger of a living inhumation, since Roussel was not buried in his vast tomb until twelve days after his decease. His body was embalmed and transported back to Paris, where his funeral service was held on 26 July. One might picture him in a state of suspense like that of the white-clad rambler dropping his pebble into the well in Zo's fifty-second illustration, which follows that of the rich suicide:

A rambler, with his arm raised and his fingers open, having just dropped a pebble (which is still visible) down a well, seems to cock an ear as if to listen for the splash (no other people).

Or perhaps Roussel's death might be seen, as Leiris suggests in his 1939 essay on *Nouvelles Impressions d'Afrique*, as at last consummating the abiding vision of his solitary life:

Voluntary death: wall of snow and of fire, fermata, ultimate ecstasy, unique means of savouring – in an instant – *la gloire*.

# A Little Posthumous Fame

In his obituary published in the September 1933 issue of *La Nouvelle Revue Française*, Jean Cocteau recalled asking Roussel if *Impressions d'Afrique* harboured some private meaning or code. 'I will explain myself after my death,' he peremptorily replied. Roussel's novels and plays are full of astounding testaments and communications from beyond the grave that prefigure the disclosures of 'Comment j'ai écrit . . .', which first appeared – rather fittingly – on 1 April 1935. The essay, although no hoax, seems to invite Roussel's admirers to turn his writings inside out in the vain hope of discovering ever deeper – or at least less arbitrary – patterns of significance. The revelation of the *procédé* can also be seen as Roussel's final act of doubling, for it imposes upon the reader Roussel's personal obsession with duality: by alerting us to the existence of source texts underlying each prose narrative, Roussel induces an uncanny, bicameral awareness of a submerged, alternative linguistic world we can neither drag to the surface nor simply ignore. Every word comes to seem potentially a pun, a clue to the secret web of double entendres that lie buried within each episode. However seemingly innocent the surface narrative, we become conscious it is all the time subliminally haunted by some unfathomably distant, parallel system of language.

Although the original phrases Roussel inverts or deforms and the achieved stories to which they give rise have certain sounds or words in common, they are not otherwise connected. It is the disjunction between these realms which creates what Ashbery has called 'the "stereo" effect' of Roussel's prose: 'we are following him on one level and almost but not entirely missing him on another, a place where secrets remain secret.' Characteristically, the essay itself falls into two halves, as if defying us to discover links between the workings of the *procédé* and the autobiographical sections that follow. Overall, the essay provides no means of mediating between the triumphant tale of Roussel's artistic development and the 'hostile incomprehension' that greeted his every work. Only when pretending to be someone else altogether, while performing his famous impersonations, did he achieve the acceptance he yearned for.

As Michel Leiris pointed out in his essay introducing 'Comment j'ai écrit...' in *La Nouvelle Revue Française*, two writers connected to the Surrealist movement, Roger Vitrac and Jean Ferry, had both alluded in essays written before the publication of 'Comment j'ai écrit...' to the significant role played by puns in the imaginative logic of Roussel's prose. Reciprocally, Roussel seems to have felt that it was writers belonging to the Surrealist group who were most likely – at least in the immediate future – to exploit his method fruitfully; of the twenty-two writers mentioned in his testament, nearly all were members – or at one time had been members – of Breton's revolutionary cadre. In his 1924 *Manifeste du Surréalisme* Breton had co-opted Roussel into his fledgeling movement by declaring him 'a Surrealist as a storyteller', and in his 1937 lecture that was eventually to preface the entries in his *Anthologie de l'humour noir* he linked Roussel with his other favourite proto-Surrealist: 'Roussel,' Breton declared, 'along with Lautréamont, is the greatest hypnotist of modern times.' The anthology did not, in the event, appear until 1940, and did not then include any extracts from Roussel's œuvre: Michel Ney, in the role of Roussel's literary executor, had decided that his uncle's ill-fated literary career had brought the family into enough disrepute, and he denied Breton permission to reprint the passages he had selected from *Impressions d'Afrique*, *La Poussière de soleils* and *Nouvelles Impressions d'Afrique*. They were, however, incorporated into the third edition of 1966, by which time Roussel's complete works had been republished by Jean-Jacques Pauvert, and Ney had been persuaded that the black sheep of his family was a literary genius (and a potential source of income) rather than a mere embarrassment.

━━━━━

It seems likely that Roussel, ever the positivist, genuinely hoped subsequent writers would employ the *procédé* just as he had revealed it, as if it were a discovery equivalent to the combustion engine or penicillin. Paradoxically, the appeal of Roussel's work to the writers and artists who have been inspired by him has been its complete originality, the extent to which, beyond the pale itself, it has licensed their own experiments. Marcel Duchamp has perhaps expressed the aesthetic excitement to be derived from Roussel's writings most eloquently:

> Roussel was another great enthusiasm of mine in the early days. The reason I admired him was because he produced something I had never seen. That is the thing that brings admiration from my innermost being – something completely independent – nothing to do with great names or influences. Apollinaire first showed Roussel's work to me. It was poetry . . .

In an interview with Pierre Cabanne conducted in 1966, Duchamp explained in greater detail why he felt it was Roussel, more than any other artist, who had decisively liberated him from the burdens of tradition. 'What mattered', Duchamp suggested, 'was an attitude, more than an influence':

> That man [Roussel] had done something which really had Rimbaud's revolutionary aspect to it, a secession. It was no longer a question of Symbolism, or even of Mallarmé – Roussel knew nothing of all that . . . But he gave me the idea that I too could try something in the sense of which we were speaking; or rather anti-sense . . .

At the time of the gestation of his *Large Glass* (1912–22), Duchamp could have known nothing of the *procédé*, but he shared with Roussel not only an interest in the precise description of obscure mechanisms, most fully explored in his 'Notes' on the *Large Glass*, but also in the aesthetic possibilities of the pun. Indeed, Duchamp might be said 'to have found his way' through word pairings that are essentially similar to Roussel's: Rrose Sélavy ('Eros, c'est la vie', appropriated from Desnos), L.H.O.O.Q. ('Elle a chaud au cul', at the bottom of a picture of the Mona Lisa), Anemic cinema, and all his other *morceaux moisis* are vital catalysts in the Duchampian project of undermining all certainties, just as his ready-mades are analogous to what Foucault described as the 'found' or 'ready-made language' inherent in Roussel's use of the *procédé*. Foucault's summary of the overall effect of Roussel's œuvre might easily be transferred to that of Duchamp:

> His work as a whole . . . systematically imposes a formless anxiety, diverging and yet centrifugal, directed not towards the most withheld secrets but towards the imitation and transmutation of the most visible forms: each word at the same time energized and drained, filled and emptied by the possibility of there being yet another meaning, this one or that one, or neither one nor the other, but a third, or none.

Historically, Roussel and Duchamp can both be placed in the tradition of the extreme dandy whose immaculate surfaces teasingly confound our yearning for interiority or transcendence. One suspects, on the other hand, that Duchamp's eagerness to acknowledge Roussel as a precursor owes more to his sense of their being complementary opposites; for, once viewed through the pure lens of Duchampian irony, Roussel's inviolable naïvety emerges as the polar antithesis to Duchamp's equally inviolable sophistication. Intriguingly, although both were championed by Breton, in their radically different ways both Roussel and Duchamp fought to preserve their distance from the Surrealist movement; and if Roussel found their productions 'un peu obscur', Duchamp might be said to have found their work not obscure enough.

Prompted by Leiris, Roussel had in fact dabbled a little in the avant-garde art market of the mid-1920s. In 1924 he bought a small still life by André Masson, attracted, he told his friend, by its 'transparency'. Later the same year he acquired a canvas by Joan Miró, and then in 1926 attended the first important exhibition of the work of Max Ernst. Ernst happened to be in the gallery himself that afternoon, and Roussel, taking him for an employee, inquired into the artist's methods:

> Among other questions, the visitor asked – all the time apologizing for his curiosity – if the painter did not make

use of certain particular technical methods to create his works . . . He [i.e. Ernst – the account is written in the third person] was more than happy to explain to him the 'procedures' of his painting. Then the 'client', turning to the gallery secretary, purchased *Le rossignol chinois*, gave his name and address, and left. It was Raymond Roussel.

It would, however, be a mistake to deduce from these forays into modernism that Roussel had any significant interest in experimental art of the early twentieth century; though his work may herald, as Duchamp suggested, a revolutionary 'secession' from the past, Roussel's 'Notes prises sur les œuvrages de divers écrivains'* suggest that his aesthetic preferences were stubbornly conservative. In an interview of 1986 Leiris recalls asking him why he refused to switch publishers:

> I know that Gallimard would willingly have published him. 'Why do you remain with Lemerre; Lemerre is not the publishing house for you, but for the likes of François Coppée [a thumpingly ordinary Parnassian]'. Then Roussel looked at me, and I saw him go pale, his face froze and hollows appeared in his cheeks, as he replied, 'But . . . François Coppée is a very great poet.'

Roussel's dubious taste – like his naïvety – has always been part of his attraction to radicals like Duchamp, and can even be seen to have resulted in effects curiously similar to those consciously engineered by the avant-garde. Zo's illustrations for *Nouvelles Impressions d'Afrique*, for instance, are disquieting in a manner that oddly resembles Ernst's more or less contemporaneous collage novels, such as *La Femme 100 têtes* (1929) or *Une Semaine de Bonté* (1933), created from cut-ups of nineteenth-century engravings. It was the unintentionally subversive aspect of Zo's pictures which most appealed to Robbe-Grillet, who at

---

* Of the thirty-nine contemporary authors whose work Roussel ponders, only Paul Valéry and Michel Leiris could be considered innovative. Roussel's critical comments throughout are strikingly unilluminating: his entry on Valéry, for instance, consists of copious quotations and the terse observation that Valéry has written 'several admirable sonnets' (FR, cat. no. 4508, f. 149v).

one time planned to write a novel based on them; in the 1977 Roussel special issue of *L'Arc* he reflects on this aborted project:

> the engravings of Zo have always fascinated me by their total nullity, their flagrant inutility and, I should say, even by their emptiness: not only a rare and complete absence of pictorial interest, but also a remarkable anecdotal poverty, desired, it seems, by Roussel.

And from a similar perspective, Ashbery has suggested that the 'militant banality' of the scenes and Zo's pedestrian draughtsmanship significantly contribute to the poem's 'mysteries of construction'.

In the years immediately following Roussel's death, it was Leiris who was the principal keeper of the Roussel flame. The essays he published in 1935, 1936 and 1939 skilfully present Roussel as both an extraordinary person and a major writer. It was during this period also that Roussel's influence on Leiris's own work begins to become apparent, as for instance in a text such as *Glossaire, j'y serre les gloses* (1939), a catalogue of words defined in surreally punning terms:

> CIEL – si elle? où elle? ré-elle ou irré-elle? (SKY – if she? where she? re-al or unre-al?)
> MALHEUR – mâle heurt? (UNHAPPINESS – man knocks into something?)

Leiris had been compiling this *glossaire* for many years; indeed, he sent several early examples to Roussel, and was gratified when the older writer reported himself greatly 'struck' by them. 'The method evolved', to borrow a phrase from 'Comment j'ai écrit . . .', and soon came to underpin Leiris's entire conception of literature, as is perhaps most apparent in his four-volume autobiography, written over almost three decades, and published under the collective title *La règle du jeu*. In *Biffures*, for example, the first of these volumes, Leiris exhaustively explains his own development in relation to *procédé*-style misunderstandings of words that, as in Roussel's fiction and plays, fuse the ordinary and the irrational. One of his first examples concerns a chant sung by his older brother – 'Blaise qui partait,/ En guerre s'en

allait' (Blaise who was leaving,/ Was going off to war) – but this
is not what the young child hears:

> Between his lips and my ears, the second line changed, and
> what reached me, the problem I had to unravel, was: 'Blaise
> qui partait/ En berçant la laisse' (Blaise who was leaving/
> Rocking the leash). A fragment of an old-fashioned,
> ordinary song from the *Dragons de Villars* was thus
> transformed by my mishearing into a mystery I had
> somehow to solve.

These 'fiches' (slips), as Leiris calls them, are treated as clues to
his inner workings and a means of plotting his early life. 'It was
a question,' he explained in an interview of 1986, 'as for
Roussel, of "equations of facts" which I was seeking to
resolve . . . Just as he was obliged to use the elements furnished
by his word games, so I established as a rule that, when I had
a slip, I should never just put it to one side.'

*Biffures* appeared in 1948, the same year in which *Cahiers de
la Pléiade* published essays by Jean Ferry and André Breton on
Roussel's second play. Both articles were reprinted five years
later in the first of Ferry's three book-length studies of Roussel's
work. Taken together, these two pieces can be seen as
dramatizing the very particular problems posed to criticism by
Roussel's writings. Jean Ferry, one of Roussel's most dedicated
advocates, offers an accurate, indeed meticulous, account of the
play, but makes no attempt to justify it in terms beyond those
set out by Roussel himself.\* Breton, by contrast, clearly dissatis-
fied with the pure self-referentiality of the *procédé*, claimed to
have discovered within the play's tableaux a series of references
to the arcana of alchemy; his essay argues that *La Poussière de
soleils* furnishes 'the rudiments necessary for undertaking what

---

\* The bulk of *Une étude sur Raymond Roussel* consists of a line-by-line
explication of Canto II of *Nouvelles Impressions*. In *Une autre étude sur
Raymond Roussel* (1964) he offers a similarly detailed exegesis of Cantos I,
III and IV of the poem, and in his third book on Roussel, *L'Afrique des
impressions* (Paris: Jean-Jacques Pauvert, 1967), he explains in great detail,
and often with the aid of illustrations, the technical aspects of the various
machines and performances presented in *Impressions d'Afrique*.

the alchemists mean by the Great Work'. If, on the one hand, Roussel's œuvre is so rigorously constructed it reduces all comment to mere paraphrase, on the other it can appear like a tantalizing enigma waiting to be deciphered by the discovery of some extra-literary purpose or motivation. It is on this paradox that Louis Aragon's discussion of Roussel comes to rest in *Je n'ai jamais appris à écrire, ou les Incipit*:

> For me, Roussel remains the man of the great secret. But this secret is one that no one will ever pierce.

The attraction of Roussel to French writers who came of age in the 1950s and 1960s was markedly different from that which he had to the generation that embraced Surrealism. Both Michel Butor and Alain Robbe-Grillet, for instance, are intrigued not so much by the marvels thrown up in the course of Roussel's narratives, as by the repetitiveness inherent in his methods and the precision, or 'demented acuity', to borrow Robbe-Grillet's phrase, of his descriptive techniques. The *nouveaux romanciers* found in Roussel's neutral, exhaustively accurate style a prefiguration of their own obsessive denotations of the objective world. As previously mentioned, *La Vue* was considered by Robbe-Grillet a crucial influence on his second novel, *Le Voyeur* (1955). It was the anti-metaphysical implications of Roussel's aesthetic procedures that most struck the young novelist:

> To borrow one of the favourite expressions of academic literary criticism, Roussel doesn't seem to have 'anything to say'. No transcendency, no humanist 'going beyond' can be imputed to the series of objects, exploits and events which, at first sight, make up his universe.

Roussel's books, Robbe-Grillet contends, should be seen as 'direct ancestors of the modern novel' principally because of the depthlessness that results from their systematic self-enclosure:

> The greater the accumulation of precise minutiae, of details of form and dimension, the more the object loses its depth. So this is an opacity without mystery, just as there is nothing

behind the surfaces of a backcloth, no inside, no secret, no ulterior motive.

While Breton and Aragon were convinced that Roussel's work contained some perhaps irrecoverable but particular secret, Robbe-Grillet and Butor represent him as a post-modernist *avant la lettre* whose elaborate inventions preserve their disconcerting strangeness by, in the end, always proving ineffably banal. In an interview conducted in 1983 on the influence of Roussel on his own work, Butor argues that Roussel's descriptive methods are essentially a means of 'hollowing out reality'. Pondering the dental mosaic and aerial pile-driver in Chapter 2 of *Locus Solus*, Robbe-Grillet observes:

> Now this chain of extraordinarily complex, ingenious and far-fetched elucidations seems so ludicrous and so disappointing that it is as if the mystery were still intact. But from now on it is a cleansed, eviscerated mystery that has become unnameable. The opacity no longer hides anything. It's like finding a locked drawer, and then a key, and the key opens the drawer impeccably . . . and the drawer is empty.

Although he never mentions Foucault in the piece, Robbe-Grillet's article was in fact a review of his friend's study of Roussel published in France in 1963 and in English translation in 1986, two years after Foucault's death. In an interview appended to the text, conducted in 1983 with its translator Charles Ruas, Foucault reminisced about the origins of his infatuation with Roussel. It is worth, I think, quoting at length:

> I wrote this study of Raymond Roussel when I was quite young. It happened completely by chance because I have to admit that I had never heard of Roussel until the year 1957. I can recall how I discovered his work: it was during a period when I was living abroad, in Sweden, and returned to France for the summer. I went to the librairie José Corti to buy I can't recall what book. Can you visualize that huge bookstore across from the Luxembourg Gardens? José Corti, publisher and bookseller, was there behind his enormous desk, a distinguished old man. He was busy

speaking to a friend, and obviously he is not the kind of bookseller that you can interrupt with a 'Could you find me such and such a book?' You have to wait politely until the conversation is over before making a request. Thus, while waiting, I found my attention drawn to a series of books of that faded yellow colour used by publishing firms of the late nineteenth, early twentieth centuries; in short, books the likes of which aren't made any more. I examined them and saw 'Librairie Lemerre' on the cover. I was puzzled to find these old volumes from a publishing firm as fallen now in reputation as that of Alphonse Lemerre. I selected a book out of curiosity to see what José Corti was selling from the stock of the Lemerre firm, and that's how I came upon the work of someone I had never heard of named Raymond Roussel, and the book was entitled *La Vue*. Well, from the first line I was completely taken by the beauty of the style, so strange and so strangely close to that of Robbe-Grillet, who was just beginning to publish his work. I could see a relation between *La Vue* and Robbe-Grillet's work in general, but *Le Voyeur* in particular. At that point José Corti's conversation came to an end, I requested the book I needed, and asked timidly who was Raymond Roussel, because in addition to *La Vue* his other works were on the shelf. Corti looked at me with a generous sort of pity and said, 'But, after all, Roussel . . .' I immediately understood that I should have known about Raymond Roussel, and with equal timidity I asked if I could buy the book since he was selling it. I was surprised, or rather disappointed, to find that it was expensive. José Corti probably told me that day I should read *Comment j'ai écrit certains de mes livres*. Raymond Roussel's work immediately absorbed me: I was taken by the prose style even before learning what was behind it – the process, the machines, the mechanisms – and no doubt when I discovered his process and his techniques, the obsessional side of me was seduced a second time by the shock of learning of the disparity between this methodically applied process, which was slightly naïve, and the resulting intense poetry. Slowly and systematically I began to buy all of his works. I developed an affection for his work, which remained secret, since I didn't discuss it.

The strange thing is that I met Robbe-Grillet for the first time in Hamburg in 1960 and we became friends and went to the Hamburg Fair together, going through the fun house maze of mirrors. It's the starting point of his novel *Dans le Labyrinthe.* By a mental lapse that can't have been entirely innocent on my part, I never spoke of Roussel with him, nor asked about his relationship to Roussel. That's how things stood for several years until one day during vacation I decided to write a small article on Roussel, but by then I was so absorbed by Roussel and his work that I isolated myself for two months and in fact wrote what turned out to be this book.

With a telling poetic logic, Roussel's own reticence seems to infect his readers and render them unwilling to share their admiration even with each other. Later in the interview Foucault elaborates on the peculiar nature of his relationship with the only author to whom he ever devoted a literary monograph:

I have kept my love for Roussel as something gratuitous, and I prefer it that way . . . My relationship to my book on Roussel, and to Roussel's work, is something very personal, which I remember as a happy period. I would go so far as to say that it doesn't have a place in the sequence of my books. No one has tried to explain that I wrote it because I had already written a study of madness and that I would write on the history of sexuality. No one has paid much attention to this book, and I'm glad; it's my secret affair. You know, he was my love for several summers . . . no one knew it.

To have written on another author afterwards would have felt like 'betraying' this intense, clandestine passion and compromising Roussel's own 'unique[ness]'.

Nevertheless, Foucault does acknowledge that it was only his familiarity with the *nouveaux romanciers,* in particular Robbe-Grillet and Butor, which enabled him to respond so positively on that first occasion in José Corti's bookshop; without this 'previous conditioning' he would have 'slammed [the book] shut with a good laugh'. Roussel, of course, would have found *Les Gommes*, *Le Voyeur* or *La Modification*, or for that matter *Les Mots et les choses* as 'obscure' as he found the work of the Surrealists, but by a curious loop of literary history his œuvre, destined, as he thought, to conquer the masses, has been kept alive only by the interest of successive avant-gardes.

And, infuriatingly for Roussel's shade, despite the fact that these avant-gardes have themselves in turn become institutionally sanctioned, it might be argued that none has yet really succeeded in dragging Roussel with them once and for all into the canon. Hence the peculiar position occupied by Foucault's study of Roussel in relation to his overall project: it has no real place in the sequence of his books, and he concomitantly suggests that Roussel has no real place in the French literary tradition. 'I have to admit,' he muses

> I would not dare to compare Roussel to Proust . . . I would remain very cautious about Roussel's historical place. His was an extremely interesting experiment; it wasn't only a linguistic experiment, but an experiment with the nature of language, and it's more than the experimentation of someone obsessed. He truly created or, in any case, broke through, embodied and created a form of beauty, a lovely curiosity, which is in fact a literary work. But I wouldn't say that Roussel is comparable to Proust.

'A form of beauty, a lovely curiosity . . .' One can't help noticing that the emotive, even sensuous charge of Foucault's language is intrinsically linked to his figuration of Roussel as marginal, fundamentally beyond the reach of a canon catholic enough to include such figures as the Marquis de Sade and Lautréamont. Although Foucault's delight in Roussel eventually resulted in the book that has proved the most instrumental of any in winning for Roussel the 'little posthumous fame' he hoped for, two decades later Foucault appears to have wished he had kept this early love strictly to himself.

Yet this uncertainty, or self-division, is of course itself wholly Rousselian, as the feverishly multiplying paradoxes of Foucault's original analysis insistently prove:

All of Roussel's language, in its reversal of style,
surreptitiously tries to say two things with the same words.
The twisting, slight turn of words which ordinarily allows
them to make a tropological 'move' that brings into play
their fundamental freedom is used by Roussel to form an
inexorable circle which returns words to their point of origin
by force of his constraining rules . . .

In their basic function Roussel's machines make all speech
undergo a moment of annihilation, in order to rejoin the
language divided from itself – and yet identical to itself – in
so perfect an imitation that between that imitation and its
model only the thin black blade of death has been able to
penetrate . . .

Language has become circular and all-encompassing; it
hastily crosses distant perimeters, but it is always drawn by
a dark centre, never identified, always elusive – a perspective
extended to infinity in the hollow of words, just as the
perspective of the whole poem ['La Vue'] opens to the
horizon at the very centre of the text . . .

Paradoxically, for Roussel this hollowness is the sun, a sun
which is there but which remains unattainable. It shines,
but its rays remain contained within its sphere; it dazzles,
but it cannot be seen through; from the core of this sun
words rise, but the words cover it up and hide it; it is unique
and yet it is double, and twice duplicated since it is its own
mirror and nocturnal opposite.

These brilliant, self-completing rhetorical pirouettes emulate the
manner in which Roussel's *procédé* 'disconnect[s] the language
from all contact, induction, surreptitious communication and
influence, giving it an absolutely neutral space in which to fully
develop.' This neutral space, Foucault later explains, 'is not
where the canonical figures of speech originate,' for Roussel's
texts, whether viewed as the impersonal products of a pre-
existing formula, like Duchamp's ready-mades, or – at the
opposite extreme – as Nietzschean acts of pure self-creation,
allow for no mediation with the evolving tradition of the canon.
Accordingly, the ultimate paradox of Foucault's impassioned

analysis of Roussel is that it not only marginalizes its subject, but itself. In the later interview Foucault confesses it was the book he wrote 'most easily, with the greatest pleasure', and yet it ends, almost on the note of the morning after, jokily disavowing its own intensities: 'So you think this has justified your spending so many pages . . .'

———

Roussel's work first appeared in English in a 1928 edition of the avant-garde magazine *Transition*, which ran an extract of *Impressions d'Afrique* translated by Maria Jolas. Fifteen years later, the autumn 1943 and spring 1944 issues of the New York Surrealist magazine *View* also included the opening chapters of Roussel's first prose novel. *View* was edited by Charles Henri Ford and Parker Tyler, who had both fallen under the influence of André Breton during his wartime years in America; its managing editor was one John Bernard Myers, who later opened the Tibor de Nagy Gallery and in the early 1950s began publishing in Tibor de Nagy pamphlets and in his broadside newspaper *Semi-colon* the work of four young poets recently arrived in Manhattan: John Ashbery, Frank O'Hara, Kenneth Koch and James Schuyler. In 1961 Myers published an article acclaiming them as the New York School of Poets, although Ashbery had by this time been resident in Paris for over five years, where he'd become known as 'that crazy American who's interested in Roussel'.

Although *View* was a prestigious and influential publication, Édouard Roditi's version of the opening chapters of *Impressions d'Afrique* attracted no discernible attention. Kenneth Koch was in the army when the issues featuring Roussel appeared and – in his own words – 'probably the only soldier in the Philippines with a subscription to *View*'. It was not, however, until 1950 that the truly decisive moment of transatlantic initiation occurred. That autumn Koch left America for Europe on a two-year Fulbright scholarship; in the course of a trip to Paris he paid the avant-gardist's obligatory visit to José Corti's bookshop, where he asked the proprietor for something 'really exciting and crazy'. José Corti reached down a faded copy of *Nouvelles*

*Impressions d'Afrique* which Koch purchased, and later lent to Ashbery when he arrived back in New York.

The influence of Roussel can be traced in a number of the poems Ashbery and Koch composed in the mid-1950s. Ashbery's 'The Instruction Manual', for instance, exploits descriptive techniques similar to those utilized by Roussel in *La Vue*. The poem is a pastiche travelogue in which Ashbery indulges in an extended daydream about Guadalajara, the city he 'wanted most to see, and most did not see, in Mexico!' Immured in a Manhattan office block, the poet is supposed to be working on an instruction manual explaining the uses of a new metal, but soon finds himself magically transported to a Mexican city of the mind:

> But I fancy I see, under the press of having to write the
>     instruction manual,
> Your public square, city, with its elaborate little
>     bandstand! . . .
> The couples are parading; everyone is in a holiday mood.
> First, leading the parade, is a dapper fellow
> Clothed in deep blue. On his head sits a white hat
> And he wears a mustache, which has been trimmed for the
>     occasion.

The pun on press further links the poems: Ashbery's fantasy is generated by the exigencies of commercial publishing, just as in 'La Vue', 'Le Concert' and 'La Source' Roussel purports to describe mechanically produced, mass-circulation images. The point is made again in the poem's final lines:

> What more is there to do, except stay? And that we cannot
>     do.
> And as a last breeze freshens the top of the weathered old
>     tower, I turn my gaze
> Back to the instruction manual which has made me dream
>     of Guadalajara.

Kenneth Koch, on the other hand, was inspired by Roussel's work to experiment with the misprisions inherent in language. In 'Days and Nights' he most clearly illustrates the origins of the surreal conjunctions and dislocations that characterize his poetry in the 'evolved' form of the *procédé*:

> Sweet are the uses of adversity
> Became Sweetheart cabooses of diversity
> And Sweet art cow papooses at the university
> And Sea bar Calpurnia flower havens' re-noosed knees

For Roussel, of course, there remained the business of inventing a narrative capable of connecting the resulting elements, whereas Koch developed his Rousselian programme of Chinese Whispers in the hope it would result in a revolutionary poetry *per se* – a kind of linguistic equivalent of an Abstract Expressionist canvas.

Soon after composing 'The Instruction Manual' in the summer of 1955, Ashbery escaped the 'press' of his office job for good. He set sail for France in September of that year, sponsored, like Koch, by a Fulbright Fellowship, and ended up spending most of the following decade in Paris. His literary sleuthing into his hero's life and works did not begin in earnest until 1958, when he embarked on a PhD thesis on Roussel. In the event this was never completed, but during the course of his researches Ashbery discovered the suppressed introduction to the *Documents pour servir de canevas* ('À la Havane...'), a series of letters from Roussel to Pierre Frondaie written during the period of their ill-fated collaboration and various photographs of Roussel and Charlotte Dufrène, whom he visited in her nursing home in Belgium in 1961. Like Édouard Roditi, he published a translation of the opening chapters of *Impressions d'Afrique* (1962) and almost thirty years later, a translation of the full text of the *Documents* (1991). His introductions and essays repeatedly make clear that his fascination with Roussel's work derives from its disquieting fusion of the astringently correct and the wholly unfathomable. Like Joyce and Mallarmé, Ashbery argues at the conclusion of an article published in 1967, Roussel

> tried to raise the word to a new power; in Roussel's case one feels that it is about to break open, to yield true meaning at last; that it is the lead which alchemy is on the verge of translating into something far more interesting than gold. The miracle does not take place, the surface of

his prose remains as stern and correct as the façade of a French prefecture or the gold-lettered bindings of the *Grand Larousse*. But the attentive reader will have glimpsed the possibility, and his feelings about language will never be the same again.

In 1961 Ashbery co-founded a small magazine that was edited in turns by himself, James Schuyler, Kenneth Koch and Harry Mathews. It was called *Locus Solus* in honour of Roussel, and it was here that Harry Mathews's first novel, *The Conversions*, appeared in instalments. Soon after they'd first met in Paris in 1956, Ashbery had suggested that Mathews might find inspiration in Roussel's writings. As Mathews has acknowledged on a number of occasions, Roussel's work proved as vital an influence on his artistic development as it had on Duchamp's forty-five years earlier. 'Roussel was the man who allowed me to write fiction,' he declared in a recent interview. In his 1987 *Autobiography* he discussed in detail the impact of Roussel's work:

> Reading Roussel brought me several revelations. He demonstrated to me that psychology was a dispensable fashion, that the moral responsibilities of writing did not lie in a respect of subject matter, and that the writing of prose fiction could be as scrupulously organized as Sir Philip Sidney's double sestina. Roussel taught me that I did not have to write out of my 'experience' (the quotation marks indicate: what one thinks one has been able to avoid); that I had the universe to play with, not merely the pieties of a late-capitalist society; that writing could provide me with the means of so radically outwitting myself that I could bring my hidden experiences, my unadmitted self into view. I have sometimes felt that the aim of Roussel's imperturbable and arbitrary procedures was to supply the truths of paradox (such as 'life after death') with the unchallengeable evidence of tautology (make a machine to revive the dead and they will 'by definition' show signs of life). Such a project suggested that his methods were powerful and original enough to accommodate my own, as yet undiscovered ambiguities.

In a short text published in the Roussel issue of *Digraphe*, Mathews recalls that Roussel's *procédé* served as both a model for and a catalyst of his own search for innovative literary techniques:

> Roussel's methods led me to discover others for myself; I began my first novel (*The Conversions*); the book wrote itself.

In 1972 Mathews became the first English-speaking member of the Ouvroir de Littérature Potentielle, to which he was introduced by Georges Perec. Roussel might again be said to have served as a vital line of communication between experimental artists, for Roussel, as we shall see, was a significant precursor of the ideals of constraint celebrated by Oulipo, and one of Perec's most cherished, and alluded-to, authors. In the 1977 issue of the magazine *L'Arc*, Perec and Mathews published a fiendishly entertaining parody of a scholarly article on Roussel that claims to decode a fragmentary Roussel manuscript containing the outline of a verse drama set in nineteenth-century Venice. This manuscript was discovered in the binding of a copy of *La Tragédie du Doge Partibon* (1532), and Roussel's play was to describe a mysterious assault on Sib, the daughter of a prominent Venetian family. Sib has been found unconscious in the bathroom clutching a handkerchief embroidered with her fiancé's initials; he is accused and arrested, but as the authorities examine the scene of the crime they hear a series of thumps from the floor above, and the words 'GOB! ... LAISSE! ...' emanating from the shower attachment. Sib's younger brother and sister have been playing leapfrog in the room directly above the bathroom, and their jumps have released Sib's cries of protest trapped in the water in the shower pipes. This 'liquid revelation' points to the family boatman, Gobbo, and to the deformation of the title of the book in which the manuscript was found that determined the contents of the story: *La Tragédie du Doge Partibon – L'outrage est dit de douche par petits bonds* (the outrage is said from the shower by little leaps). From this unfinished narrative Perec and Mathews proceed to deduce that Roussel visited Venice with his mother in 1895, and there met a certain Ascanio Grifalconi, the one and only love of his life, who, alas, fell ill and died the following year. Accordingly, they map the topography of Venice on to that of the various sites featured in Roussel's succeeding works, which they read as a cryptic commemoration of the few weeks of bliss he enjoyed with his Venetian lover. This brilliant collaborative text illustrates not only the futility of the Rousselian critic's quest for some ultimate 'liquid revelation' secreted in his writings, but the power of Roussel's work to 'accommodate', in Mathews's phrase, 'as yet undiscovered ambiguities':

> It is ultimately of no importance whether one can discover, running through these paltry fragments, the thread of a project on which Roussel might have laboured all his writing life with a view to making it his crowning work, the 'masterwork' that would have won him general recognition. There is no Roussel mystery; his work is not a riddle that we must solve. It is only our reading of it, our thirst for explanation, our love of complexity that creates the impression that there is a secret to be cracked. If secret there is, it will not be found where we look for it.

━━━━━

In an article published in the *Nouvelle Revue Française* the year after Raymond Queneau's death in 1976, François Le Lionnais recalled the origins of the movement they co-founded in 1960, partly in opposition to the moribund excesses and internecine court politics of the Surrealist movement, which was still spearheaded by Breton but with which Queneau had broken some three decades earlier:

> During luncheon in a little bistro where one could talk peacefully, I decided to propose to Raymond the creation of a workshop or seminar of experimental literature, which would address in a scientific manner that which the troubadors, the Rhétoriqueurs, Raymond Roussel, the Russian formalists and a few others had merely adumbrated. He would never have approved this project had we not been viscerally in agreement about radically warding

off any group activity that might engender fulminations, excommunications or any other form of terror.

Whereas for Breton, Roussel was, despite himself, a Surrealist excavator of the unconscious, an unknowing black humorist, the Oulipians considered him one of the assorted 'plagiarists by anticipation' who prefigured their deliberate experiments with restrictive form. As for Mathews, Roussel's *procédé* illustrated for the Oulipians the literary possibilities of rigorous compositional constraints. Over the years Oulipians have frequently appropriated the title of Roussel's posthumous essay to explain the methodology underlying particular texts: in 'Comment j'ai écrit un de mes livres' (*Bibliothèque Oulipienne*, No. 20) Italo Calvino revealed the complex mathematical equation governing the relations between reader and book in *Se una notte d'inverno un viaggiatore* (1979); in a lecture called 'Comment j'ai écrit un chapitre de *La Vie mode d'emploi*', Perec discussed the various laws operative within chapter 73 of his *magnum opus*; and in the paradoxically entitled *Pourquoi je n'ai écrit aucun de mes livres* (1986), Marcel Bénabou offered a witty and intricately patterned account of his struggles to write anything at all.

It was Bénabou, in a 1983 essay called 'Rule and Constraint', who outlined the principal appeal of Roussel's work for Oulipians most directly:

> Roussel, like Mallarmé, elaborates from the lexicon alone his own universe; and from the arbitrary choice he imposes upon himself, he brings into being a second nature.

Roussel's linguistic researches were frequently adopted and modified by Oulipians as a means of presenting language as a series of equations. Perec, for instance, developed an exercise he illustrated by taking the first and last sentences of Roussel's 'Parmi les Noirs' and by a process of associative word-plays showing how both could be made to yield the same intermediary sentence: 'Les bandes de la lettre sur les pillards du vieux blanc' (the borders of the letter about the pillagers of the old white). Another Perecquian *procédé* involved replacing each noun in the two sentences with synonyms, thus mutating 'les lettres du blanc sur les bandes du vieux billard' into 'les caractères du fard sur les rebords de la vieille table d'opération' (the characters of the make-up on the rims of the old operating-table), which is in turn processed into 'les énergies de l'artifice sur les ourlets du vieil abaque' (the energies of the artifice on the hems of the old abacus), and so on. Roussel's talismanic sentence also crops up in Perec's lipogramatic novel, *La Disparition* (1969), where it again undergoes a subtle alteration, this time to remove the offending *es*: 'L'inscription du Blanc sur un Bord du Billard.'

Towards the end of the semi-fictional, semi-autobiographical *W ou le souvenir d'enfance* (1975), Perec discusses the pleasures he has derived from his favourite authors:

> I do not read much, but I have never stopped rereading Flaubert and Jules Verne, Roussel and Kafka, Leiris and Queneau; I reread the books I love and I love the books I reread, and each time it is the same enjoyment, whether I reread twenty pages, three chapters, or the whole book: an enjoyment of complicity, of collusion, or more especially, and in addition, of having in the end found kin again.

Perec has signalled his kinship with Roussel on numerous occasions in his novels: the boat that founders in the first part of the fiction in *W*, for instance, is called the *Sylvandre*, after the ship whose wreck off the coast of Ponukélé enabled Rul to plunder the fatal corset and gold hairpins from the drowned Swiss nurse; one of the pictures in the *catalogue raisonné* that occupies most of *Un cabinet d'amateur* (1979) is entitled 'The Bewitched of Lake Ontario', a reference to the second of the Incomparables' spectacular tableaux vivants, while among the many literary 'kin' evoked in this text are the Belgian Cuijper (here an art historian rather than Roussel's operatic tenor), the ultrarealist painter Baron Gros and the famous dandy, the Viscount de Timbert, who is the subject of one of Gros's most immaculately lifelike portraits in *L'Étoile au front*.

Roussel is also one of the twenty authors whose work Perec borrows as part of a mathematically determined system of allusions in *La Vie mode d'emploi* (the references are in chapters 7, 18, 26, 36, 47, 55, 63, 65 and 91). In chapter 87, when Perec comes to describe Bartlebooth's drawing-room, the furnishings and artworks are mainly taken from the catalogue of the sale

of Madame Roussel's possessions after her death: an exception
is a landscape called *L'Île mystérieuse* (one of Roussel's favourite
Verne novels) and signed L.N. Montalescot, a yoking together
of the siblings Louise and Norbert, architects of Roussel's most
notorious construction, the whalebone statue on the rails made
of calves' lungs. In the novel's index Montalescot's dates are
given as 1877–1933.

As his name suggests, the novel's central character, Bartlebooth, is an amalgam of Valéry Larbaud's globetrotting
millionaire Barnabooth and Melville's uncooperative legal clerk
Bartleby. The peculiar project that dominates his life, on the
other hand, is in many ways an extension of Roussel's *procédé*.
The immensely wealthy Bartlebooth

> wishes to fix, to describe and to exhaust not the whole world
> – merely to state such an ambition is enough to invalidate
> it – but a constituted fragment of the world: in the face of
> the inextricable incoherence of things, he will set out to
> execute a (necessarily limited) programme right the way
> through, in all its irreducible, intact entirety.

> In other words, Bartlebooth resolved one day that his
> whole life would be organized around a single project, an
> arbitrarily constrained programme with no purpose outside
> its own completion.

Bartlebooth travels the world for twenty years, each fortnight
completing a watercolour of a randomly chosen seascape. These
pictures are sent back to Paris, where Gaspard Winckler, a
craftsman in Bartlebooth's pay, attaches each to a wooden board
and carves it into a jigsaw puzzle of 750 pieces. The following
twenty years Bartlebooth will spend solving these 500 jigsaws
of his own paintings. When a puzzle is finished, Winckler must
seal its joins and then separate the picture from its backing; this
process completed, each seascape is returned to the site it depicts,
and there dipped in a detergent solution that entirely erases the
original watercolour.

Bartlebooth's elaborate, pointless scheme can be seen as a
literal enactment of the autism inherent in Roussel's compositional methods, the way, in Bénabou's words, that Roussel
'elaborates from the lexicon alone his own universe'. Arbitrarily

selected phrases and locations are fixed, fragmented and then reconstituted as part of a wholly self-enclosed ulterior plan. Bartlebooth aims to reduce time and space to 'abstract co-ordinates' of his ongoing enterprise, just as Roussel fractured language into abstract sounds before recombining them according to the demands of his similarly inscrutable aesthetic compulsions. Roussel, of course, hoped his labours would result in writings that would irradiate the entire world, while Bartlebooth's project is motivated by the opposite ideal of pure self-negation. And unlike the relentlessly triumphant Incomparables or the omnipotent Canterel, Bartlebooth fails to accomplish his self-imposed task: he dies having all but completed the 439th puzzle. Only one space remains, in the almost perfect shape of an X:

> But the ironical thing, which could have been foreseen long ago, is that the piece the dead man holds between his fingers is shaped like a W.

───

Roussel has not as yet found his niche in the puzzle of literary history, and it remains to be seen whether the current revaluation of his works prompted in France by the discovery of his manuscripts will convert his little posthumous fame into the sort of celebrity that he felt to be his due. It seems unlikely, and certainly, despite the best efforts of Ashbery, Mathews and Koch, and of second-generation New Yorkers such as Ron Padgett and the English-born painter Trevor Winkfield, Roussel is still pretty much a well-kept secret in the English-speaking world. In 1962 Ashbery suggested he was 'an obscure figure known only to a few initiates', and nearly forty years on this situation still pretty much obtains in Britain and America. 'If the age in which he wrote was not ready for him,' the critic Ian Pindar noted sceptically in a review in the *Times Literary Supplement* of the first volumes of the new Pauvert/Fayard edition, 'the truth is we are no more so today; we may never be ready.' 'Amen,' *roussellâtres* might well murmur in response to this diagnosis; for it is precisely because no age could ever be ready for a wind-powered roadmender's tool capable of making a mosaic out of human teeth, or hairs dancing the jig 'Sir Roger de Coverly' from root to root across a man's bald pate, or tarot cards containing tiny insects that perform 'The Bluebells of Scotland', or a furless cat who transforms himself into a living battery and stimulates the remnants of Danton's head to fresh flights of oratory, that Roussel so fully deserves the title bestowed on him by Louis Aragon: 'The President of the Republic of Dreams'.

# Roussel Archives

The Fonds Roussel in the Bibliothèque Nationale at rue de Richelieu

Cat. no.

3024, Notes et cahiers personnels – notes prises durant un voyage en Égypte

4195, *Claude et Luce* (i.e. Les Noces) (En bateau-mouche)

4199, *La Seine*

4201, *La Seine*

4203, *Claude et Luce* (À l'Ambigu – first version)

4204, *Claude et Luce* (À l'Ambigu – first version)

4205, *Claude et Luce* (À l'Ambigu – first version)

4206, *Claude et Luce* (À l'Ambigu – second version)

4207, *Claude et Luce* (À l'Ambigu – first version)

4208, *Claude et Luce* (Au bois de Vincennes – après diner)

4209, *Claude et Luce* (Au bois de Vincennes – après midi)

4210, *Claude et Luce* (Au bois de Vincennes – après midi)

4211, *Claude et Luce* (Au bois de Vincennes – après midi)

4212, *Claude et Luce* (Au bois de Vincennes – après midi)

4290, *Locus Solus*

4291, *Locus Solus*

4292, *Locus Solus*

4293, *Locus Solus*

4294, *Impressions d'Afrique*

4295, *Impressions d'Afrique*

4296, *Impressions d'Afrique*

4297, *Impressions d'Afrique*

4298, *Impressions d'Afrique*

4443, *La Doublure, La Vue, L'Inconsolable*

4444, *La Doublure* (proofs)

4484, *Une Page du Folk-lore Breton*

4485, *Textes de Grande Jeunesse ou Textes-genèse*

4486, *Têtes de Carton du Carnaval de Nice*

4487, *L'Étoile au front*

4488, *Impressions d'Afrique* (playscript)

4489, *Le Mystère de Locus Solus*

4490, *La Poussière de soleils*
4491, *Poèmes Inachevées*
4499, *Registre de signatures aux obsèques de sa mère*
4500, *Lettres reçues*
4501, *Dossier familial*
4509, *Documents concernant ses propriétés*
4510, *Documents le concernant*
4875, *L'Allée aux lucioles*
4881, *Cahier de copies de ses envois*
4508, *Notes prises sur des ouvrages d'auteurs contemporains*
4511, *Documents concernant ses œuvres*
4512, *Lettres reçues*
5752, *Locus Solus*
The manuscript of *Nouvelles Impressions d'Afrique* is being restored
and has not yet been catalogued.


The Fonds Rondel in the Bibliothèque Nationale de l'Arsenal

An archive of theatrical programmes, tickets, and newspaper reviews
of his plays:
*Impressions d'Afrique* (1911–12), Rf 71.821
*Locus Solus* (1922), Rf 71.823
*L'Étoile au front* (1924), Rf 71.827
*La Poussière de soleils* (1926), Rf 71.830
General newspaper articles relating to the life and death of Roussel,
Rf 71.835

# Two menus of meals served to Roussel in October and November 1926

## First menu

Framboises au sucre
Soupe au chocolat
Fromage bondon
Huîtres royales marine
Talmouses (marzipan turnovers) de Saint-Denis au brie de Meaux
Filets de merlan (whiting) à l'anglaise, beurre noisette, persil frit
Cailles (quails) au foie gras à la Cambacérès
Compote de raisin chasselas de Thomery au coulis
Noisette de Béhague à la Doria
Sorbet au Champagne
Cœur de filet à la broche
Pommes soufflées
Salade de laitue
Pêche impératrice Eugénie
Religieuse au café (coffee éclair)
Bombe Nélusko
Consommé Monte-Carlo, crème princesse
Vol-au-vent de filet de sole Walewska
Suprême de perdreau (partridge) souveraine
Spoom
Poulet de grain à la broche
Salade caprice de reine
Ananas voilé à l'orientale

## Second menu

Fruits de la propriété
Soupe au thé
Fromage bondon
Clams
Laitance (roe) de carpe à la Villeroy
Cromesquis de filets de grives (thrushes)
Subric d'épinards (spinach)
Menus droits de volailles en Brézolles
Champignons de prairie sautés
Sorbet au citron
Saint-Honoré Chiboust
Gâteau Succès
Glace feuillantine
Consommé racines tapioca
Crème d'huîtres
Pilaff de homard
Escalope de ris de veau à la maréchale
Laitues braisées
Oranges givrés
Cavansback à la broche (Cavansback, Guillot informs us, 'is an
extremely rare bird first found in the United States; it's a wild duck
whose flesh is extremely tender; it cooks very quickly on a spit, and
is delicious'.)
Pommes Anna
Oxalis (wood sorrel) à la crème
Soufflé glacé Rothschild

Source: André Guillot, *La Grande cuisine bourgeoise* (Paris: Flammarion, 1976)

# Illustrations to *Nouvelles Impressions d'Afrique* referred to in this book

4    A man taking a dried flower from a book.

6   A wall which a slatted shutter bangs in the wind (somewhere
in the picture a tossing tree giving the impresssion of a storm).

20   A goatskin in the desert from which water is escaping
through a hole which seems to have been made by the sword
of a traitor. No people.

27  A truce bearer with his eyes blindfolded (an officer)
escorted by two soldiers in uniforms different from his. No
other people.

28  A man seated at a table on which a book is placed vertically: he is parting two of its uncut leaves so as to read a passage.

33   A woman lowering the Venetian blind of a window. The
blind is already half-closed, the slats almost horizontal.

40  A waiter in a restaurant holding two knives in the form of
a cross with which he is preparing to cut a chicken. No other
people.

43   A parrot on its perch seeming to talk to a passer-by. No
other people.

51   An elegantly dressed man pointing the barrel of a revolver
to his temple, his finger on the trigger.

52   A rambler, with his arm raised and his fingers open, who
has just dropped a pebble (which is still visible) down a well;
he seems to cock an ear as if to listen for the splash (no other
people).

53 A portrait (unnamed) of Amerigo Vespucci. You might base the picture on that in the *Nouveau Larousse illustré*.

58    A plain wall on which the words 'Mane Thecel Phares' are
written as if in letters of flame. Nothing else, no people, no
feast. Letters of the period.

59 A section of starry sky without any earthly landscape as if seen from some vantage point in space and giving the impression of infinity.

# Bibliography

## Works by Roussel

Roussel's works were all originally published at his own expense by Éditions Lemerre (21–31 passage Choiseul). In 1963 Jean-Jacques Pauvert began republishing Roussel's texts, and it is to these editions that I mainly refer. However, the discovery of Roussel's manuscripts in 1989 has prompted a new edition of Roussel's works jointly undertaken by Jean-Jacques Pauvert and Éditions Fayard. At the time of writing, five volumes of this new edition have appeared. Of the texts published during Roussel's lifetime, however, only *Mon Âme*, *La Doublure* and *La Vue* have so far been re-edited and republished in this new edition: references to these poems are keyed to the line numbers provided by this new edition. U after a title denotes the text referred to in this book.

### Lemerre editions of Roussel

*La Doublure* (1897)
*Chiquenaude* (1900)
*La Vue* (1904)
*Impressions d'Afrique* (1910)
*Locus Solus* (1914)
*Pages choisies d'Impressions d'Afrique et de Locus Solus* (1918)
*L'Étoile au front* (1925)
*La Poussière de soleils* (1927)
*Nouvelles Impressions d'Afrique* (1932)
*Comment j'ai écrit certains de mes livres* (1935)

### Pauvert editions of Roussel

*La Doublure* (1963)
*La Vue* (1963)
*Impressions d'Afrique* (1963) U
*Locus Solus* (1965)
*L'Étoile au front* (1963) U
*La Poussière de soleils* (1964) U

*Nouvelles Impressions d'Afrique* (1963) U

*Comment j'ai écrit certains de mes livres* (1963) U

*Épaves* (1972), a collection of miscellaneous items by Roussel:

i) the role of Juillard in a version of the play of *Impressions d'Afrique*

ii) various versions of Pierre Frondaie's adaptation of *Locus Solus*

iii) 'À la Havane', the suppressed introduction to *Documents pour servir de canevas*

iv) a facsimile of a draft of Canto I of *Nouvelles Impressions d'Afrique*

v) Roussel's instructions to Zo for the illustrations for *Nouvelles Impressions d'Afrique*

Gallimard edition of Roussel

*Locus Solus* (1963) U

Pauvert/Fayard editions of Roussel

*3uvres I: Mon Âme, Poèmes inachevés, La Doublure, Chroniquettes*, ed. Annie Le Brun (1994) U

*3uvres III: La Seine, La Tonsure*, ed. Patrick Besnier (1994) U

*3uvres IV: La Vue, Poèmes inédits*, ed. Patrick Besnier (1998) U

*3uvres V: Les Noces*, ed. Pierre Bazantay, preface Annie Le Brun (1998) U

*3uvres VI: Les Noces*, ed. Pierre Bazantay, preface Annie Le Brun (1998) U

Popular editions of Roussel

*Locus Solus* and *Comment j'ai écrit certains de mes livres* have been reprinted in the series L'Imaginaire Gallimard (nos. 230 and 324), and *Impressions d'Afrique* in the Biblio series of Le Livre de Poche

## Roussel's publications in newspapers and magazines during his lifetime

'Mon Âme', *Le Gaulois du Dimanche*, 12 July 1897

'Chroniquettes', *Le Gaulois du Dimanche*, 2/3 Oct. 1897

'La Vue', *Le Gaulois du Dimanche*, 18–19 April 1903

'Le Concert', *Le Gaulois du Dimanche*, 27–8 June 1903

'L'Inconsolable', *Le Gaulois du Dimanche*, 10–11 Sept. 1904

'Têtes de Carton du Carnaval de Nice', *Le Gaulois du Dimanche*, 26–7 Sept. 1904

'Nanon', *Le Gaulois du Dimanche*, 14–15 Sept. 1907

'Une Page du Folk-Lore Breton', *Le Gaulois du Dimanche*, 6–7 June 1908

*Impressions d'Afrique*, *Le Gaulois du Dimanche*, 10 July – 13 Nov. 1909

*Quelques heures à Bougival* (i.e. *Locus Solus*), *Le Gaulois du Dimanche*, 6 Dec. 1913 – 28 March 1914

Acts II and III of *L'Étoile au front*, *Comœdia*, 12–22 May 1924

'Correspondence pour mettre en rapport Benjamin Péret et Raymond Roussel', *La Révolution surréaliste*, no. 1, Dec. 1924

'Admirations et Haines', *Le Figaro Illustré*, Feb. 1933

'Chronique de Raymond Roussel', *Le Figaro Illustré*, April 1933

## Publications of Roussel texts in magazines, journals and pamphlets since his death

'Comment j'ai écrit certains de mes livres', *Nouvelle Revue Française*, no. 259 (introduced by Michel Leiris), 1 April 1935

'Indications pour 59 dessins', *Cahier G.L.M* (introduced by Michel Leiris), March 1939

'Lettre à Eugène Leiris (1921)', *Arts et Lettres*, no. 15, 1949; reprinted in *L'Arc*, no. 29, 1966

'À la Havane' (introduced by John Ashbery), *L'Arc*, no. 19, summer 1962

'Flio' (introduced by Michel Leiris), *Bizarre*, no. 34–5, 1964

'Lettre au secrétaire de Pierre Loti (1922)', *Prisme*, no. 18, 1980

'Trois lettres au secrétaire de Pierre Loti (1922–23)', *Prisme*, no. 21, 1981

'An Unpublished Note' (undated), *Atlas Anthology* 4, (1987)

'Deux chroniques retrouvées', *Europe*, no. 714, Oct. 1988

'Lettre inédite à Léon-Paul Quint (1924)' ed. J-P. Goujon, (Paris: À l'Écart), 1991

'Deux passages de *Locus Solus*', ed. Annie Angrémy, *Revue de la Bibliothèque Nationale*, no. 43, 1992

'Le Carnet gris d'Égypte (1906)' ed. Philippe Kerbellec, *Digraphe*, no. 67, Feb. 1994

'Une lettre inédite' (not dated), *Digraphe*, no. 67, Feb. 1994

## Translations of Roussel into English

*Impressions of Africa*, extract trans. Maria Jolas, *Transition*, no. 12, 1928

*Impressions of Africa*, extracts trans. Édouard Roditi, *View*, Series III, no. 4, 1943, Series IV, no. 1, 1944

*Impressions of Africa*, extract trans. John Ashbery, *Portfolio and ARTnews Annual* no. 6, Autumn 1962, reprinted in *How I Wrote Certain of My Books* (1977, 1995)

*Locus Solus*, extract trans. Harry Mathews, *Locus Solus*, V, 1962, reprinted in *How I Wrote Certain of My Books* (1977, 1995)

*The Star on the Forehead*, extract (Act I, Scene 3), trans. Rayner Heppenstall, *New Directions*, no. 8, 1964

'The Greenish Skin' (i.e. 'La peau verdâtre de la prune' from 'Textes de grande jeunesse ou textes-genèse'), trans. Rayner Heppenstall, *New Directions*, no. 18, 1964

*New Impressions of Africa*, extract (Canto III), trans. Kenneth Koch, *Art & Literature*, no. 2, 1964, reprinted in *How I Wrote Certain of My Books* (1977, 1995)

*Impressions of Africa*, trans. Lindy Foord and Rayner Heppenstall (London: Calder & Boyars,1966/Berkeley: University of California Press,1967); reprinted in paperback (London: John Calder, 1983/New York: Riverrun Press, 1983)

'Among the Blacks', trans. Ron Padgett, *Bones*, no. 2, 1968

'The Gentleman's White Curls' and 'The Skate's Scales' (i.e. 'Les boucles du petit rentier' and 'La peau de la raie' from 'Textes de grande jeunesse ou textes-genèse'), trans. Rayner Heppenstall, *London Magazine*, vol 8, no. 5, 1968

'The Stopping-Place' (i.e.'La Halte' from 'Textes de grande jeunesse ou textes-genèse'), trans. Trevor Winkfield, *Juillard*, no. 7, 1968–9

*Locus Solus*, trans. Rupert Copeland Cunningham (London: Calder & Boyars,1970); reprinted in paperback (London: John Calder, 1983/New York: Riverrun Press, 1983)

*The Star on the Forehead*, extract (Act I, Scenes 1 and 2), trans. Paul Hammond, *Juillard*, no. 8, 1971

'Among the Blacks', trans. Ron Padgett and Trevor Winkfield, *Juillard*, no. 8, 1971

'Correspondence with Charlotte Dufrène', *Juillard*, no. 8, 1971

'Among the Blacks', trans. Alastair Brotchie and Cecilia Muir, *Art Exchange Anthology* (1973)

'Instructions for 59 Drawings', trans. Trevor Winkfield, *Sun*, vol 4, no. 2, 1975, reprinted in *How I Wrote Certain of My Books* (1977, 1995)

*How I Wrote Certain of My Books*, ed. Trevor Winkfield (New York: Sun, 1977):

i)'On Raymond Roussel' by John Ashbery (first published as 'Re-establishing Raymond Roussel' in *Portfolio and ARTnews Annual* no. 6, Autumn 1962)

ii) 'In Darkest Language' by John Ashbery (review of Rayner Heppenstall and Lindy Foord's translation of *Impressions d'Afrique* and Rayner Heppenstall's *Raymond Roussel* first published in *The New York Times Book Review*, 29 Oct. 1967)

iii) 'How I Wrote Certain of My Books', trans. Trevor Winkfield

iv) Chapter 1 of *Impressions d'Afrique*, trans. John Ashbery

v) Chapter 1 of *Locus Solus*, trans. Harry Mathews

vi) Canto III of *Nouvelles Impressions d'Afrique*, trans. Kenneth Koch

vii) 'Instructions for 59 Drawings', trans. Trevor Winkfield

'Second Document to Serve as an Outline', trans. Joe Hedges, *Atlas Anthology* 1 (1983)

*L'Étoile au front*, extract (Act II scene 4), trans. John Harman, *Atlas Anthology* 3 (1985)

'In Havana', trans. John Ashbery, *Atlas Anthology* 4 (1987)

*Among the Blacks*, by Raymond Roussel and Ron Padgett (Bolinas: Avenue B, 1988)

*Raymond Roussel: Selections from Certain of His Books*, ed. Alastair Brotchie et al (London: Atlas Press, 1991):

i) *Documents to Serve as an Outline*, trans. John Ashbery

ii) *The Dust of Suns*, trans. Harry Mathews

iii) *The Star on the Forehead*, trans. Martin Sorrell

iv) *The View*, trans. Antony Melville

*How I Wrote Certain of My Books*, ed. Trevor Winkfield (Boston: Exact Change, 1995):

i) 'Introduction' by John Ashbery (i.e. a reprint of 'On Raymond Roussel')

ii) 'How I Wrote Certain of My Books', trans. Trevor Winkfield

iii) Chapter 1 of *Impressions d'Afrique*, trans. John Ashbery

iv) Chapter 1 of *Locus Solus*, trans. Harry Mathews

v) Act V of *The Dust of Suns*, trans. Harry Mathews

vi) Canto III of *Nouvelles Impressions d'Afrique*, trans. Kenneth Koch

vii) 'Instructions for 59 Drawings', trans. Trevor Winkfield

viii) *Documents to Serve as an Outline*, trans. John Ashbery

## Select Bibliography of books and articles on Roussel

Adamson, Ginette, 'Raymond Roussel: pillier inconnu des mouvements modernes?', *Language Quarterly*, XIV, nos. 1–2, 1975
- *Le procédé de Raymond Roussel* (Amsterdam: Rodopi, 1984)
Amiot, Anne-Marie, 'Valeur métaphysique et esthétique de l'insolite dans le théâtre de Raymond Roussel', *Publications du Centre de philologie et de littérature romanes de l'Université de Strasbourg*, 1972
- *'Un mythe moderne'*: Impressions d'Afrique *de Raymond Roussel* (Paris: Minard, Archives des lettres modernes, no. 76, 1977)
- 'Roussel et la science, Trois figures de l'imaginaire littéraire', *Annales de la Faculté des lettres de Nice*, 1982
- 'L'idéologie roussellienne dans *Locus Solus*: Raymond Roussel et Camille Flammarion', *Mélusine*, no. 3, 1982
- *Nouvelles Impressions d'Afrique*: texte, blanc et image', *Mélusine*, no. 4, 1982
- 'Roussel le mal-aimé', *Impressions du Sud*, no. 2, June 1983
- 'Roussel à la scène', *La Quinzaine littéraire*, no. 407, 15–31 Dec. 1983
- 'Roussel en gloire', *Raymond Roussel en gloire* (1984)
- 'Romans d'aventures et aventures du roman rousselien', *Europe*, no. 714, Oct. 1988
André, Robert, 'La stèle de Raymond Roussel,' *Bizarre*, no. 34–35, 1964
Angrémy, Annie, 'La malle de Roussel. Du bric-à-brac au décryptage', *Revue de la Bibliothèque Nationale*, no. 43, 1992
- 'Le déménageur et la bibliothécaire', *Raymond Roussel: perversion classique ou invention moderne?* (1993)
Angrémy, Annie, and Besnier, Patrick, *'La Seine*, le manuscrit fleuve d'une pièce abandonnée', *Genesis*, no. 5, 1994
Anon, 'La Doublure', review in *L'Illustration*, 17 July 1897, reprinted in 'Quatre critiques retrouvées', *Europe*, no. 714, Oct. 1988
- 'La maison roulante de M. Raymond Roussel', *La Revue du Touring Club de France*, August 1926, trans. Antony Melville, *Atlas Anthology* 4 (1987); also included in Georges Perec's *Espèces d'espaces* (Paris: Galilée, 1974), trans. John Sturrock as *Species of Spaces and Other Pieces* (London: Penguin, 1997)
Aron, Jean-Paul, 'Raymond Roussel: *L'Étoile au front*', *Les cahiers du chemin*, no. 13, 1971
Arthaud, Christian, 'L'État de Cédille (Raymond Roussel et les peintres)', *Pictura/Edelweiss*, no. 3, Feb. 1984
Ashbery, John, 'Re-establishing Raymond Roussel', *Portfolio and*

*ARTnews Annual* no. 6, Autumn 1962; reprinted in *How I Wrote Certain of My Books* (1977 and 1995), ed. Trevor Winkfield, and *Death and the Labyrinth: The World of Raymond Roussel* by Michel Foucault, trans. Charles Ruas

– 'Les versions scéniques d'*Impressions d'Afrique* et de *Locus Solus*', *Bizarre*, no. 34–35, 1964

– 'In Darkest Language', *The New York Times Book Review*, 29 Oct. 1967; reprinted in *How I Wrote Certain of My Books* (1977)

– 'The Bachelor-Machines of Raymond Roussel', *Other Traditions* (Cambridge: Harvard University Press, 2000)

Atlas, Anatole, 'Spectre nègre: Nouvelles Nouvelles Impressions d'Afrique', *Digraphe*, no. 67, 1994

Baronian, Jean-Baptiste, 'Roussel: Un certain fantastique né du langage', in *Panorama de la littérature fantastique de la France* (Paris: Stock, 1978)

Basset, Anne-Marie, 'La genèse de quelques noms dans *Locus Solus*', *Raymond Roussel: perversion classique ou invention moderne?* (1993)

Bazantay, Pierre, 'Montesquiou, lecteur sans procédé', *Europe*, no. 714, Oct. 1988

– 'Le Grand théâtre du monde', *La Quinzaine littéraire*, no. 598, 1–15 April 1992

– '*Claude et Luce*, un mélodrame inachevé', *Revue de la Bibliothèque Nationale*, no. 43, 1992

– 'Mais c'est un très grand poète!', *Raymond Roussel: perversion classique ou invention moderne?* (1993)

Bauer, George, 'Roussel–Duchamp', *La Quinzaine littéraire*, no. 407, 15–31 Dec. 1983

– 'La jolie roussel brisée: les vairs du chant', *Raymond Roussel en gloire* (1984)

Behar, Henri, 'La gloire théâtrale de Raymond Roussel', in *Étude sur le théâtre dada et surréaliste* (Paris: Gallimard, 1967)

– 'Heureuse méprise: Raymond Roussel et les surréalistes', *Raymond Roussel en gloire* (1984)

Berger, Pierre, 'Avec Raymond Roussel, au seuil du surréalisme', *Les Lettres Françaises*, no. 981, 6–11 June 1963

Bernart, Maurice, 'Discussion avec Elisabeth Roudinesco sur le film *Mort de Raymond Roussel*', *L'Arc*, no. 68, 1977

Berton, Patrice, and Lefrère, Jean-Jacques, 'Un grand et riche malade', *Le Magazine littéraire*, no. 186, July 1982

Besnier, Patrick, 'Souvenirs de Byzance', *Europe*, no. 714, Oct. 1988

– 'Claude et Luce, nouveau continent roussellien', *La Quinzaine littéraire*, no. 598, 1–15 April 1992

– 'La Seine: les confidences de la foule', *Revue de la Bibliothèque Nationale*, no. 43, 1992
– 'Une enfance malheureuse', *Raymond Roussel: perversion classique ou invention moderne?* (1993)
– 'Les profondeurs du parc', *Digraphe*, no. 67, 1994

Besnier, Patrick, and Bazantay, Pierre, *Petit dictionnaire de Locus Solus* (Amsterdam: Rodopi, 1993)
– 'Impressions d'Europe', *Europe*, no. 714, Oct. 1988

Bilous, Daniel, 'Pasticher Roussel', *Raymond Roussel en gloire* (1984)

Blanchot, Maurice, 'Le problème de Wittgenstein, Flaubert, Roussel', *L'Entretien infini* (Paris: Gallimard, 1969)

Bonnaut-Lamotte, Danielle, Rispail, Jean-Luc, and Rojas, Waldo, 'La lexicologie de *Locus Solus* ou Roussel pris au(x) mot(s)', *Raymond Roussel en gloire* (1984)

Bonnefoy, Claude, ed., La galaxie Roussel, Les Nouvelles littéraires, no. 2575, 10–17 March 1977

Borzic, Jean, 'Roussel en Sorbonne', *Bizarre*, no. 34–35, 1964

Bourque, Ghislain, 'De Triomphe pour le cas Roussel', *L'Arc*, no. 68, 1977
– 'Les répliques de l'épissure', *Raymond Roussel: perversion classique ou invention moderne?* (1993)

Breton, André, 'Fronton-Virage', *Les Cahiers de la Pléiade* (1948); reprinted in *Une étude sur Raymond Roussel* by Jean Ferry, and collected in *La Clé des champs* (Paris: Gallimard, 1953), reprinted in *Digraphe*, no. 67, 1994, and trans. Michel Parmentier and Jacqueline d'Amboise in *Free Rein* (Lincoln: University of Nebraska Press, 1996)
– 'Anthologie de l'humour noir: Raymond Roussel', *Le Minotaure*, no. 10, 1937, collected in *Anthologie de l'humour noir* (Paris: Sagittaire, 1940), trans. Martin Sorrell, *Atlas Anthology* 4 (London: Atlas Press, 1987)

Bulteau, Michel, 'Roussel à l'unanimité', *Digraphe*, no. 67, 1994

Bustarret, Claire, and Basset, Anne-Marie, 'Les cahiers d'*Impressions d'Afrique*: l'apport de la codicologie à l'étude génétique', *Genesis*, no. 5, 1994

Busine, Laurent, *Raymond Roussel: Contemplator enim* (Brussels: La Lettre volée, 1995)

Butor, Michel, 'Sur les procédés de Raymond Roussel' (1950) collected in *Répertoire I* (Paris: Minuit, 1960), trans. Roderick Masterton as 'The Methods of Raymond Roussel' in *Atlas Athology* 4 (London: Atlas Press, 1987)
– 'Comment écrire Boomerang', *Les Nouvelles littéraires*, no. 2575, 10–17 March 1977
– 'Archipel Shopping 1', *L'Arc*, no. 68, 1977

- 'Entretien sur Raymond Roussel avec Anne-Marie Amiot et Jean-Louis Meunier', *Raymond Roussel en gloire* (1984)
Caburet, Bernard, *Raymond Roussel* (Paris: Seghers, 1968)
Calvino, Italo, 'La Narration des figures croisées', *Les Nouvelles littéraires*, no. 2575, 10–17 March 1977
Caradec, François, 'La Machine à Imprimer Raymond Roussel', *Bizarre*, no. 34–35, 1964
- 'La tombe de Raymond Roussel', *Bizarre*, no. 34–35, 1964
- 'Balises', *Épaves* (Paris: Jean-Jacques Pauvert, 1972)
- *Raymond Roussel* (Paris: Jean-Jacques Pauvert,1972, updated and revised, Paris: Fayard,1997)
- 'Le Grand Infusoire', *Les Nouvelles littéraires*, no. 2575, 10–17 March 1977
- 'Un roussellâtre: Raymond Queneau', *La Quinzaine littéraire*, no. 256, 16–31 May 1977
- 'Vide Raymond Roussel', *Raymond Roussel en gloire* (1984)
- 'Faut-il avoir lu Schopenhauer pour lire Roussel?', Interview with François Caradec, *Europe*, no. 714, Oct. 1988
- 'La malle à Gouffré', *La Quinzaine littéraire*, no. 597, 17–31 May 1992
- 'Images, visages et voyages de Raymond Roussel', *Revue de la Bibliothèque Nationale*, no. 43, 1992
- 'L'inspiration', *Raymond Roussel: perversion classique ou invention moderne?* (1993)
Carrouges, Michel, 'Raymond Roussel', *Les Machines Célibataires* (Paris: Arcanes, 1954)
Caws, Mary Ann, 'À double vue, ou les artifices en plein jour roussellien', *Raymond Roussel en gloire* (1984)
Chambers, Ross, 'Literature as Parenthesis: Raymond Roussel', *Meanjin Quarterly*, no. 29, March 1970
Charbonnier, Alexandra, 'Histoire d'Étoiles: Une rencontre Roussel-Milosz', *Digraphe*, no. 67, 1994
Chatard, Jean, and Morneux, Robert, 'Interview de Michel Ney, duc d'Elchingen', *Bizarre*, no. 34–35, 1964
- 'L'homme étincelant', *Bizarre*, no. 34–35, 1964
Cocteau, Jean, 'Raymond Roussel', *Bizarre*, no. 34–35, 1964
- 'Raymond Roussel', *Poésie Critique I* (Paris: Gallimard, 1959)
Cornille, Jean-Louis, 'Réimpressions d'Afrique. Légende ou conte d'auteur', *Raymond Roussel: perversion classique ou invention moderne?* (1993)
Dalí, Salvador, 'Raymond Roussel, *Nouvelles Impressions d'Afrique*', *Surréalisme au Service de la Révolution*, no. 6, 1933, trans. Martin Sorrell, *Atlas Anthology* 4 (London: Atlas Press, 1987)

Decaudin, Michel, 'Le Secret de *La Doublure*', *La Quinzaine littéraire*, no. 407, 15–31 Dec. 1983

– 'Raymond Roussel et le roman en vers', *Raymond Roussel en gloire* (1984)

Desmille, Sylvain, 'De tous ces voyages je n'ai rien tiré pour mes livres . . .', *Digraphe*, no. 67, 1994

Desnos, Robert, '*L'Étoile au Front*', *391*, no. 17, 1924\*

– 'Raymond Roussel ou coïncidences et circonstances de la destinée', *Paris-Journal*, 8 Feb. 1924\*

– '*L'Étoile au Front* par Raymond Roussel', *La Revue Européenne*, no. 28, 1 June 1925\*

– 'Raymond Roussel et son action sur le public', *Europe*, no. 517–518, May-June 1972\*

– 'Une vie excentrique: Raymond Roussel le mystérieux', *L'Intransigeant*, 7 August 1933

[Essays marked \* collected in *Nouvelles Hébrides et autres textes, 1922–1930* (Paris: Gallimard, 1978)]

Dhainaut, Pierre, 'Raymond Roussel oseur d'influence', *Bizarre*, no. 34–35, 1964

– 'Les lecteurs de Roussel', *La Quinzaine littéraire*, no. 256, 16–31 May 1977

Dinguirard, Jean-Claude, 'La logique de Roussel', *Subsidia Pataphysica*, no. 6, 1968

Dormoy, Denis, 'Intertexte associatif Verne/Roussel', *In'hui*, no. 3, 1978

Duboy, Philippe, ' "Vers une architecture": Raymond Roussel inventeur', *Digraphe*, no. 67, Feb. 1994

Dujardin, Édouard, 'Le cas de *Locus Solus*', *Revue de l'époque*, May 1923; reprinted in *Bizarre*, no. 34–35, 1964

Dumas, Marie-Claire, 'Robert Desnos et Raymond Roussel', *Europe*, no. 517–518, May-June 1972

Durham, Carolyn, *L'Art romanesque de Raymond Roussel* (York, USA: French Literature Publications Company, 1982)

– 'Sur les impressions rousseliennes. Les stratégies de la réception', *Raymond Roussel en gloire* (1984)

Éluard, Paul, 'Raymond Roussel, *L'Étoile au front*', *La Révolution surréaliste*, no. 4, 1925, reprinted in *Bizarre*, no. 34–35, 1964

Eruli, Brunella, 'Le moule et le clou. Les objets idiots chez Roussel', *Raymond Roussel: perversion classique ou invention moderne?* (1993)

Ezine, Jean-Louis, 'Treize cases d'une vie', *La Quinzaine littéraire*, no. 256, 16–31 May 1977

Fassio, Juan-Esteban, 'La Machine à Lire *Nouvelles Impressions d'Afrique*', *Bizarre*, no. 34–35, 1964

Faussot, Jean-Jacques, 'Quand Roussel rime avec universel', *Digraphe*, no. 67, 1994

Ferry, Jean, 'Raymond Roussel', *Documents 34*, no. 9–10 (under the name Jean Lévy)

– Analyse de deux ouvrages de Raymond Roussel, *Documents 34* (new series), no. 1, 1934; reprinted in *Bizarre*, no. 34–35, 1964

– 'La chaîne de *La Poussière de Soleils*', Les Cahiers de la Pléiade, summer 1948, reprinted in *Une étude sur Raymond Roussel* (Paris: Arcanes,1953)

– *Une étude sur Raymond Roussel* (Paris: Arcanes,1953)

– *Une autre étude sur Raymond Roussel* (Paris: Publications du Collège de Pataphysique,1964); reprinted in *Bizarre*, no. 34–35, 1964

– 'En Afrique sur les traces de Roussel: A la recherche d'Ejur perdue', *Dossiers du Collège de Pataphysique*, no. 26, 8 June 1964

– 'Premières constatations à propos de Flio', *Bizarre*, no. 34–35, 1964

– *L'Afrique des impressions* (Paris: Jean-Jacques Pauvert,1967)

– 'Roussel revient', *Subsidia Pataphysica*, no. 14, 1972

Finter, Helga, 'L'offrande langagière: scènes', *Raymond Roussel: perversion classique ou invention moderne?* 1993)

Ford, Mark, 'John Ashbery and Raymond Roussel', *Verse*, Autumn 1986, vol 3, no. 3

– 'Genius in Its Pure State', *The London Review of Books*, Vol 19, no. 10, 22 May 1997

Formentelli, Éliane, 'Notes sur la pensée rhapsodique: Roussel, Ernst, Ponge', *Revue d'esthétique*, no. 3–4, 1978

Foucault, Michel, 'Dire et voir chez Raymond Roussel', *Lettre ouverte*, no. 4, 1962

– *Raymond Roussel* (Paris: Gallimard,1963), trans. Charles Ruas as *Death and the Labyrinth: The World of Raymond Roussel* (London: Athlone Press,1987)

Foulc, Thieri, 'Quelques exemples du procédé roussellien hors de Roussel', *Subsidia Pataphysica*, no. 14, 1972

Fremon, Jean, 'L'homme caché', *Les Nouvelles littéraires*, no. 2575, 10–17 March 1977

– 'L'exhibitionnisme et sa pudeur', *L'Arc*, no. 68, 1977

Goodman, Lanie, 'Le marteau et son mètre', *La Quinzaine littéraire*, no. 407, 15–31 Dec. 1983

– 'La résurrection de Narcisse: Fogar au clair de lune'

– 'Le corps-accord Rousselien: machines à composer', *L'Esprit créateur*, vol 26, no. 4, 1986

– 'Roussel, forban', *Europe*, no. 714, Oct. 1988

– 'La fantasque cuisine de Raymond Roussel: les mots plats',

*Raymond Roussel: perversion classique ou invention moderne?*
(1993)

Grossel, Hanss, 'La fiction dans la vie', *La Quinzaine littéraire*, no.
256, 16–31 May 1977

Hallier, Jean-Edern, 'D'un art sans passé', *Tel Quel*, no. 6, Summer
1961

Harig, Ludwig, 'La mise à l'envers des eurocrates', *Les Nouvelles
littéraires*, no. 2575, 10–17 March 1977

Henein, Georges, 'Un dandy caché, Raymond Roussel', *Gulliver*, no.
4, Feb. 1973

Heppenstall, Rayner, 'Raymond Roussel: A Preliminary Study', *New
Directions*, no. 18, 1964

– *Raymond Roussel* (London: Calder and Boyars, 1966)

Heroult, Michel, 'Ciel natal et position astrologique de Raymond
Roussel', *Bizarre*, no. 34–35, 1964

Herrmann, Claudine, 'La gigue de Sir Roger', *Sub-stance*, no. 10,
1974

Houppermans, Sjef, *Raymond Roussel: Écriture et désir* (Paris:
Librairie José Corti, 1985)

– 'Autour des canevas', *Raymond Roussel: perversion classique ou
invention moderne?* (1993)

Jean, Raymond, 'Il a porté haut et loin le sens de l'inutilité', *La
Quinzaine littéraire*, no. 256, 16–31 May 1977

Jenny, Laurent, 'Structure et fonctions du cliché', *Poétique*, no. 12,
1972

– 'Le discours de carnaval', *Littérature*, no. 16, 1974

– 'Le double et son théâtre', *L'Arc*, no. 68, 1977

Juin, Hubert, 'Raymond Roussel a-t-il créé le roman blanc?', *Les
Nouvelles littéraires*, 5 Sept. 1963

– 'Raymond Roussel et ses énigmes', *Le Magazine littéraire*, no. 70,
Nov. 1972

Kerbellec, Philippe G., *Comment Lire Raymond Roussel* (Paris: Jean-
Jacques Pauvert,1988)

– Raymond Roussel, presque', *Europe*, no. 714, Oct. 1988

– *Raymond Roussel: au cannibale affable* (Monaco: du Rocher, 1994)

– 'Who's Who,' *Digraphe*, no. 67, 1994

Kitayama, Kenji, 'Raymond Roussel au Japon', *Raymond Roussel:
perversion classique ou invention moderne?* (1993)

– 'Pourquoi et comment R.R. au Japon', *Digraphe*, no. 67, 1994

Kristeva, Julia, 'La productivité dite texte', *Semiotikè, recherches pour
une sémanalyse* (Paris: Le Seuil, 1969)

Lascault, Gilbert, 'Quatorze notes sur le nombre deux chez Raymond
Roussel', *Raymond Roussel: perversion classique ou invention
moderne?* (1993)

Laplace, Jean, 'Raymond Roussel et le merveilleux', *Prisme*, no. 15, Spring 1980

Lautier, Claudine, 'Chant et champ', *Raymond Roussel en gloire* (1984)

Lazareff, Pierre, 'Raymond Roussel, curieux homme', *Paris-midi*, 3 August 1933; reprinted in *Bizarre*, no. 34–35, 1964

Lebrun, Annie, *Vingt mille lieues sous les mots, Raymond Roussel* (Paris: Pauvert/Fayard, 1994)

– 'Des étoiles sous la poussière', *La Quinzaine littéraire*, no. 598, 1–15 April 1992

– 'Un obus formidable qui n'a pas encore éclaté', *Revue de la Bibliothèque Nationale*, no. 43, 1992

Leiris, Michel, 'Le Voyageur et son ombre', *La Bête noire*, no. 1, 1 April 1935

– 'Documents sur Raymond Roussel', *La Nouvelle Revue française*, no. 259, 1 April 1935

– '*Comment j'ai écrit certains de mes livres*', *La Nouvelle Revue française*, no. 268, 1 Jan. 1936; collected in *Brisées* (Paris: Mercure de France, 1966), trans. Lydia Davis as *Brisées: Broken Branches* (San Francisco: North Point Press, 1989)

– 'Autour des *Nouvelles Impressions d'Afrique*', *Cahiers GLM*, no. 9, March 1939

– 'Conception et réalité chez Raymond Roussel', *Critique*, no. 89, October 1954; trans. John Ashbery as 'Conception and Reality in the Work of Raymond Roussel', *Atlas Anthology* 4 (London: Atlas Press, 1987)

– 'Entretien sur Raymond Roussel', *Le promeneur*, no. 50, Oct. 1986

– *Roussel l'ingénu* [includes all essays above] (Paris: Fata Morgana, 1987)

– 'L'œil de l'ethnographe', *Europe*, no. 714, Oct. 1988

– *Roussel & Co.* ed. Jean Jamin and Annie Le Brun [includes all essays above, Leiris's *Cahier Raymond Roussel*, correspondence with Roussel and extracts from his journals and other texts relating to Roussel] (Paris: Fata Morgana/Fayard, 1998)

Le Roy Ladurie, Emmanuel, 'À la découverte du fonds Roussel', *Revue de la Bibliothèque Nationale*, no. 43, 1992

Leveque, Jean-Jacques, 'Du côté de chez Roussel', *Les Nouvelles littéraires*, no. 2371, 5–11 March 1973

– 'Vous reprendrez bien un peu d'hermétique Roussel', *Les Nouvelles littéraires*, no. 2892, 23–29 June 1983

London, Geo, 'Les impressions du dramaturge Raymond Roussel chef de jury aux Assises de la Seine', *Le Journal*, 12 Jan. 1928; reprinted in *Bizarre*, no. 34–35, 1964

Lorin, François, 'Raymond Roussel ou l'irrémédiable extase', *Bizarre*, no. 34–35, 1964

Lovitt, Carl, 'Locus Solus; Literary Solitaire', *Sub-stance*, no. 10, 1974

Machia, Giovanni, 'La lumière, l'extase et le sang', *Europe*, no. 714, Oct. 1988

Magné, Bernard, 'Perec, lecteur de Roussel', *Raymond Roussel en gloire* (1984)

– 'De Roussel et Perec, derechef: à propos des procédés', *Raymond Roussel: perversion classique ou invention moderne?* (1993)

Magny, Olivier de, 'Les jouets de génie', *La Quinzaine littéraire*, no. 161, April 1973

Martins, Fernando Cabral, 'Les caractères psychologiques de l'extase', *Raymond Roussel: perversion classique ou invention moderne?* (1993)

Mathews, Harry, 'En 1956 . . .', *Digraphe*, no. 67, 1994

Mathews, Harry, and Perec, Georges, 'Roussel et Venise', *L'Arc*, no. 68, 1977; trans. Harry Mathews and Alastair Brotchie as 'Roussel and Venice', *Atlas Anthology* 3 (London: Atlas Press, 1985)

Mathews, Harry, and Brotchie, Alastair, eds, 'Roussel and his methods', *Oulipo Compendium* (London: Atlas Press, 1999)

Mathews, J. H., *Le Théâtre de Raymond Roussel, une énigme* (Paris: Minard, Archives des lettres modernes,1977)

Montesquiou, Robert de, 'Un auteur difficile', in *Élus et appelés* (Paris: Emile-Paul frères, 1921); reprinted in *Digraphe*, no. 67, 1994, and as *Un auteur difficile* (intro Gilbert Lascaux, Paris: Fata Morgana, 1999); trans. Catherine Allan as 'A Difficult Author', *Atlas Anthology* 4 (London: Atlas Press, 1987)

Noailly, Michèle, '*Locus Solus*, une apothéose de l'adjectif', *Europe*, no. 714, Oct. 1988

Parisier-Plottel, Jeanine, 'Roussel's Mechanisms of Language', *Dada/Surrealism*, no. 5, 1976

– 'Lecture psychanalytique des parenthèses des *Nouvelles Impressions d'Afrique*', *Raymond Roussel en gloire* (1984)

– 'Traditions ésotériques et populaires chez Raymond Roussel', *Raymond Roussel: perversion classique ou invention moderne?* (1993)

Pauvert, Jean-Jacques, 'Histoire de lectures', *Raymond Roussel en gloire* (1984)

Perriault, Jacques, 'Informaticien sans le savoir', *Les Nouvelles littéraires*, no. 2575, 10–17 March 1977

– 'Algorithmes dans le texte roussellien', *Raymond Roussel en gloire* (1984)

Pierssens, Michel, 'La maison de Roussel', *La Quinzaine littéraire*, no. 256, 16–31 May 1977

Pindar, Ian, 'Roussel, the eternal unread', *Times Literary Supplement*, 6 October 1995

Porush, David, 'Roussel's Device for the Perfection of Fiction', *The Soft Machine* (London: Methuen, 1985)

Queneau, Raymond, '*Nouvelles Impressions d'Afrique*', *La Critique sociale*, no. 7, 1933

Raillard, Georges, 'Un homme en gazon', *L'Arc*, no. 68, 1977

– 'Par où commencer la lecture', *La Quinzaine littéraire*, no. 407, 15–31 Dec. 1983

– '472', *La Quinzaine littéraire*, no. 407, 15–31 Dec. 1983

Raymond, François, 'Roussel et le récit d'énigme', *Europe*, no. 714, Oct. 1988

Rebourg, Michel, 'Entre graphe et scope – Roussel au cinéma', *Europe*, no. 714, Oct. 1988

Ricardou, Jean, 'L'activité roussellienne', *Pour une théorie du Nouveau Roman* (Paris: Le Seuil, 1971)

– 'Disparition élocutoire', in Leonardo Sciascia's *Actes relatifs à la mort de Raymond Roussel* (Paris: L'Herne, 1972); trans. Alec Gordon as 'Elocutory Disappearance', *Atlas Anthology* 4 (London: Atlas Press, 1987)

– 'Le Nouveau Roman est-il roussellien?', *L'Arc*, no. 68, 1977

– 'Raymond Roussel: Un académisme démesuré', *Raymond Roussel: perversion classique ou invention moderne?* (1993)

Richard, Elie, 'Raymond Roussel ou le génie ne fait pas le bonheur', *Paris-midi*, 9 Oct. 1927; reprinted in *Bizarre*, no. 34–35, 1964

Robbe-Grillet, Alain, 'Énigmes et transparence chez Raymond Roussel', *Pour un nouveau roman* (Paris: Minuit, 1963; reprinted Paris: Gallimard, 1970); trans. Barbara Wright as 'Riddles and Transparencies in Raymond Roussel', *Atlas Anthology* 4 (London: Atlas Press, 1987)

– 'Page décollée', *L'Arc*, no. 68, 1977

– 'Les procédés sont faits pour être détruits', *Les Nouvelles littéraires*, no. 2575, 10–17 March 1977

Roche, Denis, 'Ma mort, mon cher Roussel!', *Le Monde*, 22 Feb. 1973

– '10/18', *Louve basse* (Paris: Le Seuil, 1976)

– 'Considérons froidement l'exercise de la poésie', *Les Nouvelles littéraires*, no. 2575, 10–17 March 1977

Roscioni, Gian Carlo, 'Comment naissent les mythes', *Europe*, no. 714, Oct. 1988

Rosset, Clément, 'Une littérature pour rire', *Raymond Roussel en gloire* (1984)

Roubaud, Jacques, 'Queneau, Roussel', *La Vieillesse d'Alexandre* (Paris: Maspéro, 1978)

Roudinesco, Elisabeth, 'La mort de Raymond Roussel', *L'Arc*, no. 68, 1977

Salceda, Hermès, 'Cases et folios', *Raymond Roussel: perversion classique ou invention moderne?* (1993)

Schneider, Pierre, 'La fenêtre, ou piège à Roussel', *Les Cahiers du Sud*, nos. 306–307, 1951

Sciascia, Leonardo, *Actes relatifs à la mort de Raymond Roussel* (Paris: L'Herne, 1972); trans. Alec Gordon as 'Acts Relative to the Death of Raymond Roussel', *Atlas Anthology* 4 (London: Atlas Press, 1987)

Sola, Agnès, 'Raymond Roussel: gallop d'essai avant Dada', *Raymond Roussel en gloire* (1984)

Sollers, Philippe, 'Logicus Solus', *Logiques* (Paris: Le Seuil, 1968)
– 'Un procédé très spécial', *Le Monde*, 4 Feb. 1977

Sorin, Raphaël, 'La Pendule de Foucault', *Bizarre*, no. 34–35, 1964

Soupault, Philippe, 'Raymond Roussel,' *Littérature*, 1 April 1922; reprinted in *Digraphe*, no. 67, 1994; trans. Antony Melville, *Atlas Anthology* 4 (London: Atlas Press, 1987)

Starobinski, Jean, 'Raymond Roussel et le mythe de la défaillance fatale', *Les Lettres nouvelles*, no. 39, Oct. 1963

Sturrock, John, 'Raymond Roussel', *The Word from Paris* (London: Verso, 1998)

Tani, Masachika, 'La mort et le temps: Raymond Roussel et Camille Flammarion', *Europe*, no. 714, Oct. 1988

Touttain, Pierre-André, 'Le destin d'un prophète', *Les Nouvelles littéraires*, no. 2371, 5–11 March 1973,

Thomson, Andrew, 'Selections from the critical writings about Roussel's theatre', *Atlas Anthology* 4 (London: Atlas Press, 1987)

Valaoritis, Nanos, 'Dioptrique: Réflexions sur l'œuvre de Raymond Roussel', *Digraphe*, no. 67, 1994

Veschambre, Christiane, 'Sur les *Impressions d'Afrique*', *Poétique*, no. 1, 1970

Villani, Arnaud, 'De la métagrammatologie: Roussel et la philosophie contemporaine', *Raymond Roussel en gloire* (1984)

Villetard, Xavier, 'Raymond Roussel', *La Nouvelle Revue française*, no. 173, 1 Feb. 1928; reprinted in *Bizarre*, no. 34–35, 1964

Vitrac, Roger, 'Joueur d'échecs', *La Nouvelle Revue française*, no. 173, 1 Feb. 1928; reprinted in *Bizarre*, no. 34–35, 1964, and *Digraphe*, no. 67, 1994; partially trans. Kathleen Cannell and Antony Melville as 'Raymond Roussel', *Atlas Anthology* 4 (London: Atlas Press, 1987)

## Special Issues of Magazines Devoted to Roussel and Collections of Essays on Roussel*

Raymond Roussel, *Bizarre*, no. 34–35, 1964

La Gloire de Raymond Roussel, *Le Monde*, 22 Feb. 1973

Du côté de chez Raymond Roussel, *Les Nouvelles littéraires*, no. 2731, 5–11 March 1973

La galaxie Roussel, *Les Nouvelles littéraires*, no. 2575, 10–17 March 1977

Raymond Roussel, *L'Arc*, no. 68, 1977

Raymond Roussel, *La Quinzaine littéraire*, no. 256, 16–31 May 1977

Raymond Roussel, *La Quinzaine littéraire*, no. 407, 15–31 Dec. 1983

Raymond Roussel en gloire, *Mélusine* no. VI, (Lausanne: L'Age d'Homme,1984)

*Raymond Roussel: Life, Death and Works, Atlas Anthology 4*, ed. Alastair Brotchie et al (London: Atlas Press, 1987)

Raymond Roussel, *Europe*, no. 714, 1988

Découvrir Raymond Roussel, *Revue de la Bibliothèque Nationale*, no. 43, Spring 1992

Raymond Roussel, *La Quinzaine littéraire*, no. 598, 1–15 April 1992

*Raymond Roussel, perversion classique ou invention moderne?* (Rennes: Presses Universitaires de Rennes, 1993)

Raymond Roussel, *Digraphe*, no. 67, Feb. 1994

## Other Works Cited

Aragon, Louis, *Je n'ai jamais appris à écrire, ou les incipit* (Paris: Les Sentiers de la création/Skira, 1969)

– *Chroniques* (Paris: Stock, 1998)

Ashbery, John, *Some Trees* (New Haven: Yale University Press, 1956; reprinted New York: Ecco Press, 1978)

Barthes, Roland, *Sade/Fourier/Loyola* (Paris: Éditions du Seuil, 1971); trans. Richard Miller (London: Jonathan Cape, 1977)

Bataille, Georges, *3uvres complètes* (Paris: Gallimard, 1970)

Breton, André, *Anthologie de l'humour noir* (Paris: Sagittaire, 1940)

– *Manifestoes of Surrealism*, trans. Richard Seaver and Helen R. Lane (Ann Arbor: The University of Michigan Press, 1969)

– *3uvres complètes*, ed. Marguerite Bonnet et al (Paris: Gallimard, 1992)

* Authors and titles of individual essays are given in the previous section.

Brotchie, Alastair, and Green, Malcolm, *Atlas Anthology 3* (London: Atlas Press, 1985)

Butor, Michel, *Portrait de l'artiste en jeune singe* (Paris: Gallimard, 1967)

– *Matière de Rêves* (Paris: Gallimard, 1975)

Cocteau, Jean, *Opium. Journal d'une désintoxication* (Paris: Stock, 1930) trans. Margaret Crosland (London: Peter Owen, 1990, first published 1957)

– *Entretiens avec André Fraigneau* (Paris: Éditions du Rocher, 1988)

Coppée, François, *Le Cahier Rouge* (Paris: Lemerre, 1891)

Chaleyssin, Patrick, *Robert de Montesquiou – mécène et dandy* (Paris: Somogy, 1992)

Desnos, Robert, *Nouvelles Hébrides et autres textes, 1922–30* (Paris, Gallimard, 1978)

Desnos, Youki, *Les Confidences de Youki* (Paris: Fayard, 1957)

Duchamp, Marcel, *The Essential Writings of Marcel Duchamp*, ed. Michel Sanouillet and Elmer Peterson, (London: Thames and Hudson, 1975)

*Dialogues with Marcel Duchamp* by Pierre Cabanne, trans. Ron Padgett, (London: Thames and Hudson, 1971)

Ernst, Max, *Écritures* (Paris: Gallimard, 1970)

Flaubert, Gustave, *Flaubert in Egypt*, trans. and ed. Francis Steegmuller (London: Penguin, 1996, first published 1979)

Guillot, André, *La Grande Cuisine bourgeoise* (Paris: Flammarion, 1976)

Hugo, Victor, 'Les Chants du Crépuscule', *3uvres poétiques*, ed. P. Albouy et al (Paris: Gallimard,1968)

James, Henry, *Roderick Hudson*, ed. Tony Tanner (Oxford: Oxford University Press, 1980, New York edition first published 1908)

Janet, Pierre, *De l'angoisse à l'extase* (Paris: Alcan, 1926)

Koch, Kenneth, *Selected Poems* (New York: Vintage, 1985)

Lehman, David, *The Last Avant-Garde: The Making of the New York School of Poets* (New York: Doubleday, 1998)

Leiris, Michel, *Glossaire, j'y serre mes gloses* (Paris: 1939); collected in *Mots sans mémoire* (Paris: Gallimard, 1969)

– *Biffures* (Paris: Gallimard, 1948)

Loti, Pierre, *Le Mariage de Loti* (Paris: Calman Lévy, 1880); trans. Clara Bell as *The Marriage of Loti* (New York: Gottsberger, 1890)

Martin, Andrew, *The Mask of the Prophet: The Extraordinary Fictions of Jules Verne* (Oxford: Oxford University Press, 1990)

Mathews, Harry, *The Way Home* (London: Atlas Press, 1989)

Mirbeau, Octave, *Le jardin des supplices* (Paris: 1890); trans. Alvah C. Bessie as *Torture Garden* (Sawtry: Dedalus, 1990)

Montesquiou, Robert de, *Les Délices de Capharnaüm* (Paris: Émile-Paul frères, 1921)

– *Les Pas effacés* (Paris: Emile-Paul frères, 1923)

Moré, Marcel, *Le Très Curieux Jules Verne* (Paris: Gallimard, 1960)

Motte, Warren F., Jr, ed. and trans., *Oulipo: A Primer of Potential Literature* (Lincoln: University of Nebaska Press, 1986)

Nabokov, Vladimir, *The Stories of Vladimir Nabokov* (London: Weidenfeld & Nicolson, 1996)

Perec, Georges, *La Disparition* (Paris: Denoël, 1969)

– *W ou le souvenir d'enfance* (Paris: Denoël, 1975); trans. David Bellos as *W or the Memory of Childhood* (London: Collins Harvill, 1988)

– *La Vie mode d'emploi* (Paris: Hachette, 1978); trans. David Bellos as *Life, a User's Manual* (London: Collins Harvill, 1987)

– *Un cabinet d'amateur* (Paris: André Balland, 1979); trans. Ian Monk as 'A Gallery Portrait' and published in *Three* (London: Collins Harvill, 1996)

– *Cahiers Georges Perec 3: Presbytère et Prolétaires* (Paris: Éditions du Limon, 1989)

– *Vœux* (Paris: Éditions du Seuil, 1989)

Polizzotti, Mark, *Revolution of the Mind: The Life of André Breton* (New York: Farrar Straus & Giroux, 1995)

Rainwater, Robert, ed., *Max Ernst: Beyond Surrealism* (New York and Oxford: The New York Public Library and Oxford University Press, 1986)

*La Révolution Surréaliste* (Paris: no. I, 1924; no. IV, 1925)

Sade, Marquis de, *Les 120 Journées de Sodome* (Paris: 1935); trans. Austryn Wainhouse and Richard Seaver as *The 120 Days of Sodom* (New York: Grove Weidenfeld, 1966)

Sawyer-Lauçanno, Christopher, *The Continual Pilgrimage: American Writers in Paris 1944–1960* (New York: Grove Press, 1992)

Sedgwick, Eve Kosofsky, *Epistemology of the Closet* (London: Penguin, 1994, first published 1990)

Seigel, Jerrold, 'Avoiding the Subject: A Foucaultian Itinerary,' *Journal of the History of Ideas* (1990)

Verne, Jules, *Le tour du monde en 80 jours* (Paris: 1873), trans. P. Desages, ed. Peter Costello as *Around the World in 80 Days* (London: Everyman, 1994)

Winkfield, Trevor, *Pageant*, text by Jed Perl, introduction by John Ashbery (West Stockbridge: Hard Press, 1997)

# References and Additional Notes

## Introduction

xxii 'total transparency': *Pour un nouveau roman* (Paris: Minuit, 1963; reprinted Paris: Gallimard, 1970), hereafter RG, p. 71.

'what he leaves us with': *How I Wrote Certain of My Books*, ed. Trevor Winkfield (Boston: Exact Change, 1995), hereafter HIW, p. xxii.

xxiii 'n'est-ce rien?': Georges Pioch in *Ère Nouvelle*. An extract from this article is included in Roussel's compilation of critical responses to his work, which is reprinted in Philippe G. Kerbellec's *Comment Lire Raymond Roussel* (Paris: Jean-Jacques Pauvert, 1988), hereafter CL, p. 252.

'il ne se classe': *La Révolution surréaliste*, no. 1, Dec. 1924, p. 32.

xxiv 'his life was constructed': *Roussel & Co.* (Paris: Fata Morgana/ Fayard, 1998), hereafter R & CO, p. 251.

'feel bound to attempt': *Raymond Roussel* (London: Calder & Boyars, 1966), p. 88.

xxv 'ensure that his next relapse': *The Word from Paris: Essays on Modern French Thinkers and Writers* (London: Verso, 1998), p. 168.

xxvii 'is like trying to summarize': *How I Wrote Certain of My Books*, ed. Trevor Winkfield (New York: Sun, 1977), hereafter HIW 77, p. 60.

'then instantly, I abandoned myself': CL, p. 248.

xxviii 'under a spell': *Opium: The Illustrated Diary of His Cure*, trans. Margaret Crosland (London, Peter Owen, 1990), hereafter O, p. 114.

xxviii 'there is hidden in Roussel': HIW, p. viii.

## CHAPTER 1: How He Wrote Certain of His Books

1 'An accompanying letter stipulated': R & CO, pp. 74–5. This letter was transcribed by Michel Leiris into his *Cahier Roussel*, a notebook in which he collected information about Roussel and wrote drafts of his essays. This notebook has now been

published in *Roussel & Co*. Also included in this collection are all Leiris's previously published writings on Roussel, extracts from his journal relating to Roussel and a selection of their correspondence.

'I have always intended to explain': *Comment j'ai écrit certain de mes livres* (Paris: Lemerre, 1935; reprinted Paris: Jean-Jacques Pauvert, 1963; all references are to the Pauvert edition), hereafter CJ, p. 11. The essay 'Comment j'ai écrit . . .' has been translated into English by Trevor Winkfield and published in *How I Wrote Certain of My Books* (1977), then reprinted in *How I Wrote Certain of My Books* (1995), p. 3. All references will be to the later volume.

' "Parmi les Noirs", for example, begins': CJ, p. 163, p. 170. 'Parmi les Noirs' has been translated into English by Ron Padgett in a small book including an autobiographical essay entitled *Among the Blacks* (Bolinas: Avenue B, 1988), hereafter AB, p. 3, p. 13.

2 'the two phrases found': CJ, p. 12/HIW, p. 4.
'now it was from the resolution': ibid.
'I would choose a word': CJ, pp. 14–15/HIW, p. 7.

3 'The *procédé* developed': CJ, p. 20/HIW, p. 12.

4 'this prospecting did not proceed': CJ, p. 29/HIW, p. 23.
'As Robbe-Grillet noted in his essay': RG, p. 72. This essay has been translated by Barbara Wright and published in an anthology of writings on Roussel entitled *Raymond Roussel: Life, Death and Works*. *Atlas Anthology 4* (ed. Alastair Brotchie et al, London: Atlas Press, 1987), hereafter AT4, p. 101.

5 'At last, when I was nearly thirty': CJ, p. 30/HIW, p. 23.
'The *nouveau romancier* Michel Butor has argued': 'Sur les procédés de Raymond Roussel', first published in 1950, is collected in *Répertoire I* (Paris: Minuit, 1960), p. 184. This essay has been translated by Roderick Masterton, AT4, p. 70.
'Eut reçu pour hochet la couronne de Rome': Hugo's poem is included in his 1835 collection *Les Chants du Crépuscule* (*Œuvres poétiques*, Vol 1, ed P. Albouy, Paris: Gallimard, 1968), hereafter VH, p. 839.
'like a horse loosed in a gigantic hippodrome': *Impressions d'Afrique* (Paris: Lemerre, 1910; reprinted Paris: Jean-Jacques Pauvert, 1963; all references are to the Pauvert edition), hereafter IA, p. 252. This novel has been translated into English by Lindy Foord and Rayner Heppenstall (London: Calder & Boyars, 1966; Berkeley: University of California Press, 1967); reprinted in paperback (London: John Calder, 1983; New York: Riverrun Press, 1983), hereafter EIA, p. 231.

6 'for just as one can employ rhymes': CJ, p. 23/HIW, p. 16.
'written immediately after *Locus Solus*': CJ, p. 25/HIW, p. 18.
'if the manuscript could be retrieved': CJ, p. 34/HIW, p. 27.

9 'The two most startling additions': these have now been
published as volumes III (*La Seine/La Tonsure*, ed. Patrick
Besnier, Paris: Pauvert/Fayard, 1994), V and VI (*Les Noces*, ed.
Pierre Bazantay, Paris: Pauvert/Fayard, 1998) of Roussel's
ʒuvres, hereafter 3 III, 3 V, 3 VI.

10 'rhyme never played for Roussel': R & CO, p. 253. The essay
from which this quotation is taken, 'Conception et réalité chez
Raymond Roussel', was first published in *Critique*, no. 89,
October 1954. It has been translated into English by John
Ashbery and published in AT4, p. 77.
'it is, truly, difficult to grasp': CJ, p. 33/HIW, p. 27.
'the initial work completed': CJ, p. 34/HIW, p. 27.

11 'I would like to draw your attention': CJ, p. 26/HIW, p. 19.

12 'Martial, a young neuropath': CJ, pp. 129–130. The section of
*De l'angoisse à l'extase* included in CJ has been translated by
John Harman and included in AT4, pp. 39–40.

13 'He was a positivist': this interview appeared in *Le Promeneur*,
no. 50, Oct. 1986, and is reprinted in R & CO, p. 267.
'This glory bursts forth': Not all of Janet's discussion of Roussel's
case appears in CJ. This quotation comes from Volume I of *De
l'angoisse à l'extase* (2 vols., Paris: Alcan, 1926), hereafter AE,
p. 460.

14 'when *La Doublure* appeared': CJ, p. 29/HIW, p. 23.
'the sublime mark of the great creators': *L'Étoile au front* (Paris:
Lemerre, 1925; reprinted Paris: Jean-Jacques Pauvert, 1963; all
references are to the Pauvert edition), hereafter EF, p. 225. This
has been translated by Martin Sorrell and published in
*Raymond Roussel: Selections From Certain of His Books; Atlas
Anthology 7*, ed. Alastair Brotchie et al. (London: Atlas Press,
1991), hereafter AT7, pp. 225–226.

15 'an almost unbearable brightness': *Locus Solus* (Paris: Lemerre,
1914; reprinted Paris: Gallimard, 1963; all references are to this
edition), hereafter LS, p. 57. *Locus Solus* has been translated into
English by Rupert Copeland Cunningham (London: Calder &
Boyars, 1970; reprinted in paperback, London: John Calder,
1983; New York: Riverrun Press, 1983), hereafter ELS, p. 51.
'ah! that sensation of moral sunlight': CJ, p. 131/AT4, pp. 40–41.
'poor little invalid': R & CO, p. 251/AT4, p. 76.
'I shall reach immense heights': CJ, p. 128/AT4, pp. 38–39.

16 'As the poet says': Roussel scholars have not located the source

of this quotation. My own guess is that 'the poet' is Roussel himself.

'To Pierre Loti': Fonds Roussel, hereafter FR, cat. no. 4881, f. 42v.

'offered, on bended knee': ibid.

'you who have the great happiness': The letter was first printed in *Prisme*, no. 18, Winter 1980–81, p. 59.

17 'raised himself to the highest peaks': CJ, p. 26/HIW, p. 20.

18 'Ask of me my life': This letter is reprinted in *L'Arc*, no. 29, 1966, p. 82.

'These literary works': CJ, p. 127/AT4, p. 38.

'Martial has a very interesting conception': CJ, p. 132/AT4, p. 41.

'If there was anything real in those descriptions': AE, Vol. II, p. 514.

19 'It is also important that I mention': CJ, p. 27/HIW, p. 20.

'serenity': R & CO, p. 250/AT4, p. 75.

'Everything that is new': ibid.

20 'Dear Master/I send you these flowers': Cited in François Caradec's biography *Raymond Roussel* (Paris: Jean-Jacques Pauvert, 1972, updated and revised, Paris: Fayard, 1997), hereafter FC, p. 202.

'Here I am in Baghdad': R & CO, p. 251/AT4, p. 76.

'Here I am in Constantinople': FC, p. 334.

'Roussel never really travelled': This essay was published in *La Bête noire*, no. 1, April 1935, and reprinted in R & CO, p. 213.

'brief biographical notes': CJ, p. 27/HIW, p. 20.

21 'Raymond Roussel, Brother-in-law of the Prince of Moscow': R & CO, p. 169.

22 'In the bookshops, nothing': CJ, p. 30/HIW, p. 23.

'Why aren't I as famous as Loti?': *Bizarre*, no. 34–35 (Roussel special issue), 1964, hereafter BZ, p. 85.

23 'an operetta then playing at the Variétés': CJ, p. 29/HIW, p. 22.

'La Vue' was first published in *Le Gaulois du Dimanche* over the weekend of 18–19 April 1903. We know from Madame Roussel's agendas that she attended *Sire de Vergy* with Raymond on 4 May 1903. For a full list of the plays, operas and operettas they attended together, see Philippe G. Kerbellec's *Raymond Roussel: au cannibale affable* (Monaco: du Rocher, 1994), pp. 219–221.

'The affair created an immense stir': CJ, p. 31/HIW, p. 24.

'People say I'm a Dadaist': R & CO, p. 205.

'I feel that your work': FR, cat. no. 4512, 257r.

24 'Thinking of the good will': Cited in FC, p. 394.

'only for the pleasure of being present': CJ, p. 32/HIW, p. 25.
'There's a bit of a row, isn't there?': Vitrac's 'Joueur d'échecs'
was first published in the *Nouvelle Revue Française* in 1928;
it was reprinted in *Digraphe*, no. 67, February 1994 (a Roussel
special issue), henceforth DG, p. 140. It has been translated by
Kathleen Cannell and Antony Melville, and published in AT4, p.
45.

25 'The play was wholly misunderstood': CJ, pp. 32–33/HIW, p.
26.
'Despite his constant disappointments': R & CO, p. 208.
'In bringing this essay to a close': CJ, p. 34/HIW, p. 28.
26 'a complete illusion of reality': IA, p. 35/EIA, p. 33.
'And so I seek comfort': CJ, pp. 34–35/HIW, p. 28.


CHAPTER 2: Many Years of Perfect Bliss

27 'I have preserved of my childhood': CJ, p. 28/HIW, p. 21.
'I was brought up with my sister Germaine': CJ, pp. 27–28/HIW,
pp. 20–21.
28 'Sylvestre was madly in love with Nanon': CJ, p. 51.
'he came to loathe the places': IA, p. 163/EIA, p. 168.
'Certain towns which evoked particularly happy memories': R &
CO, p. 213.
29 'People will research the acts of my childhood': CJ, p. 128/AT4,
p. 38.
'Another photo reveals her': These photos are in the Biblothèque
Nationale, département des Estampes et de la Photographie, Cat.
nos. NA 471, NA 472.
30 'Each evening the servants would gather': *Je n'ai jamais appris à
écrire, ou les Incipit* (Paris: Les Sentiers de la création/Skira,
1969), p. 141.
'the Proust of dreams': HIW, p. ix.
'They were from the same epoch': R & CO, pp. 175–176. In a
journal entry of 1964 Leiris writes: 'If between Roussel and Proust
there exists a strong connection, it could be said that the
objectivity of the former is opposed to the subjectivity of the latter,
and this is expressed in the radical opposition of their styles (the
one geometric, the other all winding [*flexueux*]) (R & CO, p.
312).
31 'a shrewish character': R & CO, p. 86. Leiris would have been
only ten when Madame Roussel died.
'All the world agrees': Cited in FC, p. 24.
'My mother adored music': CJ, p. 28/HIW, p. 21.
32 'savagely dramatic range': IA, p. 64/EIA, p. 58.

'creating the effect of a choir': IA, p. 96/EIA, p. 87.

33 'good only for concierges': R & CO, p. 203.
'had never counted for much': R & CO, p. 309.

34 'At the twenty-first attempt': CJ, p. 306. The *Documents* have been translated by John Ashbery and published in AT7, p. 55, and reprinted in HIW, p. 240.

35 'When I was sixteen': CJ, p. 28/HIW, pp. 21–22.
'–Comment, disaient-ils': CJ, p. 33/HIW, p. 26.

36 'M. Raymond Roussel is the celebrated author': this note is reprinted above the poem in the new complete edition of Roussel's works, *3uvres I* (ed. Annie Le Brun, Paris: Pauvert/ Fayard, 1994), hereafter 3 I, p. 41.
'Mon âme est une étrange usine': quotations from poems reprinted or appearing for the first time in the new complete edition will be referenced by line numbers in the text.

43 'One night I dreamed': *Nouvelles Impressions d'Afrique* (Paris: Lemerre, 1932; reprinted Paris: Jean-Jacques Pauvert, 1963; all references are to the Pauvert edition), hereafter NIA, p. 123.
'Sans souci de ces     lâtres': ibid., p. 143.
'A cette explosion voisine': ibid., p. 171.
'This poem made up part of a collection': 3 I, p. 63.

45 'A couple of scattered rhyme words': 3 I, p. 101.

46 'coincided with the crisis': CJ, p. 28/HIW, p. 22.
'lost all interest': CJ, p. 130/AT4, p. 40.
'Martial wrote other volumes': CJ, p. 131/AT4, p. 40.

47 'WARNING/As this book is a novel': 3 I, p. 24.

48 'We are in a *flat* and *discontinuous* universe': RG, p. 76/AT4, pp. 104–105.
'un peu obscur': HIW, p. xiii.

49 'really, universally, relations stop nowhere': 'Preface' to New York edition of *Roderick Hudson* (ed. Tony Tanner, Oxford: Oxford University Press, 1980 [first published 1908], p. xli).
'Roussel describes': RG, p. 70/AT4, p. 100.

50 'His unpublished manuscripts include': 3 IV, p. 250, p. 268, p. 254.

52 'equations of facts': Robert de Montesquiou's discussion of Roussel was collected in *Élus et appelés* (Paris: Emile-Paul frères, 1921) and reprinted in DG, p. 22. Parts of this article have been translated by Catherine Allan and published in AT4, p. 29. Roussel himself quotes Montesquiou's formulation in 'Comment j'ai écrit . . .', CJ p. 23/HIW, p. 16.

53 'more or less unintelligible': this review is reprinted in *Europe*, no. 714, Oct. 1988, p. 94.
'fort ennuyeux': this review is reprinted in 3 I, p. 378.

'When the volume appeared': CJ, p. 130/AT4, p. 40.

CHAPTER 3: Prospecting

57 'I started working again': CJ, p. 29/HIW, p. 22.
58 'pointless to search': CJ, p. 25/HIW, p. 19.
   'The verses of the understudy': CJ, p. 39.
59 'The worms in the lining': CJ, p. 48.
60 'The skin of the skate': CJ, p. 254.
61 'A question was to be posed': CJ, p. 166/AB, pp. 7–8.
62 'The white letters on the cushions': CJ, p. 163/AB, p. 3.
   'He watches his companions rapidly disappear': CJ, p. 164/AB, p. 4.
63 'Tombola grows angry': CJ, pp. 164–165/AB, pp. 4–5.
64 'embryo': CJ, p. 162.
   'the entire genesis': CJ, p. 12/HIW, p. 4.
   'Soon his face brightened': CJ, p. 170/AB, p. 12.
65 'The details of each story': CJ, p. 222/225.
   'metrical': Sade/Fourier/Loyola (Paris: Éditions du Seuil, 1971) has been translated into English by Richard Miller and published under the same title (London: Jonathan Cape, 1977). All references are to this edition, hereafter SFL, pp. 4–5.
66 'again set about prospecting': CJ, p. 29/HIW, p. 22. For further discussion of their dating, see Pierre Bazantay's article 'Claude et Luce, un mélodrame inachevé' in Revue de la Bibliothèque Nationale, no. 43, Spring 1992, hereafter BN, p. 20, and the introductions by the editors in 3 III, 3 V and 3 VI.
71 'A silence.': 3 III, p. 456.
74 'He is made indignant': AE, vol. II, pp. 146–147.
76 'les cottes bleues': R & CO, p. 133.
   'a scandal that had to be hushed up': ibid. For further details, see FC, pp. 123–125.
   'one evening he pointed out': R & CO, p. 131.
78 'A rough outline, headed Les Noces': 3 V, p. 49.
   'Another draft of the ending'; 3 VI, p. 432.
79 'He was ... especially fond of melodramas': R & CO, pp. 203–204. La Bouquetière des Innocents (1862) was written by Auguste Bourgeois and Ferdinand Dugué, and La Tour de Nesle (1832) by Frédéric Gaillardet and Alexandre Dumas (père). Roussel was also extremely fond of children's shows, which he used to attend in the afternoons with Charlotte Dufrène. To avoid being the only adults in the theatre without children, he asked Dufrène to bring along the young daughter of a friend, and would whisper into her ear answers to the questions posed

in audience competitions. When she won a small toy as a prize, Roussel's 'joy was immense' (R & CO, p. 205).

81 'multiple drawers/episodes': R & CO, p. 220.
'He hated . . . psychological plays': ibid., p. 204.
'a scene between Claude and Luce': 3 VI, p. 432.

82 'subdividing, bifurcating and trifurcating': SLF, p. 67.
'make no use whatsoever': CJ, p. 25/HIW, p. 19.
'Roussel's poetic trilogy': of these, only 'La Vue' has been translated into English, by Antony Melville, included in AT7. Footnotes will refer to the pages on which citations appear in this translation. La Vue has been re-edited by Patrick Besnier and published as 3 IV (Paris: Pauvert/Fayard, 1998). All references are to this volume, which includes several unpublished texts from around the same period and an early draft version of 'La Vue'.

83 'noticed by certain scholars': CJ, p. 29/HIW, p. 22. In fact, no immediate responses from either scholars or reviewers have yet come to light. For further discussion of the volume's reception, or rather lack of it, on publication, see 3 IV, pp. 373–379.
'Sometimes a momentary gleam suddenly shines': AT7, p. 229.

84 'My left eye is firmly closed': AT7, p. 229.

85 'At this moment the brightness': ibid., p. 279.
'For it is the distillation': ibid., p. 280.

88 'She lowers/Her eyes towards him': AT7, p. 268.


CHAPTER 4: Impressions of Africa

91 'Crossed the Nile by boat': this journal has been published in DG, p. 130. It makes an interesting comparison with Flaubert's richly detailed travel notes and letters from Egypt. See Flaubert in Egypt (1979), translated and edited by Francis Steegmuller.
'the performers did not know their parts': ibid., pp. 133–134.
'luck favours him': 3 VI, p. 539.

92 'in this climate . . . one is drunk': 3 VI, p. 567.
'leave neither shadow nor reflection behind them': RG, p. 71/ AT4, p. 101.
'illumination' O, p. 111.

95 'a young man of twenty from Marseilles': IA, p. 148/EIA, p. 153.

96 'a piece demanding the most perilous feats': IA, p. 59/EIA, p. 60.
'In the end . . . Impressions d'Afrique leaves an impression of Africa': O, p. 110.
'an ornamental crest': DG, p. 23/AT4, p. 30.
'this morning a blind mimic': DG, p. 129.
'worked for seven years': R & CO, p. 207. In fact, not everyone

appreciated Roussel's invitations to select from his list of actors, comedians, singers and social acquaintances. In his roman à clef *Les Délices de Capharnaüm* (Paris: Emile-Paul frères, 1921), Robert de Montesquiou satirizes his wealthy neighbour's performances: while Montesquiou concedes the excellence of Roussel's mimicries, he tries to escape the clutches of his 'Proteus' as soon as he can (p. 147).

97 'complete illusion of reality'. IA, p. 32/EIA, p. 33.

'A fraternity of Reverends': IA, p. 71/EIA, p. 72. Roussel partly explains the origins of this performance in 'Comment j'ai écrit . . .': *dominos à révérences* (hooded gowns with bows) – *dominos* (game of dominoes) *à révérences* (priests); *cure à réussite* (cure leading to recovery) – *cure* (rectory) *à réussite* (the card game patience). Roussel reports himself unable, however, to remember the source of the copper coin tower, but suggests the word *tourbillon* (whirlwind) played some part: *tour*, tower, and *billon*, copper. CJ, p. 16/HIW, p. 8.

'seen as a whole': IA, p. 143/EIA, p. 148.

98 'endeavours to copy slavishly': IA, p. 208/EIA, p. 214.

'prompting bar by bar': IA, p. 59/EIA, p. 60.

'acquits himself honourably': IA, p. 224/EIA, p. 228.

'betrayed by his memory': IA, p. 82/EIA, p. 83.

99 'As regards the genesis of *Impressions d'Afrique*': CJ, p. 13/HIW, p. 5.

'I bleed over every phrase': CJ, p. 127/AT4, p. 38.

100 'a sort of African Nero': FR, Cat. no. 4297, f. 23.

'who could obtain nothing worthwhile': ibid., f. 85.

101 'Under the stiff folds of her tulle skirt': IA, p. 80/EIA, p. 81. The origins of this vignette are also explained in 'Comment j'ai écrit . . .': *toupie* (spinning top) *à coup de fouet* (lash of the whip, as given by a child to a top to make it spin more); *toupie* (old frump) *à coup de fouet* (spasm of pain). CJ, p. 17/HIW, p. 9.

'an incorrigible gambler': FR, Cat. no. 4297, f. 6.

'[he bawls] orders continually': ibid., f. 101.

'this blow completed the ruin': ibid., f.244.

103 'young author wondering': NIA, p. 15

104 'The screw and the steering were broken': IA, pp. 151–152/EIA, pp. 156–157.

106 '1 Revers à marguerite': CJ, p. 15/HIW, p. 7.

'1 Maison à espagnolettes': CJ, p. 14/HIW, p. 6.

'rest on a feeling of security': O, p. 113. The book's lack of dialogue is perhaps the most obvious formal symptom of this, and might be construed as a symptom of Roussel's fear of all social conflict. 'When Martial is in the grip of his denigration-phobia, the terror of hearing himself criticized, the fear of having to stand up for a friend or for a musician whom he loves, the fear of having to defend one of his opinions or of having to change it, leads to his avoiding all social relations' (AE, Vol. II, p. 322). In the context of his works in general, the total dominance of the narrative voice might be related to the immobility of the scenes described in *La Vue* or the anti-dramatic sharing out of the narratives in his plays.

107 'Fetching from the deserted stage-wings': IA, p. 145/EIA, pp. 150–151.

108 'Disregarding for the moment': this article, a review of Lindy Foord and Rayner Heppenstall's translation of *Impressions d'Afrique* and of Heppenstall's critical study of Roussel, was published in the *New York Times Book Review*, 29 Oct 1967, and reprinted in Trevor Winkfield's HIW77, p. 64.

109 'intending to undertake a long voyage': IA, p. 147/EIA, p. 152. 'more than anyone . . . he must have felt alone': R & CO, p. 213. 'after a cordial exchange of handshakes': IA, p. 316/EIA, p. 317. The musical Tancrède's disability derives from *tronc* (church collecting box) *à ouverture* (the slot through which the coins are dropped); *tronc* (the trunk of a man) *à ouverture* (who performs overtures).

110 'On a certain day of leisure': CL, p. 248. 'Then a single petal': IA, p. 240/EIA, p. 245. 'sustained by the dense element': IA, p. 241/EIA, p. 245. 'he had simply to stretch out his hand': IA, p. 241/EIA, p. 246.

111 'the cats, merged altogether': IA, p. 129/EIA, p. 135. 'suspended from elegance': O, p. 110. 'No, but conceive of this prodigious fact': *Le jardin des supplices* has been translated by Alvah C. Bessie and published as *Torture Garden* (Sawtry: Dedalus, 1990), p. 241.

112 'I Plante à faux': CJ, p. 19/HIW, p. 11. Mossem's death looks forward to that endured by the condemned prisoners in Kafka's *In der Strafkolonie* (*In the Penal Colony*, written in October 1914, published in 1919), who are executed by a machine that carves their sentences into their bodies. Mirbeau's novel was the principal source of Kafka's story. 'a corpse with wide-open eyes': IA, p. 100/EIA, p. 102.

113 'With both hands Rao brandished his axe': IA, pp. 22–23/EIA, p. 22.

114 'In 1918 I rejected Roussel': O, p. 114.

115 'Only Edmond Rostand': CJ, p. 30/HIW, p. 23. Roussel probably made Rostand's acquaintance at Biarritz, where the Rostands owned a villa near Villa Chaslon-Roussel.

'While reading this play': FR, cat. no. 4488, f. 1.

116  'That a creator who is at once outrageous and delicate': 'Un auteur difficile' in *Élus et appelés* (Paris: Émile-Paul frères, 1921), reprinted in DG, pp. 22–23/AT4, p. 29.
'It was fundamentally Roussel': 'The Great Trouble with Art in this Country', collected in *The Essential Writings of Marcel Duchamp*, ed. Michel Sanouillet and Elmer Peterson, (London: Thames and Hudson, 1975), hereafter MD, p. 126.

117  'that it will be possible, in case of decease': FR, cat. no. 4501, f. 120v.
'never duped into the role of the tourist': R & CO, p. 213.

118  For the complete catalogue of the sale, see FC, pp. 157–165.

119  'The earthworm that plays the zither': FRD, Rf 71. 821. For further details, see John Ashbery's 'Les versions scéniques d'*Impressions d'Afrique* et de *Locus Solus*', BZ, pp. 19–25, and FC pp. 135–139, 149–157.
'It was more than just a failure': CJ, p. 30/HIW, p. 23.


CHAPTER 5: A Solitary Place

121  'During this time, I was writing *Locus Solus*': CJ, p. 30/HIW, p. 23.

122  'because of Martial Canterel': CJ, p. 26/HIW, p. 19.
'a poor little invalid': CJ, p. 127/AT4, p. 38.
'Elle commence tôt sa tournée asticote': CJ, p. 24/HIW, p. 17.
Winged trance . . . Saturn elastic pannier. These elements are used in the cock Mopsus's divinations in Chapter 7 of *Locus Solus*.

123  'Locus Solus, as the property is called': LS, p. 9/ELS, p. 5. Locus Solus, it might be argued, thus rather resembles the Duc de Durcet's château at Silly in *Les 120 Journées de Sodome* (first published in 1935, translated by Austryn Wainhouse and Richard Seaver, New York: Grove Weidenfeld, 1966), which is described as 'a remote and isolated retreat' (p. 235) to which only select guests are invited. The château's apartments are similarly adapted to enable the libertines to conduct their experiments – which are on the whole almost as improbable as Canterel's.

124  'one of the champions of the spoken word': LS, p. 10/ELS, p. 6.
'continual discoveries': LS, p. 9/ELS, p. 5.

125  'It's you, my Gillette': LS, p. 216/ELS, p. 204.

126  'mass of enriching details': IA, p. 211/EIA, p. 217.

128  'embarrassing stock': LS, p. 38/ELS, p. 33.

130  'He peoples emptiness': O, pp. 109–110.
'a world beyond that of humanity': CJ, p. 132/AT4, p. 41.

131 'Her skin, of an unheard-of delicacy and transparency': this episode has been published in BN, p. 51.

132 'illusory happiness': LS, p. 154/ELS, p. 143.

134 'boucles', 'cercles d'or': CJ, p. 60.
'common stock': R & CO, p. 257/AT4, p. 80.

136 'marvellous piece of work': LS, p. 266/ELS, p. 253.
'Then Canterel': LS, p. 267/ELS, p. 254.

137 'I found a young man who was very polite': Gil Blas, 1 Dec. 1914. This article was the basis of Montesquiou's 'Un Auteur difficile'. It is included in the final Roussel album of the Fonds Rondel (cat. no. Rf 71. 835), which contains a number of obituaries and general assessments of Roussel's work.

138 'but how could he be?': Les Pas effacés (Paris: Émile-Paul frères, 1922), Vol. III, p. 78.
'I offer my Palais Rose to destiny': cited by Patrick Chaleyssin in Robert de Montesquiou – mécène et dandy (Paris: Somogy, 1992), p. 177.

139 'carrying only his cane and gloves': R & CO, p. 133.
'Him! Drive?': ibid., p. 313.
'Could you tell me why Rheims': DG, p. 145/AT4, p. 49.
'The cataclysm stupefied him': L'Intransigeant, 7 August 1933, FRD, Rf 71.835.

140 'in the years preceding the war': FR, cat. no. 4510, f. 30r, 31r.
'A truce bearer with his eyes blindfolded': these instructions are printed in Épaves (Paris: Jean-Jacques Pauvert, 1972), hereafter EP, p. 290.

141 'In Nouvelles Impressions the unconscious seems to have broken through': HIW, p. xxii.
'There, installed on rustic seats': FR, cat. no. 4875, f.9.

142 'a luxurious woman's wig': ibid., f. 14.
'complete absence of this cranial padding': ibid., f. 18.

144 'a sudden glory': EP, p. 68.
'as Jean Ferry first conjectured': 'Premières constatations à propos de Flio,' BZ, pp. 2–17.

145 'LA CLE DU BONHEUR': EP, p. 65.
'The idea that the act of eating is harmful': R & CO, p. 250/AT4, p. 75.

146 'Since the philosophical character of the novel': FR, cat. no. 4511, f. 57.

147 ' "But the trunks," said Passepartout': Le tour du monde en 80 jours (first published 1873), (trans. P. Desages, ed. Peter Costello as Around the World in 80 Days, London: Everyman, 1994), p. 20.
'Near here there are two bathing resorts': R & CO, pp. 210–211.

'In Papeete I live on the rue de Rivoli': ibid., p. 211.

148 'Loti was baptized': *Le Mariage de Loti* (Paris: Calman Lévy, 1880), p. 1.

149 'en sens inverse': ibid., p. 139. A number of postcards of this waterfall were preserved among Roussel's collection of photographs.

'overwhelmed by the dreadful news': These letters are printed in *Prisme*, no. 21, autumn 1981, pp. 16–17. For further details of Roussel's Loti-mania, see FC, pp. 200–212. See also Caradec's 'Images, visages et voyages de Raymond Roussel' in BN, pp. 24–35.

'exempt de charges': LS, p. 9/ELS, p. 5.

'On arrival in New York': AE, II, p. 148.

CHAPTER 6: Nous sommes la claque et vous êtes la joue

152 'Why does the play make people laugh?': FRD, Rf 71. 823.

'*Locus Solus* is at once a fairy play': ibid.

153 'Roussel had paid lavishly': FR, cat. no. 4511, f. 80v, f. 75r. Other costs listed include publicity, which came to 3,480 francs (f. 70r), and music (composed by Maurice Fouret), which cost 10,000 francs (f. 74). Roussel also paid 15,000 francs in compensation to Frondaie for allowing his very successful play *L'Insoumise*, which had been playing to packed houses at the Antoine, to have its run interrupted by that of *Locus Solus* (f. 64r).

'Is our eccentric author quite sure': FRD, Rf 71. 823.

'How awful to see so much money wasted': ibid. Antoine was particularly incensed that Roussel's folly was playing in a theatre named in tribute to himself.

'I demand the creation of a police': ibid.

'a rich lunatic is free to roam at large': ibid.

154 'Ah, if I were poor': DG, p. 139/AT4, p. 44.

'group of very lively partisans': CJ, p. p. 31/HIW, p. 24.

'to my most passionate supporter': FR, cat. no.4881, f. 42v.

'the only show': cited in FC, p. 242. Three years later, in an issue of *La Révolution surréaliste* (no. IV, 15 July 1925), Philippe Soupault asserted: 'I do not think I am being over-bold in declaring that Raymond Roussel writes his "anecdotes" (this is what he calls his series of facts) exactly as André Breton and myself wrote *Les Champs magnétiques* '(p. 8). In fact, Roussel's highly deliberative *procédé* is automatic writing's polar opposite, as Michel Leiris observed in his notebook; Rousselian inspiration 'takes place at the antipodes to that of automatic writing since it is not by the abolition of all rules that the unconsious is unleashed, but, on the contrary, by the multiplication of those rules' (R & CO, p. 107).

155 'Great numbers of students live in real poverty': FRD, Rf 71. 823.

'It is this book': ibid.

'Roussel is not an adroit millionaire': *Revue de l'Époque*, May 1923 (reprinted in BZ, pp. 56–57). Montesquiou also compares Roussel with Villiers de L'Isle-Adam (DG, p. 25), while Leiris explores at some length in his Roussel notebook what seem to him the crucial similarities and differences between Roussel and Poe: both, Leiris suggests, found themselves identifying with 'God the Father' (R & CO, p. 102). Other tendencies they have in common include 'sadism and necrophilia; intoxication; overdeveloped taste for logic; analogy between "Comment j'ai écrit..." and "The Genesis of a Poem"; Edgar Poe and Roussel and the detective novel, the cryptogram, the puzzle in general. The Blacks at the North Pole in *Arthur Gordon Pym* could have been invented by Roussel. Chess... Differences from Roussel: Poe arrives (or claims to arrive) at his elements by deductive logic – a continuation of aesthetic considerations; Roussel arrives at his by puns, a richer method, to the extent that it is more open to chance' (R & CO, p. 103, p. 106). The Blacks of Poe's novel are in fact found at the South Pole.

156 'Thinking that the incomprehension of the public': CJ, p. 31/ HIW, p. 24.

'the novel I have published': this advertisement is reprinted in DG, p. 141.

157 'The present invention': Roussel's application is reprinted, with relevant diagrams, in Philippe Duboy's ' "Vers une architecture": Raymond Roussel inventeur,' DG, pp. 174–181.

'this little building': FR, cat. no. 4509, f. 155. The whole of this certified statement is reprinted in FC, p. 353–354.

158 'in a French that is irreproachable': *Comœdia*, 8 May 1925, FRD, Rf 71. 827.

'the words *singulier* and *pluriel*': CJ, p. 25/HIW, p. 18.

159 'A rich and light food': EF, pp. 85–86/AT7, pp. 170–171.

161 'You will excuse my frankness?': EF, pp. 101–102/AT7, p. 177.

'Throw it out!': EF, p. 30/AT7, p. 149.

163 'Such energy is expressed': EF, p. 153/AT7, p. 197

164 'between the "advanced" ': FRD, Rf 71. 827.

'Another tumult, another battle': CJ, pp. 31–32/HIW, p. 25. In a review of 11 May 1924, one Léo Marchès quoted an abbreviated version of Desnos's reply and declared it 'biting, and extremely relevant'. The provocateurs, he observed, knew exactly what they were up to, as did the public 'which, in a very Christian spirit, proffered its cheek' (FRD, Rf 71. 827).

165 'A bronze plaque': R & CO, pp. 204–205. This picture has since disappeared. Hugo's *Hernani* opened at the Théâtre-Français on 25 February 1830 and caused a legendary uproar.
'After a while the atmosphere had become stormy': *Les Confidences de Youki* (Paris: Fayard, 1957), pp. 102–104.
'This time again the critics savaged me': CJ, p. 32/HIW, p. 25. It was one Jacques Florange who came up with this witticism – his phrase was in fact 'l'araignée au front', a slang term for madness – in *Paris-Midi*, 8 May 1924 (FRD 71. 827).

166 'It was an appalling scandal': 'Interview de Michel Ney, duc d'Elchingen,' Jean Chatard and Robert Morneux, BZ, p. 99.
'He was, he told me politely, flattered': DG, p. 75.
'to avoid all dangerous conversations': R & CO p. 250/AT4, p. 75.
'You think yourselves shrewd': CL, p. 258.

167 'absolute uselessness': 'Raymond Roussel', *Littérature*, 1 April 1922. This article is reprinted in DG, p. 73, and has been translated by Antony Melville, AT4, p. 37.
'Monsieur/M. Raymond Roussel received your letter': *La Révolution surréaliste*, no. 1, 1924, p. 32.

168 'Let me tell you at once how much I admire': FR, cat. no. 4500, f. 196.
'to Robert Desnos': FR, cat. no. 4881, f. 22r.

169 'I admire the astonishing genius': FR, cat. no. 4500, f. 197, 198.
'The star to whose mysterious influence he refers': this review was published on 1 June 1925, and is reprinted in a collection of Desnos' critical writings, *Nouvelles Hébrides et autres textes, 1922–1930* (Paris, Gallimard, 1978), p. 225.
'I knew him . . . as much as one could know': *L'Intransigeant*, 7 August 1933, FRD, Rf 71. 835.

170 'The authors of these articles': *Le Matin*, 13 December 1926; *Revue du Touring Club de France*, August 1926 (this article has been translated by Antony Melville and reprinted in AT4, p. 149); *L'Illustration*, 26 February 1926, FR, cat. no. 4510, ff. 178–80.
'Mussolini came'; Cited in FC, p. 318.

171 ' "It's very pleasant," he confided to me': DG, p. 149/AT4, p. 52.
'I forced myself to write each story': R & CO, p. 207.

172 'Look up there at that nebula': *La Poussière de soleils* (Paris: Lemerre, 1927; reprinted Paris: Jean-Jacques Pauvert, 1964),

hereafter PS, pp. 199–200. It has been translated by Harry
Mathews and published in AT7, pp. 137–138.

173 'Those who are for him': *La Liberté*, 27 January 1926, FRD, Rf
71. 830.

174 'There was enormous demand for places': CJ, p. 32/HIW, pp.
25–26.
'They came with the intention of kicking up a row': FRD, Rf 71.
830.
'During the interval': ibid.

175 'We had no difficulty agreeing': 'Fronton-Virage' was written in
1948 and served as a preface to Jean Ferry's *Une étude sur
Raymond Roussel* (1953). It was also collected in Breton's *La
Clé des champs* (1953), which has been translated by Michel
Parmentier and Jacqueline d'Amboise as *Free Rein* (Lincoln and
London: University of Nebraska Press, 1996), hereafter FRN,
p. 189.
'The style is less involved': FR, cat. no. 4500, f. 199.
'While the curtain was falling': CJ, p. 33/HIW, p. 26.

176 'a certain disproportion': FRN, p. 190.
'The anecdotes cast on the characters': HIW, p. xx.


CHAPTER 7: In parenthesis

178 'in his memoirs . . . Guillot records': *La Grande Cuisine
Bourgeouise* (Paris: Flaumanian, 1976) pp. 39–44.

180 'On my way to Tehran': R & Co, p. 212.
'on the advice of a respected doctor': ibid.

181 '((((pendant notre hiver notre tignasse essaime': NIA, p. 63.
'chez l'homme/Le feu d'œil s'éteint': NIA, p. 85.

183 'He had the hair': *Entretiens avec André Fraigneau* (Paris:
editions du Rocher, 1988), p. 79. This interview took place in
1951.
'*Locus Solus* is a prodigious feat': CL, p. 254.
'proves that Roussel is not unaware': O, p. 108.
'Is Raymond Roussel mad?': CL, p. 252.

184 'It concerned a tiny pair of opera-glasses': CJ, pp. 33–34/HIW,
p. 27.
'On 6 March Roussel sent Leiris a typed draft of Canto I': EP,
pp. 277–284.

185 'Truly, it is difficult to credit': CJ, p. 33/HIW, p. 27.
'Arpent drelin spirale guilledou guipure frugal': This worksheet
is reproduced in facsimile in BN, p. 44. The line 'À
prendre . . .' is on p. 27 of NIA.

'Comme si chosissant la seconde opportune': ibid. The original
line is also on p. 27 of NIA.

187 'as J.B. Brunius first pointed out in an essay in 1938': reprinted
in Jean Ferry's UE, pp. 154–156. See also François Caradec's
'La Machine à Imprimer Raymond Roussel' (BZ, pp. 58–62) and
Juan-Esteban Fassio's 'La Machine à Lire *Nouvelles
Impressions d'Afrique*' (ibid., pp. 62–66).
'Sans doute à réfléchir, à compter cela porte': NIA, p. 7.

188 'Que de mémoire, à fond, il sait sans une faute': NIA, p. 7/p. 19.
'(Comme sait l'occupant, dans une maison haute': ibid.
'((Pouvoir du retoucheur! lorsque arborant ses gemmes': ibid.

189 '–Se demandant, pour peu qu'en respirant il bouge': ibid, pp.
7–9.
'((((Tels se demandent': ibid., p. 9.
'ailleurs placé que sous l'aisselle': ibid., p. 13.

190 'l'appareil qui, trouvé par Franklin': ibid., p. 27.

191 'pour celle qu'à l'ampoule': ibid., p. 31.
'un lac de sang surgi': ibid., p. 39.

192 'Here occurs again, but transposed': R & CO, p. 220.

193 'la boule aquatique et nue': NIA, p. 29.
'faux explorateur': ibid., p. 67.
'La gloire a l'horreur': ibid., p. 15.

194 'sommité disparue': ibid., p. 77.
'le saint feu du génie': NIA, p. 83.
'S'éteint quand l'âge rend son détenteur gaga': ibid.

195 'Combien change de force': ibid., p. 79.
'(((Besoin d'aide! ô besoin sublime, universel!': ibid., p. 63.
'(((Se fait-on pas à tout? deux jours après la tonte': ibid., p. 73.

196 '–le jour du blanchisseur': ibid., p. 37.
'quand, comme il faut/Fait un cheval au vert': ibid., p. 43.
'Quand d'un bas on l'expulse, un œuf à repriser': ibid., p. 47.
'pour ce qu'orneé/De clous': ibid., p. 49.
'Qu'outre-Manche à certains essuyages intimes': ibid., p. 55.

197 'horizontal jet fort': ibid., p. 67.
'Quand, poisseuse, elle a l'heur de puer, la semelle': ibid., p. 11.
'What sluice-gates burst in him': UE, p. 59.

198 'It all adds up to a tumultuous impression of reality': HIW, pp.
xx-xxi.

199 'Rasant le Nil, je vois fuir deux rives': NIA, p. 73.
'Dont une suffirait à vingt de nos salons': ibid.
'Se fait aux profondeurs du grand vide céleste': ibid., p. 85

200 'These are not the pictures I would have made' and following
quotations from Zo, FR, cat. no. 4512, f. 311.
'Roussel's directions to Zo': see Appendix 3. These instructions

were passed on to Leiris by Lemerre's foreman Eugène Vallée after Roussel's death, and discussed in his essay 'Autour des *Nouvelles Impressions d'Afrique*' (first published in March 1939 in *Cahiers GLM*, no. 9, reprinted in R & CO, pp. 219–226). They are included in EP, pp. 287–294, and with the prints in HIW (translated into English by Trevor Winkfield), pp. 104–164. See also Laurent Busine's *Raymond Roussel: Contemplator enim* (Brussels: La Lettre volée, 1995) for an extensive discussion of their genesis and import.

201 'lowering the Venetian blind of a window': EP, p. 291.
'make us witness conflicts': *Surréalisme au Service de la Révolution*, no. 6, 1933, hereafter SD, p. 41. Dalí's review has been translated by Martin Sorrell, AT4, p. 55.

202 'He had a second life': BZ, p. 98.

204 'If I die before I finish this work': CJ, p. 264.
'many vital essences': EP, p. 266/AT7, p. 17.

205 'a sheaf of arguments for her cause': EP, p. 275/AT7, p. 21.

207 'n'est que de la boursouflure': *Le Figaro illustré*, February 1933, reprinted in *Europe*, no. 714, October 1988, p. 81.
'At the end of three and a half months': CJ, p. 133.
'The chess world should celebrate': CJ, p. 156. *Les Cahiers de l'Échiquier français* was edited at the time by François le Lionnais, who co-founded the Oulipo moivement (an organization dedicated to exploring the aesthetic possibilities of formal constraint) in 1960.
'He seemed very "strait-laced" ': *Dialogues with Marcel Duchamp* by Pierre Cabanne, translated by Ron Padgett (London: Thames and Hudson, 1971), hereafter DMD, p. 34. These interviews were recorded in 1966, two years before Duchamp's death.

208 'esprit terriblement logique': BZ, p. 104.

209 'My stupefaction in the face of such a regeneration': FR, cat. no. 4500, f. 200.
'This, of all the books of our era': SD, p. 41/AT4, p. 55. A battered copy of *Impressions d'Afrique* was one of two books on Dalí's bedside table the night he died. See also his 1938 self-portrait *Impressions d'Afrique* (Musée Boymans-van Benningen, Rotterdam).
'It is by systematic and endlessly repeated use': ibid.
'creates works with a power': *La Critique sociale*, January 1933, no. 7, FRD, 71. 835.

210 'Today, the greatest authors': *Le Matin*, 6 December 1932, *L'Excelsior, Comœdia*, 7 December 1932, FRD, 71. 835.

211 'He had not seen me for about two years': R & CO, pp. 260–261/
AT4, p. 83.

212 'Cut, cut, but give me my drug!': R & CO, p. 261/AT4, p. 83.
'Her catalogue was confiscated': a page of it is reproduced in
facsimile in AT4, p. 130. For a medical description of the drugs
taken by Roussel, see DG, pp. 184–185.
'How easy it is to open one's veins': R & CO, p. 261/AT4, p. 83.

214 'pendant l'ivresse': NIA, p. 9.
'He confided this detail': Sciascia's essay has been translated by
Alec Gordon and published in AT4, pp. 124–146.
'in France he is considered a genius': AT4, p. 129.

215 'I absolutely insist': A facsimile of this instruction is included in
FC, facing p. 187.
'A rambler, with his arm raised': EP, p. 293.
'Voluntary death': R & CO, p. 226.

## CODA:  A Little Posthumous Fame

216 'I will explain myself after my death': *La Nouvelle Revue
Française*, 1 September 1933, no. 240, reprinted in *Poésie
Critique I* (Paris: Gallimard, 1959), p. 139.
'we are following him on one level': AT7, p. 16.

217 'As Michel Leiris pointed out': R & CO, p. 202.
'a Surrealist as a storyteller': André Breton, *Manifestoes of
Surrealism* (trans. Richard Seaver and Helen R. Lane, Ann
Arbor: The University of Michigan Press, 1969), p. 27.
' "Roussel," Breton declared, "along with Lautréamont" ': *Le
Minotaure*, no. 10, 1937, collected in *3uvres complètes*, vol. II,
ed. Marguerite Bonnet (Paris: Gallimard, 1992), p. 1068/AT 58.
'The anthology did not, in the event, appear until 1940': For
further details, see ibid., pp. 1751–1752, and Breton's
*Anthologie de l'humour noir* (Paris: Sagittaire, 1940). In this and
in the following edition of 1950, Breton briefly describes the
passages he has chosen, and prints some extracts from Jean Lévy
(i.e. Ferry)'s essay on Roussel published in the magazine
*Documents*, no. 1, 1934.

218 'Roussel was another great enthusiasm of mine in the early days':
MD, p. 126.
'That man had done something': DMD, p. 34, p. 41.

219 'His work as a whole': Foucault's *Raymond Roussel* was
published in 1963, and translated by Charles Ruas and
published under the title *Death and the Labyrinth: The World
of Raymond Roussel* (London: Athlone Press, 1987). All
references are to this edition, hereafter MF, p. 11.

'transparency': R & CO, p. 278.

'Among other questions, the visitor asked': Max Ernst, *Écritures* (Paris: Gallimard,1970), p. 51.

220 'I know that Gallimard would willingly have published him': R & CO, p. 266. And Gallimard did eventually publish him. In 1963, to accompany Foucault's critical study, they issued an edition of *Locus Solus* – without, however, having obtained Michel Ney's permission. The book was impounded and a legal wrangle ensued; eventually an agreement was reached between Ney, Gallimard and Jean-Jacques Pauvert, who had bought the rights to Roussel's complete works. This stipulated that 50 per cent of Gallimard's profits from the edition should be passed on to Pauvert.

'Zo's illustrations for *Nouvelles Impressions d'Afrique*': See Evan M. Maurer's 'Images of Dream and Desire: the Prints and Collage Novels of Max Ernst' in *Max Ernst: Beyond Surrealism*, ed. Robert Rainwater (New York and Oxford: The New York Public Library and Oxford University Press, 1986), pp. 37–93.

221 'the engravings of Zo': *L'Arc*, no. 68 (1977), p. 51. Alas, Robbe-Grillet discovered that he had lost his copy of *Nouvelles Impressions d'Afrique*, and the novel was never even begun.

'mysteries of construction': HIW, pp. xx-xxi.

'CIEL – si elle?': *Glossaire, j'y serre mes gloses* is collected in *Mots sans mémoire* (Paris: Gallimard, 1969), pp. 78, 97. See also Robert Desnos' similar string of puns in 'Rrose Sélavy' (first published in 1922) in *Nouvelles Hébrides* (Paris: Gallimard, 1978, pp. 158–160).

'struck': R & CO, p. 267.

222 'Between his lips and my ears': *Biffures* (1948) has been translated by Lydia Davis as *Scratches* (New York: Paragon House, 1991), p. 10.

'It was a question': R & Co, p. 268.

'the rudiments necessary for undertaking': FRN, p. 191. See also Jeanine Parisier-Plottel's 'Traditions ésotériques et populaires chez Raymond Roussel' in *Raymond Roussel, perversion classique ou invention moderne* (Rennes: Presses Universitaires de Rennes, 1993), pp. 183–199. Parisier-Plottel produces a number of connections between Roussel and the alchemist Fulcanelli, but it still seems to me highly unlikely that Roussel's works secrete some magic alchemical formula.

223 'For me, Roussel remains the man of the great secret': *Je n'ai jamais appris à écrire, ou les Incipit* (Paris: Les Sentiers de la création/Skira, 1969), p. 144.

'To borrow one of the favourite expressions': RG, p. 70/AT4, p.

100. See also Jean Ricardou's 'Le nouveau roman est-il roussellien?' in *L'Arc*, no.68 (1977), pp. 60–78.

'The greater the accumulation of precise minutiae': RG, p. 71/ AT4, p. 101.

224 'hollowing out reality': *Mélusine: Roussel en gloire*, No. 6 (Lausanne: Éditions l'Age d'Homme, 1984), p. 249. In the course of this interview Butor suggests that the impact of Roussel on his own literary development is most clearly discernible in *Portrait de l'artiste en jeune singe* (1967) and *Matière de Rêves* (1975).

'Now this chain': RG, p. 73/AT4, p. 102.

'I wrote this study of Raymond Roussel': MF, pp. 171–172. For further discussion of Roussel's importance to Foucault, see Jerrold Seigel, 'Avoiding the Subject: A Foucaultian Itinerary', *Journal of the History of Ideas* (1990), vol. 51, pp. 273–299.

226 'I have kept my love for Roussel': MF, p. 185.

'slammed shut with a good laugh': MF, p. 174.

227 'I have to admit, I would not dare to compare': MF, p. 175.

228 'All of Roussel's language': MF, p. 16.

'In their basic function': MF, p. 55.

'Language has become circular': MF, p. 135.

'Paradoxically, for Roussel': MF, p. 164.

'disconnect the language': MF, p. 8.

'is not where the canonical figures': MF, p. 16.

229 'most easily, with the greatest pleasure': MF, p. 184.

'So you think this has justified': MF, p. 167

'Roussel's work first appeared in English': *Transition*, no. 12, 1928.

'that crazy American': MF, p. xxvii.

'probably the only soldier in the Philippines': cited in David Lehman's *The Last Avant-Garde: The Making of the New York School of Poets* (New York: Doubleday, 1998), p. 217.

'really exciting and crazy': ibid., p. 148.

230 'But I fancy I see': *Some Trees* (first published 1956, reprinted New York: Ecco Press, 1978), pp. 14–15. For further discussion of Roussel's importance to Ashbery, see Lehman, pp. 145–149, and my 'John Ashbery and Raymond Roussel', *Verse*, autumn 1986, vol. 3, no. 3, pp. 11–23.

'What more is there to do, except stay?': ibid., p. 18.

231 'Sweet are the uses of adversity': *Selected Poems* (New York: Vintage, 1985), p. 228. He is referring in particular here to the compositional processes that underlie his long poem *When the Sun Tries to Go On*, written in 1953, soon after his return from Paris. In 1964 Koch published a translation (in rhyming

couplets) of Canto III of *Nouvelles Impressions d'Afrique* (reprinted in HIW, pp. 97–103).

'tried to raise the word to a new power': HIW77, p. 64.

232 'Roussel was the man': cited in Christopher Sawyer-Lauçanno's *The Continual Pilgrimage: American Writers in Paris 1944–1960* (New York: Grove Press, 1992), p. 250.

'Reading Roussel brought me several revelations': *The Way Home* (London: Atlas Press, 1989), p. 155.

233 'Roussel's methods led me to discover': DG, p. 46.

'In the 1977 issue of the magazine *L'Arc*': translated into English by Antony Melville in collaboration with Mathews and published in *Atlas Anthology 3* (London: Atlas Press, 1985), pp. 69–86.

234 'It is ultimately of no importance': ibid., p. 83.

'During luncheon in a little bistro': translated by Warren F. Motte Jr and published in his anthology *Oulipo: A Primer of Potential Literature* (Lincoln: University of Nebaska Press, 1986), hereafter OU, p. 77.

235 'Roussel, like Mallarmé': OU, p. 42.

'Another Perecquian *procédé* involved': *Cahiers Georges Perec 3 : Presbytère et Prolétaires* (Paris: Éditions du Limon, 1989), pp. 40–43.

236 'L'inscription du Blanc': *La Disparition* (Paris: Denoël, 1969), p. 156.

'I do not read much': W has been translated by David Bellos and published as *W, or the Memory of Childhood* (London: Collins Harvill,1988), p. 143.

'The Bewitched of Lake Ontario': translated by Ian Monk and published in a collection called *Three* (London: Collins Harvill, 1996), p. 167.

237 'wishes to fix, to describe and to exhaust': *La Vie mode d'emploi* (1978) has been translated by David Bellos and published as *Life, a User's Manual* (London: Collins Harvill, 1987), p. 117. For further discussion of the relationship between Roussel and Perec, see Bernard Magné's 'Perec, lecteur de Roussel' in *Raymond Roussel en gloire: Mélusine*, no. 6 (Lausanne: L'Age d'Homme, 1984), pp. 203–220, and his 'De Roussel et Perec, derechef: à propos des procédés' in *Raymond Roussel: perversion classique ou invention moderne* (Rennes: Presses Universitaires de Rennes, 1993), pp. 245–266.

238 'But the ironical thing': ibid., p. 497.

'Trevor Winkfield': In an attempt to further my understanding of Roussel's appeal to visual artists such as Duchamp, Ernst, Dalí, Giacometti – who once told John Ashbery that Roussel's fiction had inspired much of his early work (HIW, p. xviii) – and to Trevor Winkfield himself, I asked the New York-based painter to describe the impact of Roussel's work on his own development. He replied in the following terms: 'I was first attracted to Roussel in 1964 through his influence on Marcel Duchamp; anyone whose influence has helped form the *Large Glass* had to be special. I bought a copy of *Impressions d'Afrique* and although I had only a rudimentary understanding of French I could tell Roussel was using very unusual words, words which in isolation became objects in a sea of verbiage. I studied French in order to translate his expository essay 'How I Wrote Certain of My Books' (indeed, it was through my translation of this in 1970–73 that I found a new way of painting, after giving up art in 1967). But the deeper I went into the books, paradoxically the more impenetrable they became: the matter-of-fact manner in which the complicated machinery was described could not disguise the notion that another dimension existed behind the apparent text. In retrospect, this led to the layering of my paintings, so that what one sees is not necessarily what one gets. A single object can have multiple interpretations. And speaking of objects, I was delighted that so many abounded in Roussel's work; it's full of visual material and art objects for an artist to ponder (the ruler made of bacon, the aerial piledriver and its mosaic, the focal gaol and its fading prints, the bowler hat with the word *Pincée* traced on it, the zither played by a worm . . .). I was particularly struck by an actual Roussel object: the star-shaped biscuit which he'd kept as a souvenir of his 1923 meal with the astronomer Camille Flammarion, and the little star-shaped glass box he constructed to preserve it. I was also very attracted to the idea that Roussel had constructed a totally artificial world, self-contained and somewhat claustrophobic. As Janet so memorably put it: "the work must contain nothing real, no observations on the world or the mind, nothing but completely imaginary observations." A world verging on insanity, but delineated logically by a writer who kept regular office hours every day (in other words, who relied not so much on inspiration as on hard work). I adopted a similar working routine as a result. And although Roussel's world was artificial, he appropriated facts from the outside world to build it. I was always taken by the knowledge that he'd phonetically distorted his shoemaker's name and address (Hellstern, 5 place Vendôme) to give him "Hélice tourne zinc plat se rend (devient) dôme", which gave him the elements of one of his outlandish apparatuses. Roussel's use of the real world to fabricate an artificial one was of great consequence for me, though his eventual suicide as a result acted as a warning. Finally, *Nouvelles Impressions d'Afrique* is the only book I'd like to be marooned with. Its stories within stories within stories I still find, after thirty years, endlessly fascinating. Zo's mundane illustrations, of course, make this a perfect bedtime book' (letter to the author). For a selection of Winkfield's most Rousselian compositions, see *Pageant* (text by Jed Perl, introduction by John Ashbery, West Stockbridge: Hard Press, 1997).

'an obscure figure': HIW, p. viii.

'If the age in which he wrote': *Times Literary Supplement*, 6 October 1995, p. 9.

239  'The President of the Republic of Dreams': 'Une Vague de rêves', first published in 1924, collected in *Chroniques* (Paris: Stock, 1998), p. 198.

# Index

Abbreviations used in the index are: *CJ* for *Comment j'ai écrit certains de mes livres*; *EF* for *L'Étoile au front*; *IA* for *Impressions d'Afrique*; *LS* for *Locus Solus*; *NIA* for *Nouvelles Impressions d'Afrique*; RR for Raymond Roussel. Titles of English versions of texts by Roussel are given in brackets after their French titles.

INDEX

186–7, 190, 199–201, 209, 215, 220–1, 239n, Appendix 3
methodology 190–7
*procédé* 185
published and reviewed 186–7, 208, 209–10
scatology 195–7
and World War I 140–1, 184
writing 147–8, 184–6

O'Hara, Frank 229
Orlando (valet) 211, 212, 214
Oulipo movement 207, 209, 233, 235

Padgett, Ron xxv, 238
Palermo 210, 211–14
Paris 151, 211, 214
  Café de la Régence 206–7
  Père Lachaise cemetery 202
  Ritz hotel 181, 196
  RR's homes in 27, 118, 181–2, 201–2
  boulevard Malesherbes 27
  rue Quentin-Bauchart 7, 182, 202
  *see also* Neuilly estate
  RR's last years in 206–8
  RR leaves, *1933* 7, 211
  rue Pigalle 202
  theatre 119, 153, 175
  *see also names of theatres*
Pascal, Blaise xxviii
patent 157–8
Pauvert, Jean-Jacques xxv, 21, 217
Peking 147
Père Lachaise cemetery 202
Perec, Georges xxiii, 233–4, 235–6
  *Un cabinet d'amateur* 236
  *La Disparition* 236
  *La Vie mode d'emploi* 236–8
  *W ou le souvenir d'enfance* 236
Péret, Benjamin xxiii, 167–8
Persia 180
Picabia, Francis 120
Pindar, Ian 238
Pioch, Georges 183
Poe, Edgar Allan 155, 207
post-modernism 224
*procédé poétique* 1, 2–6, 10, 11, 18, 32, 47, 57, 58, 60–1, 64–6, 71, 72, 82, 86–7, 94, 102, 104, 108, 111, 197, 203, 207–8, 216, 218–19, 228, 235
  in *LS* 4, 122–3, 124–6, 134

in *NIA* 185, 192, 194
  *see also* puns and doubling
proof sheets 182, 186
'prospecting' xxiii, 4, 9–10, 56–7, 66, 88, 90, 94
Proust, Marcel xxvii, 10, 27, 55n, 227
  *À la recherche du temps perdu* 55n
  compared with RR 5, 30–1, 105n, 126, 183, 186n
  comment on RR's poetry 55
puns (homonyms) and doubling xxvi, 1–6, 10, 32, 51–2, 57, 59–60, 65–6, 86, 216–17, 218–19, 221, 228
  Ashbery and Koch 230–1
  in *IA* 98–100, 103
  *see also procédé poétique*

*Quelques heures à Bougival (Some Hours at Bougival*; RR) 137n
Queneau, Raymond 209, 234

Reboux, Paul 114n
religious mania 12–16, 130
Renaissance (theatre) 25
*Révolution surréaliste, La* 167
*Revue Blanche* 53
*Revue de la Bibliothèque Nationale* xxi
*Revue de l'Époque* 155
*Revue européenne, La* 169
rhyme 10, 81–2
  alexandrines 81–2, 108
Richard, Élie 210
Ritz hotel, Paris 181, 196
Robbe-Grillet, Alain 23, 48, 49, 220–1, 223–4, 226
  *Dans le Labyrinthe* 226
  'Énigmes et transparence chez Raymond Roussel' xxii, 4–5, 92
Roditi, Édouard 229
Rome 170–1, 178
Romith (chess teacher) 206–7
Rondel, M. 152n
Rostand, Edmond 22, 115, 176
Roussel, Eugène (father of RR) 27, 33
  death 34–5, 118
Roussel, Georges (brother of RR) xxiv, 27, 33, 90n
Roussel, Germaine (sister of RR)
  childhood 27
  marriages 21
  later life 118, 166, 181, 182